A Poverty of Imagination

A POVERTY OF IMAGINATION

Bootstrap Capitalism,
Sequel to Welfare Reform

David Stoesz

THE UNIVERSITY OF WISCONSIN PRESS

The University of Wisconsin Press
2537 Daniels Street
Madison, Wisconsin 53718

3 Henrietta Street
London WC2E 8LU, England

1   3   5   4   2

Printed in the United States of America

Library of Congress Cataloging-in-Publication Data
Stoesz, David.
A poverty of imagination : bootstrap capitalism, sequel to welfare reform / by David Stoesz.
pp.   cm.
Includes bibliographical references and index.
ISBN 0-299-16950-2 (cloth : alk. paper)
ISBN 0-299-16954-5 (pbk. : alk. paper)
1.   Public welfare—United States. 2.   Welfare
recipients—Employment—United States. 3.   Poor—Government
policy—United States.
I.   Title.
HV95 .S824   2000
362.5'0973—dc21   00-008036

para Julio,
bienvenido a las aventuras del mundo

Contents

Illustrations

PHOTOGRAPHS

TABLES

FIGURE

Preface

On August 22, 1996, President Clinton shocked liberals by signing the Personal Responsibility and Work Opportunity Reconciliation Act (PRWORA), a.k.a. "welfare reform." Clinton had earlier vetoed two similar congressional proposals on the grounds that they were too damaging to children. But on the eve of the 1996 presidential campaign, opportunism took over, and a 60 year-old entitlement for poor families was sacrificed on the altar of electoral expedience. As a student of social policy and the Clinton presidency, I found the president's action not particularly surprising—the facility with which Bill Clinton borrowed, manipulated, and exploited policy themes was already becoming legendary. If, to borrow Clinton's words, you couldn't "make an eagle by putting wings on a pig," could you make a president by putting a governor in the White House?

What I did find remarkable amid the liberal angst surrounding welfare reform was the stubborn longevity of public welfare, an institution that had persevered for more than a half-century, despite being held in contempt by clients, staff, and taxpayers. Having once been a welfare caseworker, and many years later a welfare department director, I could attest to the miserable state of affairs of public welfare. Yet liberals were aghast at the prospect that it would be cashiered and replaced with a conservative framework for welfare reform that was *truly* revolutionary. I found myself wondering why liberals, during the halcyon days of Democratic control of Congress and the White House, had not reformed welfare themselves. Surely they could have reinvented welfare in a way that would have prevented the calamity that was about to befall the poor because of conservative reforms. But liberals had failed to do this.

Why?

The liberal explanation for American poverty policy has been that welfare represents a token commitment to a poor, disproportionately minority population that is exploited by predatory capitalism. If, as a result, public welfare proved unpopular, that was the symbolic price accompanying the provision of benefits to the poor. That public welfare was stigmatizing, punitive, even oppressive, was unavoidable in a market economy. It may be unhappy, liberals rationalized, but it was better than nothing—and it certainly had to be better than conservative welfare reform.

The many state experiments with welfare reform that were encouraged by the 1981 Omnibus Budget Reconciliation Act were to upset the liberals' "necessary evil" assumptions. When governors and legislatures mandated work, welfare recipients responded positively, often enthusiastically. As their earnings increased, decisionmakers were often willing to elevate the earned income disregard, allowing them to keep more of their earnings. Innovations in asset-based strategies to alleviate poverty followed, such as Individual Development Accounts. There were claims that even the ambiance of the welfare department began to improve. Early returns from welfare reform validated the transition from welfare state to what Mickey Kaus called the "work ethic state."[1]

The liberal reply to this has been one of mistrust if not plangent negativism. To paraphrase Mencken's caricature of a Puritan as someone who fears that someone out there is having a good time, liberal reaction to welfare reform seems to reflect apprehension that the poor are becoming upwardly mobile. Was the crux of the matter conservative obsession with work or liberal intransigence about the capability of the poor?

If reducing poverty were the issue, both liberals and conservatives could be held culpable. A case could be made that liberals had become "welfare dependent"—that six decades of welfare policy conditioned liberals not only to expect the poor to be disabled, but also to base an entire bureaucratic apparatus upon that presumption. A different poverty policy—one that assumed competence and attempted to accelerate upward mobility—was simply inconceivable. Worse, in reaction to a competence-based alternative in the form of conservative welfare reform, liberals chose to perpetuate a despised public welfare apparatus. Welfare might be depersonalizing, stigmatizing, and aspiration-destroying, but it was "all we had"—it was, in a word, familiar.

This insistence on the familiar in opposition to constructive, plausible change was reflected in an experience I had during the early 1990s. It serves as a cautionary tale, not so much about devolution—though liberals may take it as such—as about the pusillanimity of welfare professionals: given an alternative to inferior and inadequate programming for the disadvantaged, too often welfare professionals have preferred to reaffirm the status quo. Rather than assert themselves, seize the day, and explore innovations in social policy, social welfare professionals all too often revert to toady mode.

KIDS PROP

After teaching social policy in San Diego for five years, I decided to organize a local ballot proposition that would put in place a comprehensive array of services for kids and their families. Having chaired the data subcommittee of the local United Way's "children's initiative" as well as reviewing the reports from Children Now, the statewide advocacy organization, I was aware that San Diego County was not up to par with other California jurisdictions in providing services to children. The United Way venture seemed timid, and even if a local ballot proposition for kids failed, it might put some spine into the United Way's efforts.

The timing seemed good. In 1991 San Francisco voters had passed a "children's amendment," which sequestered a portion of the city budget and reserved it for kids. The San Francisco proposal included no tax increase—a prudent strategy, given the antitax strictures of Proposition 13—yet it had been expected to fail. City officials opposed it because it interfered with their decisional prerogatives, but the organizers were clever, using little red wagons to deliver the reams of paper on which were scribbled the required signatures for their proposition. The electorate responded enthusiastically, and the amendment won easily.

If such a modest venture could pass muster in San Francisco, a city with comparatively fewer kids than San Diego, a bolder proposition seemed promising. I reviewed the latest thinking on children's services from organizations such as the Children's Defense Fund and queried a few colleagues. They were interested but cautious, as nothing of this nature had been attempted before. Local elected officials, their appointees, and civil servants had, for better or worse, called the shots in child welfare in San Diego, and this would challenge their hegemony. But a former student took to the idea instantly. Sue had a masters degree in public health and was pursuing a doctorate at the University of California. She was more aware than I of how inferior the county's child welfare patchwork had become. Probably the worst performer was Child Protective Services (CPS), an agency that had become so enamored with fashionable "issues" like satanic abuse and repressed memory that routine services had lapsed. During this period one child a week died of abuse or neglect in San Diego County, even when the case was known to CPS.

The first step for Kids Prop was to look into the technical feasibility of mounting a ballot proposition. This led me to Bob Felmuth of the Children's Advocacy Institute, an appendage of the law school of the University of San Diego. A veteran of innumerable legislative skirmishes involving the welfare of children, Felmuth listened between frequent phone calls, then walked to a cabinet and hauled out a thick file. Over the years he had considered a statewide children's proposition, but between Proposition 13 and conservative governors, the timing had never been right. He suggested, however, that we could probably amend one of those state drafts for a local proposition. But could we include increased tax revenues? I asked. That might invite a legal challenge, Felmuth indicated, but we would be on firm ground if we simply added on to an existing tax, such as the county sales tax. At that time, Proposition 13 required a two-thirds majority vote for the institution of a new tax, but a simple majority to increase an existing one. Did he have a suggested increment? I inquired. Felmuth noted that a 0.25 percent increase in the county sales tax for prison construction was expiring, and it would be a relatively simple matter to continue the revenue flow and divert it for children's services. The juxtaposition could not have been more exquisite, since prison is the ultimate and most expensive disposition for problem kids, who all too often become troubled youths, only to graduate as juvenile delinquents, eventually consolidating their careers as adult offenders. Substitute the kids' tax for the prison tax, and the public wouldn't even notice, Felmuth suspected. However, he cautioned, it would be essential to include "no supplantation" language so that new money wouldn't be used to replace existing funding. Would he work on a local ballot proposition? Reaching to intercept another phone call, he nodded.

Soon thereafter Sue and I set aside an afternoon and cobbled the children's proposition together. We drew on the San Francisco experience, the latest thinking among children's advocates, and the nuances of the local political environment. The result was not particularly simple, but it was explainable, and we thought it would work. Kids Prop would continue the 0.25 percent sales tax increase for 10 years, during which time revenues would go to a pool that would fund programs for children under four accounts: family preservation, child daycare, health and mental health, and culture and recreation. The fund would be managed by a Children's Authority, the members of which would be appointed by various elected and appointed officials. Existing agencies could request funds from the Children's Authority, but in doing so would agree to buy into the service plan designed by authority staff, who would also be responsible for putting in place performance-based budgeting. Aside from designating the communities for which services would be deployed, the Children's Authority would have complete freedom in formatting the new arrangement. By the end of the decade, we figured the new system would be in place, and the 0.25 percent tax continuation could be sunsetted. At the end of the session, Sue noted that Kids Prop was not only ingenious, it was plausible.

From previous experience planning and implementing community mental health services, I knew that Kids Prop was ambitious and bold—perhaps too bold, in which event it was quixotic. So I called the regional planning agency and asked how much was generated by the present 0.25 percent of the sales tax being diverted for prison construction. The answer was $41 million annually. I was astonished; a reasonable extrapolation suggested that Kids Prop could eventually add a half-billion dollars in new programming for San Diego children.

Among the flurry of subsequent calls were several to a political consultant who had managed campaigns for several successful Democratic candidates, including Lynn Schenk, who had just been elected to Congress. The consultant was all business; a local proposition was feasible at least as far as lead-time was concerned, but it would require thousands of voter signatures, and the cost of gathering them would run about $100,000. I registered surprise, but he wouldn't budge a nickel. That, he noted, would be a small investment, given what would be delivered in children's programming. If nothing else, Kids Prop would enhance my social skills, I figured, envisaging the innumerable lunches and receptions necessary to raise the money.

Sue and I decided to roll out Kids Prop to a select audience of child welfare professionals at a prestigious institution. Accordingly, we reserved the boardroom at Children's Hospital. The invitation included overview information and RSVP. A week before the meeting, we had commitments from 30 people to attend, most of those we'd invited. In preparation, we filled folders (complete with crayons), printed name tents, and practiced a 30-minute presentation that would leave ample time for questions. In presenting Kids Prop to the choir, we anticipated an opportunity to identify weaknesses, iron out problems, and recruit confederates. From casual conversations with child welfare colleagues, it was evident that Kids Prop was generating a lot of interest.

The morning of the rollout, Sue called, obviously disconcerted. She didn't know what had happened, but the most prominent child welfare pediatrician in San Diego had called and abruptly backed out of the meeting. Equally worrisome, child welfare managers suggested that they were being dissuaded from attending, and several canceled their reservations. Sue didn't know the source of the problem, but it was significant. Having little choice, we decided to go on with the program anyway.

Cancellations notwithstanding, we had a packed room. I gave an overview of children's services in San Diego, Sue followed with transparencies that diagrammed how Kids Prop would work, and I concluded with a summary of the new children's programming that would be generated for every community in San Diego County. We were on time to the minute, leaving an hour for discussion. Then I asked for questions.

Silence.

I was mystified. No one spoke.

Finally, Felmuth floated an observation about the process of putting a proposition on the ballot. Someone asked a vaguely worded question about the feasibility of the whole idea. And that was it. I looked at Sue; she shrugged, and I thanked everyone for attending.

As we packed up our materials, Sue expressed misgivings about the entire project. She said she would speak with administrators at the hospital; I said I'd make a few calls. We would regroup that afternoon.

My calls suggested that the chair of the County Board of Supervisors had quashed the meeting, but this was hearsay. Whatever had happened was momentous—probably lethal to Kids Prop—but its intent and shape were amorphous. "Who," I thought, "could be against better services for kids when this county loses a kid a week to abuse and neglect, even when child welfare workers are supposed to be on the case?"

At mid-afternoon Sue called to withdraw from the project. She had met with a hospital administrator who suggested that she drop out if she expected to use Children's Hospital in any way related to her dissertation. The threat was direct, brutal, and effective. She was in tears, and at a loss to explain why something of such clear benefit would generate such threats. But she had little choice.

Two days later I had enough of the picture, as sketched by the political consultant, to repeat it to a local columnist, who soon verified my version and published an account in the newspaper. Their traditional mode of decisionmaking threatened, the chief supervisor's senior staff had called prominent child welfare professionals on the morning of the meeting and suggested that they not attend. If they *did* elect to attend, as county employees or recipients of county contracts they were not free to comment about the material presented—hence the silence.

But *why*, I had asked the political consultant, would the chief supervisor object to something like Kids Prop? Easy, came the reply. Rumor had it that the chief supervisor was thinking about challenging Lynn Schenk for her seat in Congress, and he did not want Kids Prop on the ballot at the same time. If it was on the ballot, she would support it, he would oppose it, and he might lose, because it would probably prove popular.

After this conversation I wasn't sure if I should be more outraged at the chief supervisor, for his crass political ambition, or my child welfare colleagues, for being so easily muzzled.

Undaunted, I secured a grant from the Kaiser Family Foundation to survey public opinions about child welfare. The grant was modest, but it was more than adequate to pay the university's Survey Research Center to conduct a state-of-the-art phone interview with 611 San Diego County voters, assuring an error rate of no more than plus or minus 4 percentage points. Embedded in the half-hour interview were central questions about Kids Prop. The results were revealing: a majority of voters, most of whom identified themselves as "conservative" and "Republican," favored (1) a 0.25 percent sales tax reserved for children's services, (2) consolidating children's services under a Children's Authority, and (3) funding services under the four accounts we had envisioned for Kids Prop. In compliance with the Kaiser Family Foundation grant, brochures with the survey results were printed and distributed.

Hoping that broad public support would reinforce the inchoate sympathy of child welfare professionals, I sent a copy of the brochure to everyone who had RSVP'd for the rollout meeting, inquiring in a cover letter about their continued interest in Kids Prop and inviting them to contact me.

Two called.

Clearly that level of support was insufficient, so I conceded the demise of Kids Prop. Under what might seem the most propitious of circumstances— obviously needy children, available legal expertise, the support of conservative voters, a community-based format that was in tune with the times— child welfare professionals accepted the gag imposed by an elected local official and silenced themselves.

The denouement was mercifully brief. Having declined to endorse Kids Prop, the United Way unfurled its "children's initiative" and watched it flutter briefly amid the self-congratulatory plaudits of the local booboisie before floating to the ground. Its glossy and inconsequential reports could be safely interred on agency shelves.

Ever-vigilant conservatives in the state legislature bolstered Proposition 13 so that even increases in existing taxes would require a two-thirds majority of voters, effectively closing the loophole that Kids Prop had been poised to dart through.

The political consultant was correct in his reasoning that the chief county supervisor wanted Kids Prop blotted from the ballot. Brian Bilbray did challenge Lynn Schenk for her congressional seat in the next election. He won and has retained his seat in the House of Representatives ever since.

CONSERVATIVE WELFARE REFORM

But what about conservatives? Has their triumph in welfare reform translated into reductions in American poverty? The precipitous decline in the welfare caseload across the nation has allowed them to elide this question; the conservative pronouncement on welfare reform is "welfare reform works"—period. The absence of civil unrest by the welfare-poor and the inability of liberal academics to portray conspicuous damage as a result of welfare reform has given conservatives free rein in social welfare policy. Yet their conclusion that a minimalist response suffices is not only inaccurate with respect to the known facts about poor families, but immoral with respect to the American ethos. Welfare reform that offers the welfare-poor a ticket to become working-poor offers short-term gains but long-term misery.

Not long ago a colleague and I proposed using a small amount of Virginia's welfare block grant surplus for Individual Development Accounts to accelerate the upward mobility of welfare families headed by adults who had found employment. The goal was to ensure that their work efforts would not be subverted by the state's two-year time limit for public assistance. In promoting Virginia Individual Development Accounts (VIDAs), we published op-eds in newspapers, testified before legislative committees, and lunched with more decisionmakers than I can recall. We faxed copies of the proposal to lawmakers, being conscientious about including Republicans, since a member of their party was the incoming governor. Amid this flurry of activity, one afternoon I found myself at a legislative reception, copies of the proposal jammed into my suit jacket. Working the crowd, I spied Clarence Carter, the state's director of social services, a black Republican appointed by the outgoing Republican governor but likely to be retained by the incoming one. After introducing myself, I recited the VIDA mantra and handed him the proposal. He didn't miss a beat.

"We're not considering *any* allocations from the welfare block grant surplus," he said with finality.

I acknowledged his position while cursing under my breath the narrow-mindedness of executive branch appointees who were unwilling to see the virtue of policy innovations, even those that reflect conservative values. Fortunately, more imaginative minds prevailed, and the VIDA program was approved as a $500,000 demonstration project.

THE THESIS FORETOLD

The campaigns for Kids Prop and VIDA were minor events that illustrate the machinations of the poverty industry as it has evolved in this century. During the Progressive era a group of reform-minded women cobbled together a set of widows' pension programs that served as the pretext for Title IV of the 1935 Social Security Act, which would become Aid to Families with Dependent Children (AFDC). During the subsequent decades, AFDC expanded fitfully under the direction of welfare bureaucrats who aspired to replicate in the United States the northern European model of the welfare state.[2] "Welfare states," observed Linda Gordon, "after their first inauguration, have always had as their functions not only providing public aid but also empowering and supporting professionals and bureaucrats and nourishing a culture that seeks official/professional solutions to social problems."[3] The inevitability of the implementation of a full array of programs to protect citizens from insecurities related to health, unemployment, and poverty was foretold by liberal welfare philosophers, who cited the dramatic expansion of poverty programs during the War on Poverty of the 1960s as testament to their faith.

Subsequently, social work—the profession that had accepted welfare as part of its social mission—did the inexplicable: it abandoned the poor. Social workers in direct practice opted for a clinical route, mimicking psychologists and psychiatrists in private practice.[4] Social work professors in academe indulged in intellectual fashions, trumpeting the virtues of diversity as evident in race, gender, and sexual orientation. The result of this "professional involution" (described in more detail in Chapter 2) was the institutional neglect of such traditional concerns as poverty and, to a somewhat lesser extent, child welfare. For all the railing about the feminization of poverty during the 1970s and 1980s, social work failed to conduct *any* substantive research on poverty and welfare programs, leaving welfare bureaucrats to their own devices. The significance of social work's abnegation of public welfare cannot be overstated; it is as if the nation's teachers and the faculties of university schools of education decided to turn their backs on public education.

Without the corrective influences that an engaged social work could have introduced through theory and research, public welfare drifted away from its original mandate, becoming not only institutionally corrupt but also disconnected from its primary constituents: staff, clients, and taxpayers. By the 1980s, public welfare was ripe for reprisal, and conservatives seized the moment with relish. Their initial victory, the 1981 Omnibus Budget Reconciliation Act, encouraged the states to experiment with waivers, innovations that diverged from traditional program rules, and Republican governors were eager to exploit the opportunity. By the mid-1990s, so many states had been granted waivers that AFDC had ceased to exist in any practical sense. Whether we interpret his action as an election-eve capitulation to congressional conservatives or as the fulfillment of his promise "to end welfare as we know it," President Clinton signed a most un-Democratic Personal Responsibility and Work Opportunity Reconciliation Act in 1996, devolving AFDC to the states and ending the 60-year entitlement to welfare.

Yet the conservative triumph in welfare reform is not the final word in poverty policy. Conservative welfare reform has proceeded on dual tracks. First, welfare-to-work has provided a series of supports to encourage women on welfare to enter the labor market. This is the route to upward mobility, a strategy that liberals could use to reenter the debate about poverty policy, but only if they cease (1) demonizing low-wage work and (2) defending a discredited public welfare system. Second, welfare behaviorism has provided the pretext for a series of initiatives to correct the conduct of the poor. Penalties related to school attendance, childhood immunizations, family planning, and establishing paternity, plus time limits on receipt of welfare, have a superficial resonance, but they will ultimately prove futile. Fully articulated, welfare behaviorism will founder on the shoals of conservative philosophy, because of its invasive paternalism, and be finished off by fiscal imprudence, since such surveillance of the poor necessitates expanding the welfare bureaucracy.

Under these circumstances, "bootstrap capitalism" is one candidate for future poverty policy. Advocates of social justice, whether they be compassionate conservatives or recovering liberals, could use bootstrap capitalism to mainstream the poor through wage supplements, asset building, and community capitalism. As explored in the final chapter, bootstrap capitalism can replace public welfare as the programmatic basis of poverty policy, but only by networking capital, a strategy that has dual implications. Ultimately, bootstrap capitalism means mainstreaming the welfare-poor and, at the same time, deconstructing the welfare bureaucracy. In the face of the controversy that these are likely to engender, two observations are worth making. First, bootstrap capitalism has not only inspired immigrants throughout the nation's history, but has also provided the means by which poor families have entered the middle class. Second, no one of sufficient means would deign to receive cash benefits or social services from public welfare if he or she had a choice; indeed, continuing to subjugate poor citizens with public welfare only serves the interests of welfare bureaucrats while denying upward mobility to disadvantaged families.

ACKNOWLEDGMENTS

I am grateful for the institutional support afforded by the Samuel S. Wurtzel Endowment. Sandy Kramer pointed out needed corrections and secured permissions, and the editorial assistance of Rosalie Robertson and Jane Barry was much appreciated. Several colleagues have been instrumental in the emergence of this work, though the author alone is responsible for what is to follow. Foremost, David Saunders served as a catalyst for many of the ideas here, insistently pointing out guideposts to the future even as illness was robbing him of the possibility that he would ever see it; his friendship is sorely missed. As has been the case for two decades now, I look forward to further collaboration with Howard Karger in elaborating these ideas in the service of a more just and equitable social policy. Michael Sherraden, arguably the most consequential social worker of my generation, critiqued the first draft. William Epstein, the professor to whom this professor turns, aptly assessed my efforts as "knowledgeable journalism." Peter Edelman has offered patience and needed correctives as the manuscript evolved. In addition, two inspirations of the previous generation must be recognized. Harry Chaiklin's affinity for social theory, much appreciated while I was one of his students, is reflected in this work. I think he would agree that social work will not attain fruition as an intellectual discipline without an empirically testable theoretical base; this is a modest effort toward that end. Finally, during a memorable tour of Mr. Jefferson's architecture, B. J. Curry Spitler listened sympathetically to my complaints and then said, "Listen, dear, if you want this country girl's advice—if that's the way it is, then that's what you put down."

So, I did.

David Stoesz

dstoesz@saturn.vcu.edu
Richmond, Virginia

A Poverty of Imagination

1

The End of Welfare

"What took you so long to get off welfare?" Shot from the audience, the question is aimed at the lone African American woman on stage.

Stunned momentarily, Evontà Whitley composes herself and then says, "It wasn't that I waited so long to get a job; it was why someone waited so long to hire me!"

Neither question nor answer does justice to the talk show's subject that morning: welfare reform. To the white interrogator, Whitley is the stereotypical ghetto mother, breeding eight children over 14 years on public assistance before finally getting a job as a result of the state's welfare reform initiative. In counterpoint, Whitley expresses gratitude for the $5.50 per hour cleaning job that got her off welfare, even though her wages are so low that she continues to receive Food Stamps and Medicaid.

But Whitley has chosen to omit some of the details that contributed to her participation in the labor market. After an 11-month and seven-day sentence for drug possession, a job was one part of a plan that would retrieve four of her eight children from foster care. In fact, despite her television appearance as the personification of successful welfare reform, Whitley had found employment before the state's welfare reform was implemented.[1] Thus, stereotype defeated rationality in yet another performance of the nation's welfare reform melodrama.

Just beneath the surface of Whitley's accomplishment—her graduation from welfare—lurk nuances, however. On welfare, she and the four children who are living with her had been getting by on $322 per month in cash benefits, $391 per month in Food Stamps, and Medicaid—$8,556 per year. Welfare helped, she would later admit, but "it also made me lazy, waiting for the check." Whitley describes herself at the time as "wild"—involved with drugs, running a house where clients smoked cocaine. But her sentence for possession followed by the death of her 42-year-old brother from AIDS quickly sobered her up. Work became a compass pointing to the future; her family, the landmark from which all progress would be charted.

Not that finding work was all that easy. Whitley had submitted any number of unsuccessful job applications, finally resorting to a girlfriend who told her about a temporary cleaning job at Commercial Services that might convert to full-time. Whitley jumped at the opportunity. Despite having to work nights on an on-call basis, she is ecstatic: "I love my job. The best thing that ever happened to me was to get off welfare." Eventually, the cleaning job became full-time, even offering overtime, though all her hours were at night and on the weekend. With older children at home, Whitley avoids the high cost of child care. Moreover, she was able to retain Medicaid, so that her employer's failure to provide health insurance is less critical. Once she started working, Whitley's income immediately eclipsed her previous welfare benefits.

Outwardly, Whitley is a sound illustration of "making work pay." At 56 hours per week, her take-home pay minus withholding comes to $14,221.90 a year.[2] With $4,104 in Food Stamps annually, her family hurdles the poverty level of $17,900 for a family of five. In addition, Whitley is eligible for an Earned Income Tax Credit refund of $2,050, which she received for the first time when she started working. Whitley's total income for the year thus comes to $20,375.90.

In this case, however, appearances would be deceiving. Like her personal history, Whitley's economic circumstances are far from simple. She has left three teenagers in foster care with families nearby, and as a result she is paying the state 20 dollars a month per child in child support. The children are doing well, and she is reluctant to disrupt their foster families and bring them back to her; in truth, her small home (less than 1,000 square feet) lacks the necessary bedroom space for them, anyway. The cost to the state of foster care for the three teens comes to $14,400 annually, an amount the state would have saved if Whitley had stayed home and cared for all of her children. But even if she desired to, staying at home is tenable only in the short run. Welfare reform provisions dictate that if Whitley had insisted on remaining a mother, she would eventually have run afoul of the state's two-year limit on welfare receipt, and perhaps the federal five-year lifetime limit as well, and been summarily terminated from aid. Thus, her participation in the labor market seems ineluctable.

Two adults also figure prominently in the household. Her 24-year-old daughter leaves an infant in Whitley's care while at sea for the Navy. And "the man in my life," George, has become a source of stability as well as a father figure for the younger children. George, a "self-employed recycler," met Evontà Whitley while they were "in the drug world"; both have been clean since her incarceration. While George is a frequent presence in the Whitley household, he resides with his mother a few blocks away. The portrait that thus emerges is one of a family struggling in unpredictable waters;

Evontà Whitley

when the tide is out, traditional expectations and relations hold sway, but these are swept away during high-water crises.

Evontà Whitley's resurrection from a descent into the underclass is a tale of individual heroism, however tentative that may prove to be. In this respect she serves as a foil to the portraits of other African American women on welfare that have been presented to the public. The best-known of these would be Rosa Lee Cunningham, also a mother of eight, who lived in Washington, D.C., and was featured in Leon Dash's Pulitzer Prize-winning series in the *Washington Post*. As Dash poignantly recounts, Rosa Lee and six of her children succumbed to drugs, thievery, and prostitution, in the process being incarcerated and contracting AIDS.[3] If a shadowy apparition assumes residence in the family of Evontà Whitley, it will be the one that haunted the home of Rosa Lee Cunningham.

A happier outcome is depicted by Rosemary Bray. Growing up in Chicago with parents who had been sharecroppers and had migrated North to escape Jim Crow, Bray wrote her family biography—as she put it—to rebut the "ignorant and vicious ideologues who have never regarded the poor with anything but contempt."[4] The antithesis of Rosa Lee Cunningham, Rosemary Bray's mother insisted on raising her children to respect mainstream values and seize the elusive opportunities before them. Welfare supported Mrs. Bray and her children, buffering the erratic breadwinning of an abusive father, even if it aggravated his frustration and violence. One can only hope that Evontà Whitley will summon the stamina to reconcile the demands of motherhood and employment and replicate Mrs. Bray's performance.

Evontà Whitley, Rosa Lee Cunningham, and Rosemary Bray fairly reflect the reality of welfare in America,[5] and in so doing reveal it as fundamentally more complex than current slogans hyping "welfare reform." Therein lies a moral lesson that the nation will learn—soon, if Americans are studious; slowly and painfully if policymakers elect to be punitive toward the poor. In working through this lesson, Evontà Whitley and her children warrant attention because they are at the nexus of several cross-currents: poverty compounded by the effects of racism and sexism, a neighborhood infested with drugs, marginal employment, cramped housing, and an uncertain future. To the extent that Evontà Whitley continues to work, her children do well in school, and her family prospers, they will serve as beacons to others who have been socioeconomically segregated from the mainstream. If, on the other hand, the nation fails to deploy the supports essential for such success, the Whitley family will in all likelihood plunge once again into the underclass, some of its members generating a volume of social pathology that can only be managed by the most expensive of institutional programs, incarceration.

Poverty policy looms large in the destiny of the Whitleys. Having cashiered Aid to Families with Dependent Children (AFDC) in favor of Temporary Assistance for Needy Families (TANF), the nation has begun a series of state experiments to see which of these futures will predominate. Unfortunately, the justification for this policy change has been based almost entirely on ideology. Since the late 1970s, much of the understanding of welfare has evolved under the influence of two polemics: liberals have been in the trenches, defending archaic welfare based on left-wing fantasy, while conservatives have attacked social programs with data that are often transparently ideological. The liberal line on welfare has been that the poor are victims of structural defects associated with capitalism and its side effects: racism, sexism, and classism; the only way to ameliorate the predations of the labor market is to deploy public assistance through a public welfare bureaucracy that provides income benefits and social services to low-income families. Such advocates of social equality looked upon welfare as a nuisance, a temporary digression from the evolution of a European-style welfare state.

The conservative tack has been to impugn the attitudes and behaviors of the disadvantaged and rid the culture of any organized efforts to assist them. Leave the poor to fend for themselves in the marketplace, and they will be the better for it, conservatives contend. Two decades of hyperbole have left liberals treating "work" as if it were a four-letter epithet, just as conservatives have come to understand "help." Such polarization glorifies argument, the grist of pundits and policy wonks, but denies the complexity and nuance—the reality, if you will—of welfare and its relationship to poverty.

A superficial reading of welfare reform has been that work-mandates quite literally work—*period*. However easily it glides from the tongues of politicians, this is an oversimplification. Ultimately, welfare reform must contend with three exigencies if it is to enjoy long-term success.

First, liberals must acknowledge the amount of social debris generated during the past half-century by welfare. In their defense of social programs that have been savaged by conservatives, liberals have been unwilling to concede the damage associated with public welfare. After the appearance of Daniel Patrick Moynihan's report on the black family, as William Julius Wilson has pointed out, it was politically incorrect for academics to investigate the pathological impacts of chronic poverty because of their racial implications.[6] In the absence of social scientific research on the matter, during the 1970s and 1980s conservative ideologues enjoyed an open field of inquiry, producing an abundance of ideological tracts explicating the evils of welfarism. Despite the obvious motives behind conservative diatribes about welfare, social scientists with rare exceptions failed to conduct basic research on the problem—the experiences of recipients, the influences on their children, the behavior of welfare caseworkers, the perceptions of the public. Had they done so, the disastrous social, economic, and political consequences of cash assistance to the poor would have become obvious, and corrective action might have been undertaken. But this was not to be. Still pre-occupied with a "war against the poor" waged by the right,[7] liberally inclined academics remain reluctant to critically examine welfare and its metastases.

Second, conservatives must be willing to acknowledge the limitations of the low-wage labor market. Requiring welfare mothers to work makes for resonant political rhetoric, but it also precipitates a host of problems. Of immediate concern is the adequacy of wages. To the present discussion of welfare-to-work "transitional benefits"—Medicaid, childcare, and transportation—must be added the continuation of wage subsidies and benefits for the welfare- as well as the working-poor. "Making work pay" entails a fully elaborated array of work-related supports; conservatives must accept that the inception of the "work ethic state" warrants the appropriations to make this a constructive reality.[8] A related matter is the impact of welfare-mandated work on family life. Work may elevate the self-esteem of mothers long dependent on the dole, or it may overwhelm mothers who have to manage children at home, coordinate childcare and school, and then surpass a first employer's expectations in order to get a decent job paying wages that will ensure economic independence. Evidence of family stress is already apparent. "Child-only" cases have skyrocketed—instances in which the child remains eligible for aid after the mother is removed from the grant; because of the ensuing hardship, many child-only cases are children being cared for by adults other than their parents. Many families—perhaps one in four—simply disappear from the rolls after welfare is terminated because of a mother's noncompliance with welfare reform.[9] Virtually ignored in the current execution of welfare reform is the situation of black men who are out of work. If African American males are already institutionalized in disproportionate numbers, the increasing self-sufficiency of black mothers as a result of welfare reform will surely aggravate male marginalization. Irrelevant to family life, save for procreation, minority males will be left to drift into the netherworld of the underclass.[10] The only way to prevent this is to make work as meaningful, adequate, and accessible for men as it is for women.

Finally, ideologues of both camps should move beyond the significant yet modest outcomes of "welfare-to-work" and recognize that upward mobility must be accelerated for both individuals and communities.[11] The success of welfare reform, in other words, must not be gauged simply by caseload reduction, but by poverty alleviation. By devolving welfare to the states, the 1996 Personal Responsibility and Work Opportunity Reconciliation Act (PRWORA) offers wide latitude in program innovation toward this end, yet many opportunities have been lost because of ideologically induced myopia. Welfare advocates have charged that devolution is a diabolical plot to gut social programs; if this is so, it is a devilishly opportune one. For example, federal welfare reform makes provision for Individual Development Ac-

counts (IDAs), and the Assets for Independence Act makes modest appropriations for IDAs, both of which encourage the poor to accrue assets,
thereby boosting their upward mobility.[12] The aggregate effect of individual
initiative can be multiplied through community regeneration. In several
locations across the nation, Community Development Financial Institutions (CDFIs) have been deployed to provide financial services to the poor
while simultaneously capitalizing community revitalization. Optimally, such
CDFIs would replace the deadening welfare bureaucracy that has become
so perversely proficient at stunting families and their neighborhoods.

In the best of all postwelfare worlds, wage subsidies, asset building, and
community capitalism would serve as the template for a new poverty policy,
"bootstrap capitalism." Such a policy is consistent with the work ethic, would
reinforce community institutions, and unlike welfare, is resonant with the
American credo. What's more, the money to put it in place is there.[13] Since
the establishment of the budget baseline for the new welfare block grants,
caseload reductions have created an anticipated "surplus" of $9 billion annu-
ally until 2002.[14] On an annual basis, this is roughly equivalent to the total
five-year appropriation for welfare reform the last time it was undertaken in
1988 through the Family Support Act. This "surplus," in other words, could
be invested in an innovative set of initiatives that would become an alternative to welfare as it is now known. The replacement of discredited welfare
with a dynamic poverty policy is in the best tradition of American social policy, as evident in Social Security and the GI Bill. The only impediment remaining would appear to be not the destitution of the poor, but rather a
poverty of our imagination.

WELFARE AS WE KNEW IT

Welfare has been anything but a tidy program. Rather, "welfare" is an um-
brella label covering an entire collection of governmental ventures. The eligibility requirements, the reporting procedures, and the changing provisions
of welfare are the stuff of bureaucratic legend: few emerge unscathed from
the welfare swamp. The following overview highlights some prominent features of welfare as a social institution.

THE VOLUNTARY SECTOR

Welfare is not the same thing as charity. Voluntary efforts to aid the destitute
have been a tradition in the United States since the colonial era. In the nineteenth century, the social and economic dislocations that accompanied industrialization, urbanization, and immigration inspired upstanding citizens
to organize a charitable response. By 1900 virtually every metropolitan area

boasted a Charity Organization Society (COS) through which "friendly visitors" encouraged the socialization of the immigrant poor. These agents of the COS were well-educated women who acted out of a sense of *noblesse oblige,* providing moral guidance to the disadvantaged. Granting tangible assistance was frowned upon, as this subverted self-sufficiency. Indeed, the credo of the friendly visitors—"not alms, but a friend"—underlies the admonition of Josephine Shaw Lowell, director of the New York Aid Society: "Human nature is so constituted that no man can receive as a gift what he should earn by his own labor without a moral deterioration. No human being will work to provide the means of living for himself if he can get a living in any other manner agreeable to himself."[15] In addition to institutionalizing stinginess, the COS introduced a caricature that has populated American culture ever since: the friendly visitor was transmogrified into the social worker as busybody, a little old lady in sneakers with little to do but intrude upon the privacy of others.

During the early decades of the nineteenth century, the very idea of charity came under assault from Social Darwinists, who contended that social inferiors could be bloodlessly expunged by virtue of *laissez-faire* economics as well as the more sinister practices of the eugenics movement. H. L. Mencken offered this venomous judgment of COS work from a Social Darwinist perspective:

> The social worker, judging by her own pretensions, helps to preserve the multitudes of persons who would perish if left to themselves. Thus her work is clearly dysgenic and anti-social. For every victim of sheer misfortune that she restores to self-sustaining and social usefulness, she must keep alive scores of misfits and incompetents who can never, for all her help, pull their weight in the boat. Such persons can do nothing more valuable than dying.[16]

Professional condescension and Social Darwinism notwithstanding, COSs became enduring fixtures in American cities during the Progressive era. Indeed, their proliferation led more rationally minded managers to suggest systematic organization of their activities. Beginning in Denver in 1887, nonprofit service organizations consolidated their fundraising efforts, a precursor to the United Ways of today.[17] The Progressive penchant for efficiency resulted in a standardization of structure, policies, and services that still influences United Way member organizations.

Highly decentralized, community-oriented, and often semiprofessional, nonprofit social agencies still tend to provide services to the disadvantaged, as opposed to material assistance. Shelter and meals may be offered directly to the homeless, but the provision of cash by a nonprofit agency is a rarity, echoing the friendly visitors' fear of inducing dependence in the poor. Providing money, as nonprofit agency personnel understand, is not a social service—it is "welfare," the responsibility of the state.

Although charitable organizations have traditionally avoided doling out welfare, there has recently been much speculation about the extent to which they can shoulder the government's poverty burden. With annual budgets totaling $65.2 billion in 1996, nonprofit legal and social services were a fixture of the American welfare state,[18] a fact that was not missed by ideologues of the right, who suggested that the private, voluntary sector could replace government social programs.[19] "The crisis of the modern welfare state is not just a crisis of government," the conservative journalist and policy maven Marvin Olasky contended. "The more effective provision of social services will ultimately depend on their return to private and especially religious institutions."[20] Olasky's anti-welfare-state rhetoric attracted the attention of leading conservatives, such as George W. Bush and Newt Gingrich, as well as right-wing intellectual institutions, including the Heritage Foundation and the Progress and Freedom Foundation. "Private charities had succeeded in helping many individuals because they offered compassion that was challenging, personal, and spiritually based," Olasky restated in his update of *The Tragedy of American Compassion.* "Government over time proved itself incapable of doing the same; instead, governmental charity emphasized entitlement rather than challenge, bureaucracy rather than personal help, and a reduction of man to material being only."[21] Yet scholars of the voluntary sector, such as Lester Salamon, have been more skeptical about Olasky's proposal to replace the government safety net with nonprofit ventures. Assessing changes in federal support for nonprofit social service agencies since the advent of the Reagan presidency, Salamon computed a 40 percent reduction between 1980 and 1986.[22] Increases in contributions to nonprofit social service agencies failed to compensate for this massive cut.

The relationship among the primary welfare institutions—the family, government, and the voluntary sector—was explored by Rebecca Blank, who concluded that neither the family nor the voluntary sector can compensate for cuts in governmental welfare.

> Overall, no estimate of the discouraging effect of government dollars on private spending comes close to suggesting that decreases in public spending on public assistance programs will be offset by equivalent increases in family-based or voluntary charitable contributions. If government spending on the poor declines, any resulting increase in private support will make up only a small fraction of the loss of government dollars.[23]

Perhaps the best test of the social carrying capacity of the nonprofit sector was a set of initiatives undertaken by the Bush and Clinton administrations.

President Bush's "Points of Light" initiative illuminated the good works of innovative voluntary sector agencies across the nation. In the spring of 1997, former General Colin Powell, on behalf of the Clinton administration, convened thousands of volunteers in Philadelphia in order to kick off "America's Promise," an effort to enlist the corporate and civic sectors to become more involved with the poor. Despite the attendance of three presidents, half the Clinton cabinet, 30 governors, and dozens of CEOs, a review of project activities a year later was disappointing. Although summits had been convened in more than a dozen states, relatively few new volunteers had come forth. In Philadelphia, for example, 120,000 mentors had been sought for poor children, but a year after the America's Promise event, only 12,000 had stepped forward. Reports from other cities were similarly discouraging.[24] Spokespersons from America's Promise countered that more than 200 volunteer initiatives had sprung up since the 1997 summit and that Big Brothers and Big Sisters experienced a 22 percent increase in volunteers during the interim,[25] but these achievements are short of the revolution in mentoring that Powell had envisioned.

THE GOVERNMENTAL SECTOR

During the colonial period, the destitute poor were auctioned off to those in the community who might offer them room and board in exchange for work. The contract system, arguably adequate for an agricultural society, was strained by economic downswings and increasing immigration. Outsiders were urged to move along so as not to become long-term dependents, a precursor to the residency requirements for receipt of welfare that resurface periodically in discussions of welfare reform. Eventually, local governments established almshouses or poorhouses, buildings that sheltered the able-bodied poor and required them to work for aid provided. "Poorhouse" had a derogatory connotation, sufficiently uninviting to repel any but the most acutely destitute. Michael Katz, the historian of poor relief, noted that almshouses lacked the rudiments of sanitation, privacy, and resident selection. Disease was rampant, and death its frequent companion. "With almost no classification of their inmates, men and women mingled freely during the day and, even, at night. As a result, many of the births in poorhouses were 'the offspring of illicit connections.'"[26] If nothing else, the poorhouse stigmatized the receipt of public aid, at least for the able-bodied. In contrast to residents of the poorhouse, the "worthy poor"—those not considered able-bodied, such as pregnant women, widows, and the disabled—were not expected to work and were therefore entitled to modest allowances in their own homes ("indoor relief"). Given the punitive nature of the poorhouse, the discriminations between the able-bodied and the worthy poor made by local welfare officials had serious consequences.

The poorhouse as a social institution collapsed under the weight of the Great Depression. In the waning years of the Hoover administration, unemployment ballooned to 25 percent nationally, and exceeded 60 percent in some places. Growing labor militancy raised the specter of civil strife, as heralded by the rapidly increasing popularity of the Industrial Workers of the World. Immediately upon assuming office, President Franklin Delano Roosevelt brought Harry Hopkins from New York to Washington, D.C., to manage a series of public works programs. Having lived in a Settlement House, Hopkins was a social worker of a different stripe than the COS friendly visitors. For Hopkins the New Deal was a tableau of social and economic justice. He coined the phrase that operationalized the interactive formula of programs and voters that defined liberal hegemony in social affairs: "tax, tax; spend, spend; elect, elect." Tax the rich, redistribute the derived revenue to the working- and welfare-poor through social programs, and depend on the beneficiaries to vote Democratic. For a half-century they did.

The political economy stabilized through massive public works programs, Roosevelt and his lieutenants institutionalized these fledgling programs through the Social Security Act, which, among other things, announced federal dominance in social policy. The Social Security Act of 1935 introduced the American welfare state through two types of programs: "social insurance" and "public assistance." Social insurance was modeled after private insurance programs, requiring prepayment in order to receive benefits; the difference was that public participation was mandated. The primary social insurance programs are Social Security, Medicare, and Unemployment Compensation. In contrast, public assistance or "welfare" relied on public revenues and instituted a morals test as well as a "means test"—low income and negligible assets. As Linda Gordon noted, the more ample social insurance programs were designed for male workers; the inferior public assistance program, for women and their dependents.[27] The dominance of social insurance is evident in table 1.1, which presents allocations in dollars and as a percentage of gross domestic product. By the mid-1990s, social insurance consumed almost half of all social program expenditures, exceeding public assistance—"welfare"—by a factor of three.

During the recent past the prominent public assistance programs have been Aid to Families with Dependent Children (AFDC; since 1996, Temporary Assistance for Needy Families), Medicaid, Food Stamps, and Supplemental Security Income (SSI). Recent allocations for these programs are indicated in table 1.2. Tables 1.1 and 1.2 show why discussions of welfare are

Table 1.1   Gross Domestic Product and Social Welfare Expenditures (in billions)

	1965	1970	1975	1980	1985	1990	1994
Gross domestic product	$701	$1,023	$1,590	$2,719	$4,108	$5,683	$6,832
Social expenditures							
Total	77	146	289	492	732	1,049	1,435
Social insurance	28	55	123	230	370	514	684
Public assistance	6	16	41	73	98	147	238
Health and medical							
care	6	10	16	27	39	62	79
Veterans' programs	6	9	17	21	27	31	37
Education	28	51	81	121	172	258	344
Housing	0.3	0.7	3	7	13	19	27
Other	2	4	7	14	14	18	25
Social expenditures as percent of GDP							
Total	11.0	14.3	18.2	18.1	17.8	18.5	21.0
Social insurance	4.0	5.3	7.7	8.5	9.0	9.0	10.0
Public assistance	0.9	1.6	2.6	2.7	2.4	2.6	3.5
Health and medical							
care	0.9	1.0	1.0	1.0	0.9	1.1	1.2
Veterans' programs	0.9	0.9	1.1	0.8	0.7	0.5	0.6
Education	4.0	5.0	5.1	4.5	4.2	4.5	5.0
Housing	0.0	0.1	0.2	0.3	0.3	0.3	0.4
Other	0.3	0.4	0.4	0.5	0.3	0.3	0.4

Note: Totals may not match sum of subtotals because of rounding.
Source: Social Security Bulletin, Annual Statistical Supplement (Washington, D.C.: GPO, 1997).

Table 1.2   Expenditures for Major Public Assistance Programs (in billions)

Program	1970	1975	1980	1985	1990	1995	1996
AFDC	$16.4	$23.8	$21.8	$20.7	$21.8	$22.0	$20.4[a]
Medicaid	—	12.6	28.5	40.9	72.5	156.4	162.0
Food Stamps	—	—	9.6	13.5	17.7	27.4	27.3
SSI	—	—	7.9	11.1	16.6	27.0	28.3

[a] Replaced by Temporary Assistance for Needy Families in 1996.
Source: Committee on Ways and Means, House of Representatives, *Overview of Entitlement Programs* (Washington, D.C.: GPO, 1996); Committee on Ways and Means, House of Representatives, *Overview of Entitlement Programs* (Washington, D.C.: GPO, 1998).

so confusing. While the largest public assistance programs account for 97 percent of welfare expenditures, there are many, many smaller programs. A 1994 inventory of social programs revealed 336 operating under eight program domains.[28] Such expansion led conservatives like James Q. Wilson to speculate about the implications of so many poverty programs and observe that in 1992 poverty programs spent "$5,600 for every man, woman, and child in the lowest fifth of the nation's income ladder."[29] Similarly, the Cato

Institute contended that optimal exploitation of means-tested benefits in several localities resulted in an annual income equivalent to that derived from a $25,000 job;[30] the state benefits ranged from $36,400 in Hawaii to $11,500 in Mississippi.[31] Furthermore, of the four largest public assistance programs, only the smallest, AFDC, has come to be understood as "welfare," even though Medicaid, Food Stamps, and SSI are also public assistance programs. Thus, in the debate about welfare reform, conservatives have rightly complained about the seemingly endless multiplication of means-tested programs, and liberals have noted that the relatively minor AFDC program takes up only one percent of the federal budget.

Note that virtually all of the government social programs listed in table 1.1 are open-ended entitlements, meaning that the Treasury will make benefit allocations regardless of the implications for the federal budget. Since the social insurance programs are self-financing (at least ideally), the fiscal burden of open-ended entitlements falls most directly on the public assistance programs. Conservatives have complained bitterly about entitlement spending, and they have discovered how difficult it is to rein in poverty programs. As table 1.1 shows, the expansion of public assistance programs slowed only slightly during the Reagan years; after the 1980s, it started to climb once again. The optimal solution to this problem—one that liberals oppose, of course—is to convert open-ended entitlements to discretionary programs, for which the appropriations have to be determined every year in an amount that cannot be exceeded. The most recent conversion of a welfare entitlement is the replacement of AFDC with the TANF block grant, which is devolved to the states. In many ways, this transformation accurately reflected President Clinton's promise to "end welfare as we know it" insofar as it terminated the open-ended public assistance entitlement to poor families. Among the features of the PRWORA that most infuriated liberals was the proposed appropriation: $16.4 billion annually, identical to the program allocation for AFDC in 1970![32]

In addition to cash and in-kind public assistance benefits, a variety of social services are associated with public welfare. Often these focus on child welfare, and because care of children is a prominent concern in welfare reform, these programmatic supports must be acknowledged. The oldest of these is child welfare, which originated in Title IV of the 1935 Social Security Act, and covers foster care, adoption assistance, independent living for youths reaching the age of majority, and child protection. In 1996, federal funding for child welfare totaled $4.1 billion. Augmenting this funding is the Title XX Social Services Block Grant, which provides states and localities with monies they can use for a wide range of activities. Capped at $2.5 billion in 1974, Title XX declined 67 percent in value thereafter.[33] Since the 1988 Family Support Act, child care has been available for a year after a welfare recipi-

15

ent obtains private sector employment; in 1996, $1.1 billion was appropriated for this purpose. Finally, $3.1 billion is allocated for child support enforcement in order to obtain income from absent parents. Federal funding for children's programs relating to welfare reform thus totals $14.8 billion, though this almost certainly is an underestimate. The absence of reporting requirements leaves federal funding for children in the fiscal twilight. For example, an exhaustive inventory of child welfare spending under Title IV alone indicates state and federal allocations of $14.4 billion.[34] Altogether, annual allocations for child welfare probably approximate $20 billion.

Welfare reform, then, has become a term of some political convenience. If welfare includes the means-tested public assistance programs, true welfare reform would by definition incorporate these. To be sure, some conservatives have advocated this, but they have encountered stiff resistance: Medicaid is defended by the elderly and the nursing home business; Food Stamps have a strong lobby within the agriculture industry; SSI is protected by the disabled. Since AFDC is an income support program for poor families, most of its beneficiaries have been disadvantaged children, who are disproportionately minorities. Thus, the weakest welfare program has been reformed. With respect to the federal budget, the implications verge on the minuscule. Welfare reform, in this regard, has been much ado about very little. As will be explored in later chapters, the consequences for the states and welfare recipients have been anything but minor.

THE COMMERCIAL SECTOR

During the past three decades, welfare has become big business. The commercialization of public assistance programs can be fairly dated to 1965 and the enactment of Medicare and Medicaid. Rather than deploy a Veterans Administration-type health care system for the elderly and poor, these health care amendments to the Social Security Act promised to reimburse private providers. In effect, government health care programs introduced ideal market conditions, and investors with proprietary interests responded promptly. Within a decade the nursing home industry was dominated by a handful of firms. The most prominent of these was Beverly Enterprises, which controlled patient beds that numbered in the tens of thousands. Soon other markets evolved. Hospital management came under the control of what is now Columbia/HCA, the largest health corporation in the world. Passage of the Health Maintenance Organization Act of 1973 provided incentives for proprietary firms to enter the burgeoning managed care industry. Having exhausted the pool of private insurees, HMOs began to aggressively pursue Medicaid recipients, banking on their proven ability to undercut the costs of traditional fee-for-service health care providers. Commercial interests also exploited other markets related to low-income consumers, including child-care and (improbably) corrections.[35]

The scale of firms exploiting social markets is astonishing. Columbia/HCA claims more than 130,000 employees. CIGNA, the second-largest health care corporation, employs only 44,700 workers but boasts the capital of an insurance giant. For 1995, each of the top eight health and human service corporations reported annual revenues greater than the total contributions to all of the United Ways in America. And there seems to be no end to their expansion. In 1985, 66 for-profit firms reported annual revenues of at least $10 million; by 1992, the number had virtually doubled to 121.[36]

Even cash payments to the poor have become subject to corporate exploitation. The Treasury requirement that all federal benefits be electronically deposited by 1999 has diverted tens of billions of dollars to commercial banks. The largest firm in the Electronic Benefit Transfer (EBT) market is Citibank, which has already corralled over $110 billion in deposits. In order to achieve the greater efficiencies that are afforded by the technology, states are eagerly negotiating contracts with EBT firms for welfare benefits. Under EBT, welfare beneficiaries are given an Automatic Teller Card with a magnetic strip encoded to access their account; Food Stamp benefits are also encoded, but accessed through Point of Purchase scanners that automatically separate legitimate food purchases from ineligible items. As the formal banking sector exploits EBT, a "fringe banking" industry has expanded to provide services to the poor. Consisting of pawnshops and check-cashing outlets (CCOs), fringe banking has enjoyed explosive growth in poor neighborhoods, moving in as more established banks withdraw in search of bigger profits in other markets. In many poor neighborhoods, fringe banks offer the only convenient financial service available; thus, CCOs are able to charge excessive rates for limited services because they serve a captive clientele.[37]

As the experience of the nonprofit and commercial sectors instructs, welfare has become more than a government responsibility. Viewed on a larger canvas, this makes sense. Since the Second World War, the American economy has progressively shifted from heavy manufacturing to services, of which finance and retirement, education and training, health (including mental health) and physical care are central. As the demand for services has increased, public willingness to vest this responsibility with government has ebbed, contributing to a conservative vector in domestic policy. Add to the above a technological revolution that has vastly expedited the computation and transmission of data, the processing of which would have been inconceivable a generation ago. Finally, factor in the future demands of baby-boomers, a cohort that will insist on social and income security comparable to that enjoyed by their parents. The result is a dynamic human service sector that is expanding far beyond the parameters imposed by an industrial-era definition of welfare. Yet the implications of this transformation for public welfare have been largely unexplored.

THE UNDERCLASS

Programmatic welfare existed in a context of deteriorating opportunity for the poor, the severity of which is captured by the term "underclass."[38] During the half-century following the 1935 Social Security Act, significant changes occurred in the social, political, and economic circumstances of low-income families. Eventually, these overwhelmed welfare and brought it into disrepute. Public assistance to poor mothers, once a pillar of social progress, became associated with an increasingly intransigent poverty that it had been designed to ameliorate.

During the 1970s and early 1980s, substantial shifts in demography and capital affected urban America. Millions of Americans abandoned older industrial cities for the suburbs and the Sunbelt. The population loss of several older American cities exceeded one-fifth: between 1970 and 1984, St. Louis lost 31.0 percent of its population, Detroit 17.9 percent, Cleveland 27.2 percent, Buffalo 26.8 percent, and Pittsburgh 22.6 percent.[39] Residents left behind in older cities tended to be minorities. Accordingly, between 1975 and 1985 the minority population of northeastern cities increased from 33 to 42 percent.[40]

As the white population fled industrial urban areas, the economic base of America's cities changed dramatically. Blue-collar jobs requiring less education vanished and were replaced by those of the information and service sectors. This penalized particularly the unskilled and poorly educated minority population left behind in the Rustbelt. As John Kasarda concluded,

> Unfortunately, the northern cities that have lost the greatest numbers of jobs with lower educational requisites during the past three decades have simultaneously experienced large increases in the number of their minority residents, many of whom are workers whose limited educations preclude their employment in the new urban growth industries.[41]

The loss of better-paying jobs was, of course, felt most in those industrial cities that had prospered most during the latter half of the nineteenth century and the first half of the twentieth. "In the twenty-year period from 1967 to 1987, Philadelphia lost 64 percent of its manufacturing jobs; Chicago lost 60 percent; New York City, 58 percent; Detroit, 51 percent," noted William Julius Wilson. "In absolute numbers, these percentages represent the loss of 160,000 jobs in Philadelphia, 326,000 in Chicago, 520,000—over half a million—in New York, and 108,000 in Detroit."[42] As employers fled the inner city, the commercial sector that not only provided services, but also served as the foundation for the local tax base, imploded. In North Lawndale on Chicago's West Side, a population of 66,000 had a limited menu from which to access consumer goods: one supermarket, one bank, 48 lottery outlets, 50 check-cashing stores, and 99 liquor stores.[43]

The impact of entrenched poverty on minority youngsters would be indelible. "Children who lived in poverty for four or five years had IQ points lower than children who had never lived below the poverty line in their first five years."[44] Moreover, poverty was a primary contributor to physical stunting among poor children.[45] Such deficits are detrimental to school performance, concluded educational researchers: "poverty was negatively related to high school graduation, college attendance, and years of schooling obtained."[46] School is apt to be a frustrating experience for disadvantaged children, resulting in serious behavioral problems. "As early as kindergarten there are children displaying clear symptoms of chronic aggressive behavior," observed Kenneth Dodge, director of Duke University's Child Policy Center. "We know from experience that these kids—especially if they are poor—will grow up to be adolescent behavior problems."[47]

Historically, accumulated knowledge and behavior deficits have made poor youths weak competitors in the labor market. Kasarda examined the plight of poorly skilled inner-city residents in a market where many jobs had migrated to the suburbs. As table 1.3 shows, the consequences of poor education for urban residents varied considerably by race. During the past three decades, the employment prospects of black male dropouts plummeted, a drop exceeding 50 percent in every region of the United States. Yet a high school diploma was no guarantee of a job for young African Americans, either; between 1974 and 1995, the proportion of black high school dropouts who worked full-time fell from 68 to 46 percent, while their incomes plunged 43 percent.[48]

Moreover, the plight of young minority males was but one indicator of the deterioration of urban America. In his review of metropolitan poverty, Paul Jargowsky charted the magnitude of the damage that had occurred between 1970 and 1990: a more than twofold increase in the number of high-poverty communities and an increase in the number of their residents from 4.1 to 8.0 million.[49] Douglas Massey and Nancy Denton labeled the concentration of poor minorities in urban neighborhoods "hypersegregation"[50] and went so far as to suggest a recipe for creating an underclass—replicate the experiences of blacks in the United States:

> Throughout U.S. history, the wealthy of all groups have sought to put distance between themselves and the poor. As their levels of education, income, and occupational statuses have risen, Jews, Italians, Poles, Mexicans, and Asians have all sought improved housing in better neighborhoods not dominated by their own ethnic group. What distinguishes blacks from everyone else is that this process of normal spatial mobility occurs within a segregated housing market. As a

Table 1.3   Out-of-School Males Aged 16–64 Not Working and Residing in the Central City,
by Race, Education, and Region for Selected Metropolitan Areas

	1968–70	1980–82	1990–92
Northeast			
White			
Less than high school	15	34	37
High school graduate only[a]	7	17	24
Black			
Less than high school	19	44	57
High school graduate only	11	27	31
Midwest			
White			
Less than high school	12	29	34
High school graduate only	5	16	18
Black			
Less than high school	24	52	63
High school graduate only	10	30	41
South			
White			
Less than high school	7	15	18
High school graduate only	3	9	19
Black			
Less than high school	13	29	52
High school graduate only	1	19	22
West			
White			
Less than high school	18	20	26
High school graduate only	10	16	19
Black			
Less than high school	26	44	57
High school graduate only	13	14	43

Note: Northeast includes Boston, Newark, New York, Philadelphia, and Pittsburgh; Midwest
includes Cleveland, Chicago, Detroit, Milwaukee, and St. Louis; South includes Atlanta,
Dallas, Houston, Miami, and New Orleans; West includes Denver, Long Beach, Los Angeles,
Oakland, Phoenix, San Francisco, and Seattle.
[a] Completed high school, but no higher education.
Source: John Kasarda, "Industrial Restructuring and the Consequences of Changing Job
Locations," in Reynolds Farley, ed., *Changes and Challenges: America 1990* (New York:
Russell Sage Foundation, 1995), table 5.15.

result of racial segregation, middle-class blacks are less able to achieve a neighborhood commensurate with their socioeconomic status, and poor blacks are
forced to live under conditions of unparalleled poverty.[51]

In no small irony, the Eisenhower Foundation marked the twenty-fifth anni-
versary of the Kerner Commission report with an admonition: "We conclude
that the famous prophecy of the Kerner Commission, of two societies, one
black, one white—separate and unequal—is more relevant today than in

1968, and more complex, with the emergence of multiracial disparities and growing income segregation."[52]

The response of the Reagan and Bush administrations exacerbated these forces. Federal grants to cities declined sharply during the Reagan administration. In the years immediately preceding the Reagan Revolution, federal urban aid had increased dramatically; between 1975 and 1980, federal aid to subordinate levels of government for community development block grants ballooned from $38 million to $3.9 billion. Toward the end of the second Reagan term, however, federal aid to the cities actually declined—$3.3 billion by 1987. Similarly, the federal contribution for community services block grants decreased from $557 million in 1980 to $354 million in 1986.[53] The House Ways and Means Committee reported that "for HUD's programs alone, appropriations of budget authority declined (in 1989 dollars) from a high of $57 billion in 1978 to a low of $9 billion in 1989."[54] The Bush administration budget for 1991 proposed to further reduce federal assistance for low-income housing by 4.2 percent. For the same year, federal allocations for community development block grants dropped to $2.7 billion, and federal support for community services block grants plummeted to $42 million.[55]

Welfare benefits were also pared during the 1980s. Within seven months of assuming office, President Reagan showed his hand in poverty policy by signing the Omnibus Budget Reconciliation Act (OBRA) of 1981. The new AFDC eligibility guidelines established by OBRA were particularly punitive, since they were directed at poor families who were participating in the labor force. Suddenly, AFDC family heads who were trying to improve their economic lot found that (1) they could deduct only $160 per month per child for childcare, (2) the deduction for work expenses was limited to $75 per month, and (3) the earned income disregard (the first $30 per month and one-third of income thereafter) was eliminated after four months.[56] As if to strangle the welfare bureaucracy in paperwork, OBRA required the welfare department to redetermine monthly the eligibility of those on AFDC who insisted on working. These, among other measures, had an immediate impact on the AFDC rolls: 408,000 families lost eligibility altogether, and another 299,000 had their benefits reduced.[57] Significantly, OBRA disentitled working-poor families; 5 percent of the total AFDC caseload became ineligible due to OBRA, and "about 35 percent of those who were working were terminated by the legislation."[58] Contrary to the welfare reform enacted in 1988 through the Family Support Act, which encouraged adults on public assistance to work, the 1981 OBRA harshly penalized welfare families with an adult participating in the labor market.

Thus, the 1980s were particularly punishing for poor families; the erosion of family income for the working-poor seemed almost benign compared with other, more pernicious indicators of social degradation. The incomes of more prosperous families, those with a full-time worker, stagnated or fell during the decade. "By 1989, in fact, half of all household heads who worked full-time that year and were employed in 1979 either still worked for less than an adequate wage or sustained a real decline in their wage," noted the political scientist John Schwarz.[59] Rapidly declining opportunities for minority youths were expressed by sharply increasing rates of unwed births on the part of young women and drug arrests for young men. In 1980 the rate of unwed births for black women aged 15 to 44 (81.1 per 1,000 unmarried women) was four times that of whites (18.1); even in the early 1990s, the black rate remained more than double that of white women. Between 1960 and 1995, the number of black female-headed households more than tripled, and the children in single-parent households in which the adult had never married increased by a factor of 19.[60] Each year about $22 billion is expended in welfare benefits on women who were or are teen parents.[61]

Among young minority males, in the absence of legitimate ways to earn income, illicit drugs became not only a source of money, but also a symbol of oppositional culture. Jerome Miller noted that "as the drug war expanded, arrests of black youths surged from 683 per 100,000 in 1985 to 1,200 per 100,000—nearly five times the white rate—by 1989. By 1991, the rate for black juveniles was at 1,415 per 100,000."[62] This disparity in arrest rates was also evident with respect to incarceration. In 1991, the incarceration rate of white males was 352 per 100,000; for black males aged 25 to 29, it was 6,301 per 100,000.[63] The consequences were, of course, registered most directly in poorer cities.

> On an average day in 1991, more than four in ten (42%) of all the 18–35-year-old African-American males who lived in the District of Columbia were in jail, in prison, on probation/parole, or being sought on arrest warrants; on an average day in Baltimore, 56% of all its young African-American males were in prison, jail, on probation/parole, on bail, or being sought on arrest.[64]

Moreover, employment is often precluded by an arrest record. This fact was not lost on black youth. An oppositional subculture—replete with gangs, rap music, and a cultivated defiance of traditional authority—became an integral part of urban America.

Reflecting the bleak prospects for poor minority youth, these deviant career paths—public welfare for young women, drug trafficking for young men—complemented one another. As Donna Franklin observed, "The increasing reliance on welfare by young black mothers corresponded to the erosion of opportunities for young black males."[65] The policy response to these groups—enhanced opportunities for young mothers through welfare reform, incarceration of young men in new correctional institutions—is arguably the most poignant contradiction of the contemporary American welfare state.

MERTON'S CONSTANT

The interaction of public assistance and the underclass debased welfare as that institution had been understood. Indeed, the motives and behaviors of welfare administrators, advocates of social justice, and human service professionals were, in the process, contorted to the point of tragicomedy. The corruption of institutional welfare vis-à-vis the underclass parallels the deviancy thesis proposed by Robert Merton. In his classic paper, "Social Structure and Anomie," Merton proposed that society invited deviancy when structures frustrated the aspirations of its members. The interaction between "cultural goals" and "institutionalized means" in a relatively open society afforded a variety of types of responses, ranging from conformity to rebellion. Merton was enough of a realist to recognize that poverty exacerbated frustrations— "the greatest pressures toward deviation are exerted upon the lower strata"[66] —and that the poor often resorted to "illicit means" when "legitimate" strategies were not successful. The struggles of parents to reconcile social norms with available means are not lost on their children, of course. Over time, alienation is institutionalized in a manner that is contrary to traditional norms, and "cultural chaos supervenes."[67]

Failing to adjust to newer manifestations of poverty, public welfare became increasingly untenable and ultimately corrupt as its liberal defenders, chafing under the conservatism that had asserted control of social policy, attempted to maintain it. Eventually, liberal reluctance to reform welfare contributed to its association with underclass deviancy. The nature of this reciprocal process may be labeled "Merton's constant": in the absence of legitimate institutional supports, the poor will deviate from conventional norms, inventing opportunities and exploiting resources illegitimately in order to survive. In this instance, as the value of welfare benefits deteriorated, poor, disproportionately minority young adults resorted to deviant behavior—unwed pregnancy and drug trafficking—in order to survive. Thus, the integrity of a social institution tends to mirror that of the population it is designed to serve. The perversion of one engenders depravity in the other. In the case of welfare, however, discussions of reform have focused on the recipients; apart from pushing mothers into the labor market through "welfare reform," virtually no thought has been given to restructuring the welfare bureaucracy. Most insidiously, however, the welfare-poor are driven to the informal sector, essentially required to engage in illegal behaviors in order to make ends meet; and once they are enmeshed in such activities, return to the formal economy becomes increasingly difficult.

Exactly how perverse welfare had become is evident in many ways. Fundamentally, the nature of the families served changed. Under Title IV of the Social Security Act, aid for poor children was intended for their widowed mothers. As of 1970, widows accounted for no more than 5.0 percent of AFDC families; by 1994, the proportion of widows was down to 1.7 percent.[68] Moreover, while AFDC continued as a family program that unconditionally assured benefits to poor mothers, less disadvantaged women were moving in droves into the labor market. Between 1951 (the earliest date for the following data) and 1995, the number of married women in the labor market increased from 19.8 to 47.0 percent, while the number of single working mothers increased from 9.9 percent to 18.0 percent.[69] Despite these demographic shifts, AFDC remained basically unaltered for a half-century after its inception.

During the 1980s the integrity of welfare was strained beyond its institutional parameters. Because benefits were established by states that did not index them for inflation, the value of benefits, which were never particularly generous, eroded substantially (table 1.4). Clearly, states vary considerably in their generosity toward poor families, ranging from Alaska's payment of $923 monthly to Mississippi's $120. Such variation has led some critics to suggest that welfare families migrate from lower-benefit to higher-benefit states, but to date there is no evidence that welfare families from Mississippi are invading Alaska. AFDC payments for 15 states were lower than Food Stamp benefits, a good indication of state stinginess. Consequently, federal Food Stamp benefits tended to compensate for low AFDC benefits. This occurred because states were required to front about one-half of AFDC benefits, with the federal government covering the remainder, while Food Stamp benefits, completely funded by the federal government, were higher at lower AFDC levels. Hence a substantial portion of welfare benefits were federal revenues. Note also that between 1970 and 1996, the real value of AFDC benefits declined on average 51 percent. In other words, the welfare mother of the early 1990s was getting half the cash of a welfare mother a generation earlier.

As a result of low and deteriorating benefit levels, welfare mothers followed Merton's constant: given the choice between playing Mother Courage and conning the welfare department, they elected the latter. The result was fraud on a major scale. Lacking cash for necessities, by the end of the month many welfare mothers illegally sold their remaining Food Stamp coupons at a discount, often 50 percent. A burgeoning black market in Food Stamps was an embarrassment to the Agriculture Department, which operated the program, although federal officials preferred to downplay the problem. In

Table 1.4   AFDC and Food Stamp Benefits for a Three-Person Household, January 1996

State	Maximum AFDC Grant	Food Stamp Benefit	Combined Benefits	Combined Benefits as % of Poverty Level	AFDC Change in Real Value 1970–76 (%)
Alabama	$164	$313	$477	44	−33
Alaska	923	321	1,244	92	−29
Arizona	374	313	660	61	−36
Arkansas	204	313	517	48	−42
California	607	245	852	79	−18
Colorado	421	301	722	67	−45
Connecticut	636	236	872	81	−43
Delaware	338	313	651	60	−47
Dist. Columbia	420	301	721	67	−46
Florida	303	313	616	57	−33
Georgia	280	313	593	55	−34
Hawaii	712	471	1,183	95	−20
Idaho	317	313	630	58	−62
Illinois	377	313	690	64	−59
Indiana	288	313	601	56	−39
Iowa	426	299	725	67	−46
Kansas	429	313	742	69	−51
Kentucky	262	313	575	53	−55
Louisiana	190	313	503	47	−45
Maine	418	301	719	66	−22
Maryland	373	313	686	63	−42
Massachusetts	565	257	822	76	−47
Michigan[a]	459	289	748	69	−47
Minnesota	532	267	799	74	−48
Mississippi	120	313	433	40	−46
Missouri	292	313	605	56	−29
Montana	425	299	724	67	−47
Nebraska	364	313	677	63	−46
Nevada	348	313	661	61	−27
New Hampshire	550	262	812	75	−47
New Jersey	424	307	731	68	−65
New Mexico	389	310	699	65	−34
New York[b]	577	270	847	78	−48
North Carolina	272	313	585	54	−53
North Dakota	431	298	729	67	−49
Ohio	341	313	654	60	−47
Oklahoma	307	313	620	57	−49
Oregon	460	313	773	71	−37
Pennsylvania	421	301	722	67	−60
Rhode Island	554	299	853	79	−39
South Carolina	200	313	513	47	−41
South Dakota	430	298	728	67	−59
Tennessee	185	313	498	46	−58
Texas	188	313	501	46	−68

continued

Table 1.4   *Continued*

State	Maximum AFDC Grant	Food Stamp Benefit	Combined Benefits	Combined Benefits as % of Poverty Level	AFDC Change in Real Value 1970–76 (%)
Utah	426	299	725	67	−39
Vermont	650	232	882	82	−38
Virginia	354	313	667	62	−60
Washington	546	289	835	77	−47
West Virginia	253	313	566	52	−44
Wisconsin	517	272	789	73	−29
Wyoming	360	313	673	62	−57
Median state	389	310	699	65	−51

[a] Detroit.
[b] New York City.
Source: Committee on Ways and Means, House of Representatives, *Overview of Entitlement Programs* (Washington, D.C.: GPO, 1996), pp. 437–38, 446–48.

1993, trafficking in Food Stamps was estimated at $800 million, or 3.7 percent of benefits,[70] though this is surely an understatement. Five years later, the General Accounting Office reported that supplying Food Stamps to 26,000 dead people in three states had cost the federal government $8.5 million.[71]

Common sense would suggest that the typical welfare mother trying to support two children on $699 per month from AFDC and Food Stamps (let alone $433 in Mississippi) would supplement those benefits, even if failing to report income to welfare caseworkers defrauded the state. The magnitude of fraud related to such unreported income strained the credibility of public welfare. Because the federal government insisted that states make accurate payments as a condition for receipt of the federal share of benefits, states engaged in a bureaucratic fiction of quality control. Accordingly, the "error rate" for state AFDC payments was supposedly no more than 6 percent.[72] The implication that the remaining 94 percent of cases received accurate payments was absurd. In an exploratory study of Chicago families on welfare, Katherine Edin discovered that "every single mother supplemented her check in some way, either by doing unreported work, by getting money from friends and relatives, or by persuading someone else to pay a lot of her expenses." Altogether, welfare benefits covered only 58 percent of family income.[73] Further research by Edin and Laura Lein affirmed what was obvious to most observers of welfare: welfare mothers supplemented benefits in order to support their children even if doing so was a felony.[74] Significantly, the most prevalent source of unreported income was work.

26

That the official AFDC error rate more closely approximated the rate of accurate payments reflected the perversity of public welfare. For decades welfare beneficiaries had learned to hide family income—child support surreptitiously given to mothers was not credited by welfare offices, wages from regular work were squirreled away, and of course, illicit activity involving drugs and sex went unreported. Those caseworkers who were sympathetic to struggling mothers looked the other way; those who were punitively inclined had ample opportunity to make life miserable for the families for which they were responsible. Welfare administrators explained away the problem, citing the impossible intricacies of 50 state-managed welfare programs with different rules, and used the opportunity to request more revenues for the welfare bureaucracy.

None of these actors in the American welfare melodrama expected anyone to take the trouble to look backstage. But, eventually, critics did. First, neoconservatives, such as Daniel Patrick Moynihan, questioned why welfare mothers should be exempt from work while other mothers were streaming into the labor market. Then, analysts from conservative policy institutes raised questions about the probity of welfare itself, attributing to it increases in unwed births, drug abuse, and the scope of the underclass. Eventually, conservatives in Congress began to propose draconian versions of "welfare reform." The liberal rebuttal was predictable, for it had been honed for a half-century: many welfare mothers were simply unsuited for the labor market, declining benefits could not possibly have generated the increase in the number of children on aid, and (finally) the association of welfare families with a host of underclass variables was insufficient to demonstrate causation. In retrospect it is easy to see that these explanations were all lost on a public that had become fed up with what was perceived as so much liberal sophistry. Welfare no longer worked, and if that meant throwing the baby out with the bath water . . . well, where did those babies come from anyway?

THE END OF WELFARE

All of this came to a head at a time when conservative thought was ascendant and the first Democratic president in some time was on the political ropes after Congress had savaged his Health Security Act. After vetoing two conservative attempts to reform welfare, Clinton capitulated on the eve of the 1996 presidential election and signed the Personal Responsibility and Work Opportunity Reconciliation Act, or "welfare reform." Liberals were apoplectic. Senator Edward Kennedy labeled the act "legislative child abuse." Peter Edelman, one of three senior appointees who resigned in protest, characterized federal welfare reform in incendiary terms: "Congress and the President have dynamited a structure that was in place for six decades."[75] Edelman echoed the fears of many welfare advocates:

> There will be suffering. Some of the damage will be obvious—more home-lessness, for example, with more demand on already strapped shelters and soup kitchens. The ensuing problems will also appear as increases in the incidence of other problems, directly but perhaps not provably owing to the impact of the welfare bill. There will be more malnutrition and more crime, increased infant mortality, and increased drug and alcohol abuse. There will be increased family violence and abuse against children and women, and a consequent spillover of the problem into the already overloaded child-welfare system and battered women's shelters.[76]

The policy implications were comparably dire. Because states had evolved different benefit levels, researchers feared that welfare reform would set off a "race toward the bottom"—or, as professors from Harvard and Berkeley put it: "the increasing competitiveness of the federal system has forced states to set redistributive policies strategically with strong consideration of the choices made by neighbors."[77] That is, states neighboring a low-benefit state would be induced to lower benefits also to avoid becoming "welfare magnets." Immediately, the liberal Center on Budget and Policy Priorities issued a series of alarms, noting that governors, particularly those from the lowest-benefit states of the South, were preparing proposals leading to sharp reductions in welfare benefits.[78] As southern states competed with one another to lower welfare benefits, so the logic went, the undercutting would spread northward; eventually, welfare benefits in Alaska would approximate those of Mississippi.

It is a telling indicator of liberal credibility with respect to welfare that none of this has come to pass.[79] This is not to say that welfare reform has been without consequences. The drop in welfare caseloads, the increased employment and earnings of recipients, and state and federal savings have all been substantiated, and—to the glee of conservatives—they have been substantial. At the same time, the effects of the various sanctions imposed to discourage beneficiaries from continuing to receive welfare, the long-term employability of welfare mothers, and the implications of time limits on aid receipt are unknown. These—much to the distress of liberals—are also likely to be substantial. That so much assistance for poor families had been wagered on so little evidence was perhaps the most apropos epitaph for the tawdry American institution that public welfare had become.

2

The Old Maternalism

The scene is a Connecticut welfare office in 1971. The state is standardizing welfare benefits that had previously been individualized, cutting them in the process. Like bands of harpies, welfare mothers descend on the welfare department demanding hearings on their cases. Over the weeks, each welfare worker sits down with a series of protesting welfare mothers, in the presence of a "fair hearing" officer, to explain why they will get less. The welfare mothers swear that they already have less than it takes to live, and wonder aloud what the state expects them to do. The hearing officer validates the new budget, pronounces it in conformity with the new standards, and explains that the recipients have the right to redress through the courts—meaning that they will have to get by on the new grant anyway until they get an attorney. *If* they can find one willing to take on the state attorney general.

Making the trip from the waiting room to the interviewing booth, facing a welfare mother, often with kids in tow, and hearing the preordained grant reduction affirmed—all this is becoming routine. Then the receptionist calls to say that Mary Early has arrived.[1] I am perplexed: Mary Early? Here? She had been transferred to my caseload only a few months before, and I had made one home visit. Mary is 21, black, and the mother of a three-year-old toddler. Her apartment had been a disaster—little furniture, dirty dishes piled in the sink; the daughter cleaned a path by crawling across a filthy floor. On returning to the office, I reviewed the case record and discovered that Mary had been in a series of foster homes since childhood, had dropped out of school, had been hospitalized for hallucinations on more than one occasion, and had received welfare since she became pregnant at 17. Quite literally, Mary is a product of the system, and I am her most recent caseworker. She lives 30 miles away and does not have a car, so I am surprised that she has made it to the welfare department.

Waiting for the hearing officer, I offer my awkward reassurance to a woman who needs so much more. My gesture is intercepted by a voice that reeks of cheap wine.

"Stop!" she wheels around, apprehending my words. Her brilliant obsidian

29

eyes seem to clear for a moment. "Why you doin' that?" Then, with perfect diction, in a tone of dark honey: "Don't you know, there's only two things in this world—a white man and a black woman?" I am so taken aback, I forget to ask who—if anyone—is caring for her daughter.

That was my last interview with Mary Early. Department restructuring left her reassigned to a worker who was responsible for some 200 cases whose last names began with the letters *D* through *G*. Mary would receive services from that worker, provided that she was willing to wait 20 minutes on the phone or a half-day in the waiting room. If her condition deteriorated to the point where she or her daughter was endangered, services would be forthcoming only after someone filed a report with the Protective Services unit. Given changes in the welfare department, I doubted that Mary Early's family would receive any of these benefits.

Still, her words haunted me. It wasn't until many years later, when I was teaching at Howard University, the historic African American university in the nation's capital, that I could make sense of them. Welfare, she was saying, was the new plantation; poor black women were once again subjugated by white men.

Historically, the roles we played were consonant with a maternalist welfare state—one in which government and its employees served as adult surrogates for the poor who received public assistance. As welfare evolved during the decades following the 1935 Social Security Act, several features of welfare state maternalism became clearer. Foremost, many low-income families refused its benefits, despite meeting the eligibility requirements. For millions of families in poverty, being poor was humbling enough. Second, the ranks of recipients filled disproportionately with African Americans, most of them women. Thus, welfare took on overtones that were decidedly racist. Finally, the benefits offered through welfare were, over time, disastrous. As Mary Early demonstrates, there was nothing that I, the previous caseworkers, or the multiple programs from which she drew benefits did that ameliorated the social damage being inflicted upon her family. Rather than helping Mary Early and her daughter, it was evident that we were all implicated in their destruction.

MOTHERS' PENSIONS

As is noted in Chapter 1, welfare as a government activity originated in the conditions that created the Progressive era. The urbanization, industrialization, and immigration that threatened to destabilize the white, Anglo-Saxon Protestant power structure also served to liberate upper-class, educated women with the time and inclination for good works.

Indoor plumbing, electric lighting, and household laborsaving devices, and the spread of commercial canning and baking were examples of technological innovations that reduced the hours of labor for housekeeping. The falling birthrate among middle-class families as well as the availability of inexpensive immigrant and black domestic help furthered the process by which native-born, middle-class white women were released from work at home.[2]

Such women, as we have seen, organized and staffed the COSs that dispensed charity to the urban poor.

This early demonstration of women's leadership had profoundly traditional features: affluent women instructed the mothers of poor, often immigrant households about proper behavior in America. "Friendly visiting for the Charity Organization Societies could be seen as instilling the virtues of independent American family life in the poor."[3] The strategy of focusing women's influence on domestic concerns was nowhere more evident than in the "first women's mass movement," the Women's Christian Temperance Union (WCTU). By the turn of the century, the WCTU boasted 168,000 members in 7,000 local organizations in every state of the union. Women who were less politically minded but still civically oriented founded organizations that advocated for "improvements in libraries and schools, institutions close to women's proper concerns with culture and education," and eventually evolved into the Federation of Women's Clubs.[4] In assuming social responsibilities, women of the period often invoked their role in the family: "Woman's place is in the home. This is a platitude which no woman will ever dissent from," wrote the author of a book on women's clubs and politics. "But Home is not contained within the four walls of an individual home. Home is the community. The city full of people is the Family. The public school is the real Nursery. And badly do the Home and the Family and the Nursery need their mother."[5]

Yet, as the late nineteenth century saw affluent women unfettered from domestic drudgery, it also witnessed the rapid increase of industrial labor among poor, immigrant women. Appreciation for the plight of women factory workers—and even respect for the women themselves—immediately emerged among those middle-class women who opted to live in Settlement Houses. In contrast to the busybodies of COSs, Settlement House workers saw their mission politically. As Theda Skocpol observed, "American settlement houses—such as Hull House in Chicago and Henry Street Settlement in New York—became settlements from which talented women could create and pursue an alternative kind of wide-ranging career, combining social research, public education, civic activism, and intermittent periods of official service."[6] Living in the settlements, workers not only saw but also smelled and felt the degrading circumstances of poor families. Their prescriptions were also different from those of the friendly visitors. Several children living near Hull House were injured when they were left at home while their mothers worked, so Jane Addams started a kindergarten.[7] Settlement workers in America's larger cities were intimately familiar with the conditions that led to the Triangle Shirtwaist Factory fire of 1911, in which 146 women and girls were trapped in a sweatshop and killed.[8]

For Settlement House residents, effective social change came about through political mobilization and legislating policy, and organize they did. Concerned about the neglect and exploitation of children, Addams and 200 advocates met at the White House in 1909 to impress on the nation the urgent needs of America's youth, an event that led to the establishment of the U.S. Children's Bureau three years later. A decade hence, Progressives used the Children's Bureau to mount a successful initiative to promote infant and maternal welfare through the Sheppard-Towner Act. At the state level, Progressives advocated state support for widows who were left with dependent children.

> In April 1911, Missouri enacted America's first widows' pension law, a permissive statute allowing the counties to provide cash assistance to mothers who had dependent children. Two months later, Illinois followed suit, and so rapidly did the idea spread that, within two years, seventeen other states did the same. By 1919, similar statutes had been enacted in thirty-nine states, and, by 1935, all but two—South Carolina and Georgia—were extending aid to widows with children.[9]

Pioneered by the states, the surge in widows' pensions was swept into the Social Security Act under Title IV, which authorized cash benefits for destitute children.

Skocpol describes the various initiatives that Progressive women advocated as elements of a "maternalist" welfare state. The early maternalists saw women's family roles as essential to the social order, viewed themselves as nurturers of the poor, and established their campaign as a women's initiative.[10] Fundamentally, welfare legislation reaffirmed the maternal role of women in family life. To be sure, this process was not without contradictions: Progressive women advocating for poor families were establishing full-fledged careers in what would be later called social work, while the beneficiaries were expected to be grateful for being allowed to remain at home. In protecting poor working women, Progressives also advocated regulations requiring employers to limit hours, provide a safe working environment, and offer special benefits for women. Clearly, these latter objectives posed more promise for empowering women politically, but Progressive women leaders were reluctant to rush ahead. When the idea of equal rights for women first surfaced early in the century, several Progressive leaders, including Jane Addams, opposed the idea for fear that it would subvert dearly won workplace protections for women.[11] Nonetheless, for women who had yet to exercise the franchise, to leverage such legislation on behalf of their sisters was a remarkable achievement.

WORKING-POOR AFRICAN AMERICANS

African American families benefited little from Progressive advances. The Civil War had emancipated slaves, of course, but despite the efforts of the Freedmen's Bureau, which functioned from 1865 to 1872, southern Negroes were consigned to the status of peasants, eking out a living by sharecropping. Even those who migrated north were often denied COS services. Excluded from the mainstream, blacks organized their own "fraternal orders and benefit associations."[12] The institutional racism that suffused the Progressive era continued through the New Deal. To secure the support of southern legislators, Franklin Delano Roosevelt executed the most cynical of accommodations, agreeing to exclude domestic and agricultural workers from Social Security.[13] This meant that African Americans living predominantly in the South would continue to provide cheap labor—men working in agriculture, women as domestics—literally as long as they were able to. Until the Social Security Act was amended in the 1950s, there would be no public pension for them.

Securing income security for poor women through welfare was not without its costs, however. In response to concerns about the deservingness of single mothers, maternalists added a morals test to the means test. Together these assured benefits for only the most destitute, and among that group, only those with the qualities of a "fit mother."[14] These conditions provided the rationale for welfare officials to deny benefits to mothers who were perceived as undeserving. Mothers of dependent children were expected to be models of virtue. "Hardly any supporters of mothers' pensions, before or after the 1910s," noted Skocpol, "would have endorsed the notion of payments going automatically to needy mothers regardless of their personal conduct or their ability and willingness to provide a wholesome home life for their children."[15] In testimony, Edith Abbott, a pioneer of mothers' pensions, estimated that only 50 percent of poor mothers would actually receive aid, guaranteeing legislators that the beneficiaries would be "really nice children and the families are nice families."[16] As a result, many poor mothers failed to receive aid. But the brunt of the morals test fell on minority mothers: "In 1900, 97 percent of black single mothers worked on the land or in domestic service, and by 1930 this proportion remained at 93 percent."[17] Thus, on the eve of the passage of the Social Security Act, minority women had been effectively excluded from mothers' pensions, representing only 4 percent of cases.[18] "In 1937–40 only 14–17 percent of [Aid to Dependent Children] recipients were black, far below the proportion of their need."[19]

The contortion of social policy because of race would have a profound impact on the needs of poor black women. Affluent, white Progressive women had "established state Mothers' Pensions and later federal Aid to Dependent Children to allow widowed, abandoned, and divorced mothers to be full-time mothers," observed Deborah Stone. "Black reformers, by contrast, understood the necessity for women to work, and focused their energies on creating the preconditions for women as wage earners and community leaders."[20] For upwardly mobile black women, welfare was a curse— public relief was not just stigmatizing, it was also a dead-end. In an era of traditional values, the African American woman who *insisted* on escaping poverty would not only get a job, but would also consider avoiding men, matrimony, and childbearing altogether for fear of being left with dependent children who might require welfare benefits.[21] The role models of upstanding Negro women during the Progressive era were paragons of virtue. Maggie Walker, founder of Richmond's St. Lukes Penny Savings Bank, was not only the first woman bank president in the nation, but a powerful presence in the black community as well. Mary McLeod Bethune advocated educational opportunities for Negro men and women and established Bethune-Cookman College in Florida. Ida B. Wells, a vigorous champion of equal opportunity, participated in the Niagara Movement, which founded the National Association for the Advancement of Colored People, an organization she later eschewed because of its conservatism.[22]

As African American women in leadership became increasingly remote from the majority of poor black women, women who had taken more divergent paths filled the void. Flashy, independent, and defiant, female entertainers like Billie Holiday understood the predicament of their poor sisters— they had "soul"—but flouted traditional institutions such as work and family. While this offered symbolic relief, it did little for the material circumstances of poor minority women. Work offered miserable wages, but welfare was worse. Between 1973 and 1995 the number of black women working for wages up to 75 percent of the poverty level remained virtually constant at 23.0 percent, while those with wages three times the poverty level doubled from 2.2 to 4.4 percent. Over the same period the average hourly wage of young black women aged 25 to 34 declined from $7.58 to $6.19.[23]

Technically, poor blacks might have been eligible for benefits through Unemployment Compensation (if they were unemployed) and welfare (if they had dependent children). However, both of these programs were operated by state governments, and welfare officials in the South were anything but generous with respect to indigent African Americans. As Frances Fox Piven and Richard Cloward documented in their classic analysis of welfare, *Regu-*

lating the Poor, public relief benefits in the South rose and fell directly in relation to the demand for low-wage labor.[24] In investigating the relationship between welfare and work, the Illinois State Advisory Committee of the U.S. Civil Rights Commission conducted hearings during the mid-1960s and recorded the testimony of a Mr. Whitfield, a resident of Cairo, Illinois:

> Soon as the month of May, the public aid would start sending letters to the recipients. Due to seasonable work, your grant is cut and you are supposed to make it up by doing this seasonable work. This seasonable work, as we know, is farm labor. My migrant labor, that's what it is, 50 cents per hour. . . . The public aid recipient is a source of cheap labor for the farmer. We have asked a number of times. I have asked my superintendent of public aid about forcing the people into the fields, why didn't he wait and let us stay back until [wages] rise, and he said the poor farmers couldn't pay any more, we'd have to go along with this going rate, and this going rate has been the same thing ever since I have been in Cairo.[25]

Thus state welfare officials insisted on compliant behavior as a condition for receipt of public aid.

The exclusion of blacks from the benefits of the Social Security Act would prove a rationale for the War on Poverty a generation later. Although no substantial new cash benefits were authorized during the mid-1960s, the Economic Opportunity Act included establishment of the Legal Assistance Corporation, "legal aid." In skirmish after skirmish, legal aid attorneys challenged state statutes and welfare practices—"man-in-the-house" prohibitions (*King* v. *Smith*, 1968) and residency requirements (*Shapiro* v. *Thompson*, 1969)[26]—that had denied benefits to poor black families. The spirit behind such litigation was Charles A. Reich, who argued that welfare was not simply a benefit for which the poor were eligible, but an entitlement that should be regarded as a property right. Basing his case on the increasing surpluses of industrial society as well as the integration of its component sectors, Reich observed that beneficiaries of social programs were often left out when resources were distributed, a flaw that could be corrected by making welfare a property right. "Since the enactment of the Social Security Act, we have recognized that they have a right—not a mere privilege—to a minimal share in the commonwealth."[27]

> The concept of right is most urgently needed with respect to benefits like unemployment compensation, public assistance, and old age insurance. These benefits are based upon a recognition that misfortune and deprivation are often caused by forces far beyond the control of the individual, such as technological change, variations in demand for goods, depressions, or wars. The aim of these benefits is to preserve the self-sufficiency of the individual, to rehabilitate him where necessary, and to allow him to be a valuable member of a family and a community; in theory they represent part of the individual's rightful share of the

commonwealth. Only by making such benefits into rights can the welfare state achieve its goal of providing a secure minimum basis for individual well-being and dignity in a society where each man cannot be wholly the master of his own destiny.[28]

But assuring the poor access to their "new property" was another matter; toward that end he proposed "a radically new approach to the field of social welfare,"[29] a set of procedures within welfare policy that lawyers could enforce in order to guarantee the poor their share of the society's abundance.

At the same time, "welfare rights" was becoming an effective rallying cry among an incipient black leadership that used the War on Poverty as a platform for entry into the urban political arena. As class action suits removed state impediments to receipt of public assistance and the Welfare Rights Movement encouraged access, the number of families eligible for aid soared, and welfare costs skyrocketed. Between 1960 and 1970 the number of AFDC recipients increased from 3.073 million to 9.659 million (314 percent), and the cost of the program increased from $994.4 million to $4.857 *billion* (488 percent).[30] To the fury of state welfare officials, small bands of scruffy, federally subsidized legal aid lawyers were opening the sluice gates of welfare; a well-managed stream of benefits was becoming a roaring torrent. In response to the rise in welfare cases, states instituted standardized "flat" grants for families regardless of individual circumstance, and then failed to increase benefits in relation to costs. The result was a gradual, but no less effective, reduction in welfare costs; states' refusal to index welfare benefits to inflation meant that their outlays would drop over time, thereby reducing the welfare burden.[31] Two decades later poor, disproportionately minority mothers would be raising their families on half the benefits that mothers had been granted a generation earlier.

PROFESSIONAL INVOLUTION

If the Progressive era introduced government as a force for promoting the general welfare, social work was the professional means by which this end would be achieved. Certainly, leaders in social work had demonstrated their commitment to working with the poor;[32] many had become well known to the public, if not household names: Charles Loring Brace, founder of the New York Children's Society and pioneer of the "orphan trains" that transported destitute children to the Midwest; Mary Richmond, director of the Baltimore Charity Organization Society and author of *Social Diagnosis,* the first comprehensive taxonomy of the poor; Jane Addams, founder of Hull House and winner of the Nobel Peace Prize for her work as a pacifist, to name only a few. Of the many fledgling institutions, Hull House warrants mention because so many of its residents would provide the intellect and perseverance behind the social legislation of the New Deal: Edith Abbott, an author of the Social Security Act; her sister, Grace Abbott, and Julia Lathrop, who became directors of the Children's Bureau; and Frances Perkins, secretary of labor and the first woman appointed to a cabinet post.

Of primary concern to advocates for the poor was the professionalization of their work. While mothers' pensions, maternal and infant health, and workplace safety might be solutions to pressing problems of the day, Progressives viewed professional status as a way to make these achievements permanent. The professionalization of good works would integrate Progressive thought into the social order, further the cause, and preserve it well into the future. Social work thus evolved to continue the Progressive movement. The first training program in social work was a set of summer courses offered in 1898 that would eventually become the Columbia University Graduate School of Social Work.[33]

Progressive era social work paralleled the contemporaneous evolution of the social sciences. Hull House, for example, served as a de facto community laboratory for sociologists of the University of Chicago; indeed, the pragmatic philosophy of John Dewey was influenced by his work at Hull House. Among the methods that social activists employed in their work was survey research, for which social workers, equipped with keen observation and interviewing skills, were aptly suited.

Social work's maternalist impulses contained an "arrogance toward recipients" that would have annoyed contemporary feminists.[34] "Overall the continuing premise of the social work mainstream was that welfare clients could not define their own needs properly without professional expertise."[35] With the New Deal, professional condescension was institutionalized as the schools of social work proliferated. Subsequent to passage of the Social Security Act, social work would assume control of "the means of administration" for a whole range of income and social services. During the next half-century, the federal and state departments of welfare were largely managed by social workers, who exercised considerable influence, if not outright control, over public welfare. Wilbur Cohen, by way of illustration, was a social worker who, after being the first staff person hired by the newly created Social Security Administration, decades later drafted the eighteenth and nineteenth amendments to the Social Security Act, establishing Medicare and Medicaid, respectively. As Cohen's career demonstrates, the enduring accomplishments of Roosevelt's New Deal would be replicated a generation later when Medicare and Medicaid became benchmarks of Johnson's Great Society.

The New Deal provided a template for social work's orientation toward social policy. There were certain awkward contradictions. Working through the Children's Bureau, maternalist social workers accepted welfare arrangements that involved a state-federal partnership, replete with means and morals tests, expecting that the more generous federal social insurance programs would eventually solve the problem of poor mothers' dependence. As Linda Gordon observed, the maternalist social workers' vision of poor mothers was strikingly male-chauvinistic, accepting an inferior arrangement of state-managed public assistance programs whose benefits would be reserved for a small number of families who conformed with social norms. On another track altogether were the social insurance programs for male workers and their families. "Whether the Children's Bureau's efforts were timid in conception or blocked by stronger influences," assessed Gordon, "the fact remains that the women's network did not offer a welfare program equal to the proportion of the crisis" (i.e., the Depression).[36]

With a blueprint for a new social architecture in hand, social work diligently courted those influences that would most adequately articulate it. Social work thus adopted the welfare state interpretation of social policy, in the process rejecting a "welfare capitalist" orientation that would have viewed mothers as potential participants in the labor force. Prior to the New Deal, the connection of health, pension, and related benefits to workers' salaries—welfare capitalism—was expanding rapidly, though the Great Depression would retard the movement for several decades. As the Depression proved, want and suffering were handmaidens of unregulated capitalism; government was the salvation of markets run amok. Subsequently "progressive social work" vilified the business sector, proposing a radical leftist direction for social policy. Derived from a Marxist interpretation of political economy, progressive social work targeted "capitalist economies . . . that enable concentrated wealth to accumulate into the hands of a small, elite group while most people receive far less." The antidote to capitalist exploitation would be found in the left wing of the labor movement, "committed to advancing a socialist economic program that would replace the debilitated capitalist economy."[37] For radical social workers, welfare programs were a sop that a corporate-controlled government conceded to the poor; the elimination of poverty ultimately entailed not only the end of capitalist control of the means of production, but also the end of paltry welfare programs.

For more moderate social workers, the public assistance programs of the welfare state were essential instruments to alleviate poverty. However inadequate they might be, they were temporary institutions that would disappear as the northern European model of the welfare state evolved in America. From the 1930s through the 1970s, social work held dear an article of faith inspired by the left: a fully evolved welfare state, through which essential benefits would be available to the entire population as a right of citizenship, was an inevitable consequence of industrialization. For most social workers, essential benefits included employment, housing, health care, income, and personal social services. According to this scenario, social progress was pre-ordained: social policy would be the instrument for crafting a just society, and progressive taxes would pay for it. Given the presumed inevitability of the process, all American social workers had to do was beat the ideological drum; the welfare state was, after all, the final incarnation of industrial society.

The introduction of the American welfare state following passage of the Social Security Act contributed to a sharp decline in poverty, a problem that had plagued more than half the population as a result of the Great Depression. Figure 2.1 shows the marked improvement in the economic status of Americans in the decades following the 1940s. Whether such prosperity could be attributed to the obliteration of global competition during World War II, the immense public works projects introduced in the postwar era, or the expansion of the American welfare state might be disputed, of course. Yet liberal welfare philosophers of the period assumed that a full array of protections against social and economic insecurity was an inevitable comple-ment to industrialization. By 1980, it was evident that where welfare was concerned, the liberal trajectory had reached its apogee. Not only was pov-erty being experienced by an increasing number of Americans, but for a sub-set it was becoming more intractable.

Deluded by historical determinism into thinking that the northern Euro-pean welfare state had an ineluctable appeal that portended its replication in the United States, social workers failed to generate original theory and research about social policy and programs. When confronted with the need to explain new social problems—family violence, welfare dependence, chronic mental disorders—social work resorted to eclecticism, borrowing formulations from other social sciences and medicine. In matters relating to poverty, social work conceded the field of quantitative analysis to social scientists, primarily economists. Serious thought seemed irrelevant to the social work project, as long as social welfare was expanding and social work could lift ideas from other disciplines. For the half-century following passage of the Social Security Act, this proved to be the case. Despite its claim to derive its knowledge base from application of the scientific method, social work would traipse through the twentieth century "with a purposeful disre-gard for the rules of science." The result was self-defeating: "The quality of social work's contemporary research undercuts its professional ambitions for a scientifically credible practice of helping as well as its claims to serve noble social ends on behalf of the disadvantaged," observed William Epstein.[38]

Public welfare aptly illustrates social work's failure in theory and research. Content to rely on the sporadic data generated by state and federal welfare bureaucracies, social work neglected to develop an independent research capacity.[39] Perhaps the clearest evidence of this dereliction is found in *Social Work Research and Abstracts*. Beginning in 1965, articles about social wel-

Figure 2.1   Economic Status of the Total Population, 1940–1994

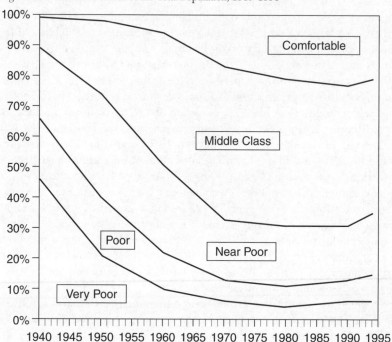

Very Poor. The percentage of the population in households with pretax cash incomes less than 50 percent of the poverty line for households of their size.

Poor. The percentage of the population in households with pretax cash incomes between 50 percent and 99 percent of the poverty line for households of their size.

Near Poor. The percentage of the population in households with pretax cash incomes between 100 percent and 199 percent of the poverty line for households of their size.

Middle Class. The percentage of the population in households with pretax cash incomes between 100 percent and 499 percent of the poverty line for households of their size.

Comfortable. The percentage of the population in households with pretax cash incomes 500 percent or more of the poverty line for households of their size.

In 1995 a four-person household fell below the poverty line if their pretax cash income was less than $15,719 (1995 dollars).

Source: Reynolds Farley, *The New American Reality* (New York: Russell Sage Foundation, 1996), p. 66.

fare were abstracted for research purposes and cross-referenced to facilitate use. In 1965, the pivotal year of the War on Poverty, 12 articles about poverty were published; the following year the number jumped to 22. Through the late 1960s and early 1970s, the number ranged between 12 in 1969 and three in 1970. In 1973 the editors added "the poor" to "poverty" as an entry, and the number of articles jumped to 11. Thereafter, social work's interest in poverty virtually flat-lined for two decades. Between 1974 and 1988, the year in which the first conservative reform of welfare was enacted through the Family Support Act, the number of articles appearing in the social work literature averaged fewer than four per year.[40]

What makes this indifference so remarkable is the dramatic increase in welfare expenditures during the period. As table 1.1 shows, between 1970 and 1985 federal expenditures for public assistance programs increased from $16 billion to $98 billion, doubling, adjusted for inflation. In contrast to their sisters' concerns during the Progressive era, social workers of the 1970s and 1980s evidently presumed that poverty had been banished by the public assistance programs of the American welfare state and turned their backs on the poor. Not until the early 1990s, when the ideological shocks of the Reagan presidency registered, would social work belatedly demonstrate a renewed interest in poverty. Even then, it was not until 1993 that the number of articles about poverty, 25, eclipsed the previous high of 1966.

Without evidence to indicate that it should do otherwise, social work un wittingly fell in line with the public welfare status quo, and it was probably inevitable that, in the absence of corrections from critical theory and research, public welfare would diverge from the social reality as perceived by recipients (whose experience no one had bothered to sample), the public (who had increasing misgivings about welfare), and even welfare caseworkers (who were abandoning the bureaucracy in droves). Social work blithely ignored the detrimental features of the welfare bureaucracy, whose organizational depravity had become notorious. If social work remained blind to the sordid nature of public welfare, however, other critics were not. In 1980 the sociologist Michael Lipsky proposed the phrase "bureaucratic disentitlement" to describe the tendency of welfare workers to deny benefits to citizens eligible for assistance. The culture of the welfare department meant that "workers on the front lines of the welfare state find themselves in a corrupted world of service. [They] find that the best way to keep demand within manageable proportions is to deliver a consistently inaccessible or inferior product."[41]

The past two decades saw a revolution in organization theory, but none of it trickled down to the local welfare department. In 1993 a journalist sketched this portrait of a Los Angeles welfare office:

> Welfare offices are so understaffed, the workers so burnt out, that some help applicants cheat just to fill unofficial quotas, avoid confrontation, get them out of their hair. It is a system so flawed that the greedy, the lazy, rip and run with ease. The attitude of both sides of the reinforced windows that separate staff from applicants is: Us against Them. The system becomes so cynical that the desperate—the great majority of applicants, by most estimates—are left under a pall of suspicion, clawing even harder to get the help to which they're entitled.[42]

41

The negative ambiance of urban welfare offices has become a caricature of disservice, as Wiseman's documentary film *Welfare* attests.[43] "Public assistance offices, particularly those in large cities that handle large caseloads, are chaotic," concluded Rebecca Blank. "Clients often talk about having to wait half a day to see a staff member, even when they were told they had an appointment at 1 P.M., then find they have to come back the next day and wait again."[44]

Whenever the perceptions of welfare recipients intruded into the literature, the portrait was nothing less than an indictment. Theresa Funiciello, an AFDC recipient, then an advocate for welfare beneficiaries, and later a staff member of a policy institute, captured the discrepancy between services provided to the poor and to the middle class:

> When affluent people decide some service they want for themselves isn't up to snuff, they vote with their feet and their pocketbooks. In that sense, markets work quite well for anyone with the power to participate in them. As long as poor people are prohibited from having a choice—a say in deciding which services they need and which providers are most capable of satisfying them—the competitive element, if there is one, is entirely in the hands of Big Brother. Most of the people in every form of this business know this: *there is no accountability in the social service field.* None demanded, none supplied.[45]

Since the Family Support Act of 1988, research on welfare reform has focused on the employment prospects of poor mothers. As a result of federal waivers granted to the states and considerable interest by the philanthropic community, many have studied the experiences of low-income mothers forced into the labor market. Most of this research—considered in more detail in later chapters—has been conducted by private organizations, such as the Manpower Demonstration Research Corporation, Abt Associates, and Mathematica, using government data on caseloads, earnings, and the like. Given its historical concern for the poor and its contemporary interest in the feminization of poverty, social work would seem particularly well suited to qualify official celebrations of progress in welfare reform with the perspectives of poor mothers, including their perceptions of and experiences with public assistance and work. Indeed, had social work professors attained the same level of research competence taken for granted by other social disciplines, the schools of social work across the nation would have undertaken the formal evaluations required under the federal welfare waivers that had been encouraged after the Family Support Act, and they would have benefited in the tens of millions of dollars. Yet, even though many graduate social work programs enjoyed monopolies in major metropolitan areas, only a handful were able to exploit these unprecedented opportunities to secure multi-million-dollar contracts to evaluate welfare reform. At the end of the

1990s, such research appears only episodically—and certainly not as a consistent demonstration of social work's declared concern for poor mothers and their children. In all likelihood, such research would raise fundamental questions about the very integrity of welfare as a public institution.[46]

The absence of extensive systematic, let alone longitudinal, data on recipient perceptions of and experiences with welfare—a program that has been operating for more than a half-century—is but one of the conundrums of American social policy.[47] When such surveys are conducted, the responses raise doubts about the services and benefits provided to the poor. In the summer of 1991, the Southport Institute for Policy Analysis conducted interviews about human services with 171 people, of whom 150 received AFDC. A sample of statements indicated that welfare was not perceived as helpful; as often as not, it was simply detested.

- I wanted to work part-time, but the social worker made it so hard with the paperwork that there was no incentive. They spend more money than the few dollars you make, by the time they finish the paperwork, letting you know that they are going to take away your benefits, when you earn that little bit.
- I'd like to work to help me out, to get a better place to live, to do better for my kids. But then they take it out [of your benefits] and you're right back where you were. You're in the same spot.
- I have had three JOBS workers. And this one tells me what I have to do or I can kiss my welfare check good-bye. All I want is to get a diploma, and get a job and get off the system.
- I don't like being on the AFDC. But my husband got disabled and he couldn't work. He draws Social Security. So I had no choice. I hate it. If you can find me a job, I'll go for it.[48]

During the early 1990s, California researchers observed the extent to which welfare caseworkers actually implemented the state's welfare reform program, GAIN (Greater Avenues for Independence), which emphasized employment. Citing caseloads exceeding 200 in some offices, the researchers noted that many caseworkers never got beyond the quotidian demands of the welfare bureaucracy to which they had become accustomed. "In over 80 percent of intake and redetermination interviews workers did not provide and interpret information about welfare reforms. Most workers continued a pattern of instrumental transactions that emphasized workers' needs to collect and verify eligibility information."[49] Only rarely did workers go beyond their own best interests and provide information that would help clients take advantage of welfare reforms.

In 1997 two social workers, Irene Bush and Katherine Kraft, investigated welfare recipients' perceptions of New Jersey's welfare reform initiative through a series of focus groups. Generally, they found that welfare clients who were supposed to be preparing for work instead expended "significant energy . . . toward maintaining welfare benefits, fighting workers, and fitting in to a one size fits all program." Instead of client deficits, they found that *"the public welfare system itself was the source of the most commonly identified barriers to self-sufficiency."* Problems included "lacking accurate information; withholding available services; and disrespecting clients."[50] The atmosphere of the welfare office was unhelpful much, if not most, of the time. "Often recipients were kept waiting long hours while caseworkers were involved in non-work-related activities. Several women reported arriving at the welfare office at 3:30 PM to be told that their caseworkers were not seeing any more recipients that day," the researchers reported. "Many spoke about telephone calls to caseworkers where they were shifted from telephone to telephone unable to make a connection with a human being who might help them."[51] Statements such as the following were "common":

- It gives me a feeling of hopelessness. Almost you feel like somebody got to listen, somebody got to listen.
- Sometimes I feel that they really don't care, you know they already have a job or whatever the case maybe, so you know [they don't care].
- . . . but they say that you know, it's hard. It's easy to give up because they're not getting help with their transportation. They don't know what to do about child care and then they're putting all these regulations in saying you have to do this now or you're getting cut off. And it's frustrating and it's very, it's very like getting hit in the head.
- The door gets slammed in your face constantly.[52]

The researchers recount this exchange in one focus group:

> QUESTION: Has the welfare office ever been helpful to you?
> PARTICIPANT: No.
> PARTICIPANT: No.
> PARTICIPANT: No.
> PARTICIPANT: We don't bother those type of people unless they call us. When I get a job and I'm ready to come off welfare, I'm gonna go down there proudly and say to my caseworker, I did it without your help. You know what? You know what? I think they need to turn the tables around and put those people that are doing this welfare thing in our shoes.[53]

It is significant that these statements were made in public, and that the private interactions between caseworker and client are almost always off the record. This message from a welfare caseworker, recorded on an answering machine, was later entered in evidence for a suit filed against a California welfare department.

> Yes, Mara Anna Young, this call is for you. This is the Department of Social Services Health and Welfare Agency, and we're in receipt of your letter saying that we have committed blatant fabrication and malfeasance.
>
> Miss Young, you're so full of shit. Why don't you get off your fat, lazy ass and get a job. You know, taxpayers like me really resent the shit out of you. What makes you so special that you don't have to get up and go to work? You just work the system and take and take and take. Why don't you get a life, get a job, and quit taking from people who do have lives and jobs. You sound plenty healthy. If you've got a disability, go to Goodwill. But quit trying to take our money.
>
> You are not special; you are a piece of shit. That's what the Department of Social Services Health and Welfare Agency thinks of you. So get off your fat, lazy ass, you bitch, because we're sick of you.
>
> And guess what? You have already lost your case. We just want to let you know what we think of you. We think you're garbage. Everybody thinks you're garbage. Go somewhere else and leech, you bitch.[54]

Of course, professional social workers have worked in welfare departments and provided substantive assistance to poor women. The welfare mothers interviewed by Bush and Kraft, for example, noted that although most caseworkers are "seen as the enemy," those who do prove helpful are frequently swamped by requests for aid, once this becomes known to the client population.[55] But such caseworkers tend to be the exception. The atmosphere of the welfare department has been hostile to welfare mothers, and this pervasive negativity subverts the intentions of human service professionals. In her in-depth studies of welfare departments, Evelyn Brodkin has found a chaotic environment in which it is difficult for managers to hold caseworkers accountable when they ignore or short-circuit formal agency policy. She summarized the experience of managers who attempted to change the bureaucratic culture of one welfare department:

> In the first two years of the program, the management structure was revised three times and top staff dismissed or reshuffled. The program's first director did not survive one year in the agency. Consequently, it was not surprising to hear top-level managers voice despair when asked about their efforts to influence bureaucratic practice. One discouraged official concluded that "lipsynching" constituted the chief product of her staff development efforts. Another, commenting on relations with staff, observed: "Sometimes it's like combat."[56]

The atmosphere within a welfare office is nowhere near what most Americans would characterize as one of public service; rather, investigations into the milieu of the welfare bureaucracy are often likened to military confrontations. Rebecca Blank noted that *"management issues are among the worst problems of the AFDC program."*[57]

Indeed, the reputation of public welfare has become so clouded that few young professionals anticipate employment in the public sector. By the end of the twentieth century, this desertion of public welfare had become a professional diaspora. "Social work has abandoned its mission to help the poor and oppressed and to build communality," wrote the late Harry Specht and Mark Courtney. "Instead, many social workers are devoting their energies and talents to careers in psychotherapy. A significant proportion of social work professionals—about 40 percent—are in private practice, serving middle-class clients."[58] Thus, professional involution provided the excuse for social work to abandon its historic association with poverty in favor of more bourgeois objectives.

CULTURAL POLITICS

While social work divested itself of responsibility for the poor, it busied itself with the politically correct. During the 1970s and with increasing urgency in the 1980s, social work's orientation to social policy focused on the grievances of "special populations": minorities of color, women, and people of alternative sexual orientation in roughly that chronology. Special sections of professional associations were designated to ensure their representation in organizational activities. Curricula in professional schools were required to include content on the attributes and needs of these groups. Positions within the welfare bureaucracy and academic institutions were effectively reserved for representatives of such groups so as to provide role models to students and ensure that programming reflected the social reality of special populations. Two decades of such preferential selection would prove consequential—social work paraded its diversity—but in the process crowded out traditional concerns. Social work courses in professional schools were required to address the needs of African Americans, gays, lesbians, and women, but classic issues such as poverty had become optional.

Social work's abnegation of poverty as a concern would be facilitated by its misplaced faith in historical determinism. Decades of neglect of theory and research left welfare departments as institutional backwaters, bastions of bureaucratic purgatory. Meanwhile, social work celebrated and indulged itself in the needs of special populations. As representatives of such groups increasingly populated welfare and academic institutions, the requirements of these groups took precedence. What little research was conducted on poverty-related matters was subjected to an ideological screen. The primary casualty of the politicization of social welfare was truth in its scientifically empirical sense. "There is, in fact, a marked hostility to science," wrote Daniel Bonevac. "Entire books have been written on child development, family relations, and so on, by people who not only have never done any empirical research on these topics themselves but who also have no familiarity with the relevant empirical research done by others."[59]

Research in transracial adoption, for example, documented that minority children who were adopted by Anglos grew up without evident impairment, but this ran counter to the political orthodoxy of African American ideologues who insisted that transracial adoption constituted "cultural genocide."[60] At the insistence of the National Association of Black Social Workers, mainstream social work organizations parroted the correct racial party line, even though empirical research indicated that transracial adoption was not disruptive for black children placed in white homes. "Our studies show that transracial adoption causes no special problems among the adoptees or their siblings," noted Rita Simon and Howard Altstein. "We have observed black children adopted and reared in white families and have seen them grow up with a positive sense of their black identity and a knowledge of their history and culture."[61] Despite such empirical evidence, social work clung to its opposition to transracial adoption. Thus, while social work abrogated its responsibility for the policies, programs, and staff serving the poor, it catered to the politically correct, sometimes assuming positions that were not only anti-intellectual but sometimes simply irrational.

Subjecting knowledge to an ideological test is antithetical to the modern idea of a profession, of course. The result was an abandonment of the empirical project by which knowledge had been generated since the Enlightenment.[62] Social work had rationalized "an insistence on ignorance, a refusal to know," in the words of Shelby Steele, eventually institutionalizing "functional areas of ignorance," all allegedly in the service of advancing the public welfare.[63] Social work's refusal to investigate the immediate circumstances of the disproportionately minority poor was paralleled by the reluctance of social scientists to examine the deteriorating environment of the black ghetto, widely attributed to the liberal reaction to Daniel Patrick Moynihan's white paper on the black family. "Indeed, after the furor over the Moynihan Report on the black family," observed Paul Jargowsky, "the topic of the values and culture of poor people became virtually off-limits to academics, especially white academics, who exercised a form of self-censorship in order to avoid being charged with 'blaming the victim.'"[64] The volatile reaction to the "Moynihan Report" on the black family and the later research of James Coleman on Head Start, school bussing, and public education transmitted a clear message that critical inquiry into ghetto life would not go unchallenged.[65] The consequence, as William Julius Wilson argued, was the failure of the academic research community to chronicle the considerable deterioration of African American institutions since the 1970s.[66]

The same period saw the rise of cultural politics on the left, from which social work derived its infatuation with specific groups. This association would neuter the profession's credibility with respect to public policy. "Leftists in the academy have permitted cultural politics to supplant real politics, and have collaborated with the Right in making cultural issues central to public debate," chastened Richard Rorty. "The academic Left has no projects to propose to America, no vision of a country to be achieved by building a consensus on the need for specific reforms."[67] Allied with the academic left, social work effectively retreated from practical action to address the worsening circumstances of the American poor.

Professional involution would eventually exact an enormous price from social work.[68] Unwilling to entertain rival explanations for the state of the poor and the programs that served them, social work stuck smugly to the welfare state paradigm. Assuming the inevitable evolution of a complete array of entitlements, social work neglected to assess the experience of clients, the outcomes of social programs, and public perception of public welfare. The social work profession had virtually abandoned public welfare by the mid-1990s, when conservatives proposed draconian welfare reform measures. Consistent with Rogers Smith's notion of "ascriptive inequality," social work, however politically correct, had become a second-rate profession serving second-class citizens.[69]

THE NANNY STATE

In the absence of rigorous professional critique and capable management, public welfare drifted along, more an article of ideological faith than anything else. Through the War on Poverty, its intellectual bulwark was at least serviceable, deriving much of its substance from British social philosophers. T. H. Marshall had set the tone grandly by portraying the evolution of the welfare state over the centuries: the eighteenth century preoccupied with establishing *civil* rights, such as freedom of speech and religion; the nineteenth delivering *political* rights via various schemes of representative democracy; leaving the twentieth to witness the establishment of *social and economic* rights through the political institution of the welfare state.[70] In their exposition of American industrialization, *Industrial Society and Social Welfare,* Harold Wilensky and Charles Lebeaux concurred, writing that "under continuing industrialization all institutions will be oriented toward and evaluated in terms of social welfare aims. The 'welfare state' will become the 'welfare society', and both will be more reality than epithet."[71] Richard Titmuss reaffirmed the trans-Atlantic welfare state accord, suggesting that the welfare state was boundless and would eventually become global, resulting in a "welfare world."[72] "Most scholars believe that the modern welfare state represents the culmination of an inevitable and desirable process of social evolution," concluded James Midgley, the philosopher of international welfare. "The liberal welfare consensus as it became known dominated American life for many years."[73]

Even after two decades of conservative hegemony in domestic affairs, liberal welfare philosophers held tenaciously to their faith. "In most ways, the welfare state is a phenomenon of the industrialized world," intoned Leon Ginsberg, Carolina Distinguished Professor in the College of Social Work of the University of South Carolina.

> It is, in many ways, the means that human societies have used to deal with exigencies of the industrial, corporate world, as humans have made the transition from rural, agrarian life to interdependence and complexity in the establishment of cities and the life of manufacturing and automation.
>
> For [liberal] thinkers, the development of the welfare state is a natural and parallel outgrowth of the industrialization of the world. Just as physical things became more complicated following the Industrial Revolution, so did social relations. The rise of metropolitan areas, the decline of the extended family, the recurring incidence of economic crises, and the increasing need for objective help from strangers in the form of government, all made the welfare state and its current patterns inevitable.[74]

Despite the evidence piling up since the 1980s, liberals insisted that the welfare state was a *fait accompli;* on institutional autopilot, its social programs would continue to expand, ensuring for larger numbers of Americans protection from a variety of insecurities.

Within this general affirmation of the welfare state, there were variations, to be sure. Upon closer scrutiny, the American welfare state seemed almost embarrassingly inadequate compared with its European counterpart, and American scholars would qualify U.S. social programs as the "semi-welfare state" or the "reluctant welfare state."[75] The historian Arthur Schlesinger, Jr., hypothesizing about 30-year ideological cycles, injected dynamism into American welfare philosophy. Drawing on the New Deal of the mid-1930s and the Great Society of the mid-1960s, Schlesinger prophesied the election of the next unapologetically liberal president—and the introduction of the next major expansion of social programs—in the early 1990s.[76] In fairness, it must be noted that Schlesinger proposed his "pendulum theory" in the waning days of the Bush administration, when it seemed possible that a populist Democrat might seize the presidency. As he was proposing his cyclic vision of social policy, "new Democrats" were busy organizing the Democratic

Leadership Council to see to it that the pendulum did *not* swing back to the political left!

As early as the 1970s, some liberal intellectuals were vocalizing misgivings about welfare programs, as evident in Moynihan's report on the black family.[77] And Moynihan was not alone. Philosophically, maternalism tended to be invasive, denying consumers of welfare the respect and dignity due them as citizens. "Paternalism is despotic," wrote Isaiah Berlin,

> not because it is more oppressive than naked, brutal, unenlightened tyranny, nor merely because it ignores the transcendental reason embodied in me, but because it is an insult to my conception of myself as a human being, determined to make my own life in accordance with my own (not necessarily rational or benevolent) purposes, and, above all, entitled to be recognized as such by others.[78]

Others began to object on utilitarian grounds. A blow-by-blow account of how an Oakland community development initiative foundered under the most propitious circumstances is tellingly subtitled: *Implementation: How Great Expectations in Washington Are Dashed in Oakland; or, Why It's Amazing That Federal Programs Work at All, This Being the Saga of the Economic Development Administration as Told by Two Sympathetic Observers Who Seek to Build Morals on a Foundation of Ruined Hopes.* In it Aaron Wildavsky and Jeffrey Pressman described an imbroglio that would have confounded the most sympathetic liberal.[79]

As disenchantment with government welfare programs spread, doubts were raised within the Democratic party, eventually attracting the attention of Charles Peters, editor of the *Washington Monthly*. An irascible journalist from the Kennedy administration, Peters was an avowed critic of bureaucracy, private or public. Peters coined the term "neoliberal" to describe those Democrats who departed from the party line with respect to social programs. "A neoconservative is someone who took a long hard look at where liberalism went wrong, and became a conservative," he explained. "A neoliberal is someone who took that same hard look at what was wrong with liberalism, and decided to correct it, but still retain his liberal values."[80] For Peters much of what was wrong with the Democratic party was its reflexive support of the welfare state and opposition to the military and business, and he proposed fundamental reforms:

> We want to eliminate duplication and apply a means-test to these programs. As a practical matter the country can't afford to spend money on people who don't need it. . . . As liberal idealists, we don't think the well-off should be getting money from those programs anyway—every cent we can afford should go to helping those in real need. Social Security for those totally dependent on it is miserably inadequate, as is welfare in many states.[81]

That Peters would choose to attack Social Security, the bedrock of the American welfare state, spoke volumes about how low liberalism had sunk.

The neoliberal disenchantment with the welfare state in general and its welfare provisions in particular resonated with younger Democrats in Congress. The apparent irrelevance of liberal domestic policy, compounded by the failed presidential candidacies of Jimmy Carter in 1980, Walter Mondale in 1984, and Michael Dukakis in 1988, provoked several prominent Democrats—Paul Tsongas, Richard Gephardt, Sam Nunn, and Bill Bradley—to found the Democratic Leadership Council (DLC) to pull the party to the right. The DLC hired Al From as its director and established a think tank, the Progressive Policy Institute (PPI), under the direction of Will Marshall. The DLC would score a major victory in 1992 when the Democratic presidential ticket featured two founders: Bill Clinton and Al Gore. In formatting its position on social policy, the Clinton administration would draw on PPI advocacy of a new social contract that included dramatic changes in welfare, such as the institution of work mandates and time limits.[82]

These political developments were profoundly unsettling for liberal welfare philosophers who sought evidence of broad public support for the welfare state. The most ambitious of these efforts was a research project undertaken by Fay Cook and Edith Barrett, who sampled over a thousand Americans as well as select members of the House of Representatives during the late 1980s. Well into the second term of the Reagan presidency, the public voiced support for social programs, though this varied significantly depending on the program. More than half of respondents, for example, favored increasing Social Security and Medicare, while half thought AFDC and Food Stamps should be maintained, with a substantial minority suggesting benefit reductions.[83] Respondents from the public and the House of Representatives favored increases in social insurance programs but preferred not to expand public assistance benefits. "The picture painted by these data is hardly what one would have expected given the so-called crisis in rhetoric of the 1980s," Cook and Barrett concluded, "when opponents of social welfare argued to the federal administration that social welfare programs had lost their legitimacy in the eyes of the public."[84]

In retrospect, Cook and Barrett seem to have sampled public support that was rapidly diminishing. The public was unwilling to increase benefits for AFDC and Food Stamps, even though these programs were among the most severely pommeled during the Reagan administration. That most Americans favored the status quo for programs as inadequate as public assistance was hardly cause for celebration. Congressional support was more problematic. To their credit, the researchers intended to survey both houses of Congress, but senators refused to participate. From 1980 to 1986, the Senate was controlled by Republicans averse to welfare programs, while the House was controlled by Democrats who favored them.

A more doctrinaire liberal approach to the plight of the American welfare state was presented by Ted Marmor, Jerry Mashaw, and Philip Harvey. In one of the surprisingly few defenses of public social programs issued toward the end of the Reagan/Bush era, these experts conceded that the United States had an inadequate configuration of social programs, but insisted that the liberal ideology that had evolved during the New Deal remained on firm footing. Marmor and his associates admitted that the public was anything but enthralled with public welfare programs. "The public has made it clear that it does not wish to roll back the clock, but the welfare state shows no signs of experiencing a renaissance either. . . . Public confidence in the durability of welfare state institutions remains low."[85] Running on empty, the welfare state was showing indications of grinding to a halt. Indeed, the response of President Clinton to the Republican congressional sweep of 1994 would dampen any remaining enthusiasm about federal social programs. Ever eager to be on the right side of public opinion, President Clinton announced in his State of the Union speech that "the era of big government is over."

In light of conservative electoral triumphs and Democratic party defections, liberals drew up a defense of social programs based on pragmatic considerations—that they simply worked. Lisbeth Schorr, by way of illustration, surveyed a variety of innovative health, welfare, and education programs and proposed that they provided lessons for national replication.[86] Sylvia Ann Hewlett presented a strategy for investing in services for children.[87] Considered on their own, these works seemed worthy, but in the context of rapidly deteriorating political and economic support for social welfare, they rang hollow. By contrast, the discouraging works of Jonathan Kozol seemed a more accurate diagnosis of the liberal predicament.[88] In reviewing the period, the welfare scholar William Epstein would assign the label "pernicious liberalism" to liberals' romantic, superficial responses to the structurally deep and confidence-shattering changes introduced by conservatives during the 1980s.[89]

In historical perspective, it appeared that the matrons who displayed such courage and imagination in fabricating the maternalist programs of the Progressive era were replaced decades later by leaders of lesser stature. Despite the dearth of leadership, professional social work expanded, battened by an evolving welfare state that presumed a continuing need for its services. Meanwhile, in the absence of any convincing evidence of its effectiveness, public welfare became a target for pundits: social workers were employed by a "nanny state," assuming that "people are too stupid or too immature to decide important things for themselves,"[90] all at public expense.

LEFT FIELD

During periods of ideological transition, leadership often shifts from the bureaucracy to the academy. So it was from the late 1970s through the 1980s and into the 1990s, when budget rescissions reduced poverty programs, that liberals looked to the left for inspiration. Leftists had long contended that the American welfare state did not go far enough in creating equality by redistributing income. Accordingly, leftist academics had indicted the nation's political economy for denying opportunity to the poor and other disadvantaged populations. In their critique of welfare, *Regulating the Poor,* Frances Fox Piven and Richard Cloward had argued that relief programs expanded and contracted in cycles related to unemployment and resultant civil disorder; even in periods of expansion, public assistance benefits were meager. William Ryan furthered leftist analysis by theorizing that the antisocial behaviors of the poor were rooted in a dysfunctional economic system that had to produce social programs in order to control poor deviants.[91] Having attributed poverty and the other problems of the poor to the American political economy, the left waited for democratic capitalism to self-destruct. The burden of socializing the cost of so much poverty-related deviance would eventually crush the political economy, leading to a complete overhaul of social policy and welfare programs, they averred; the contradictions of capitalism would result in its demise. Accordingly, on the eve of the 1980 presidential election, the prominent leftist intellectual Irving Howe charged that Ronald Reagan's candidacy was an "over-heated reaction to the welfare state" and predicted that Reagan's defeat would "prove the last gasp of the American right."[92] Later, liberal poverty researchers would express relief that federal welfare programs had emerged unscathed from Reagan policy initiatives. "Following the cutbacks achieved in the first two Reagan administration budgets," concluded David Ellwood and Lawrence Summers, "there are few proponents of further major reductions of antipoverty spending."[93]

The left was understandably flummoxed during the 1980s. Quickly, Piven and Cloward reversed field and embraced the relief programs of the welfare state for the essential economic security they provided to the poor. "The emergence of the welfare state was a momentous development in American history," they admitted. "It meant that people could turn to government to shield them from the insecurities and hardships of an unrestrained market economy."[94] Although their appreciation of welfare programs had increased in response to conservative threats, the devil in the machinery remained (capitalism), along with its institutional manifestation (the corporation), and its agents (politicians and the generals of the military-industrial complex). These interests had collaborated to revive a hoary rhetoric about the sloth-

fulness of the poor, self-serving bureaucrats, dependency-inducing professionals, and a duped public that financed the entire scheme. The true victims,
Piven, Cloward, and their collaborators insisted, were the poor and working
class, who were manipulated by a corporate-dominated power structure.

> The current ideological attack on the welfare state is a continuation of the re-
> peated efforts of the American business elite to limit the gains not only of the
> most vulnerable but of the majority of working people. In fact, the contemporary
> arguments against the welfare state are remarkably similar to those that have
> been employed decade after decade by business interests and their intellectual
> representatives.[95]

Conceding that "many of the liberal intelligentsia [were] unprepared to respond to the conservative assault with a strong defense of the welfare state,"
Piven, Cloward, and associates countered, as late as 1987, not with an alternative framework for social programs, but with vitriolic rhetoric.[96]

Throughout the 1980s, America's leading leftists failed to generate original
research that would help reverse the diminishing economic circumstances
of the welfare- and working-poor. In light of the considerable research that
went into Piven and Cloward's *Regulating the Poor* this is baffling, but it was
not without consequence. "The best-known radicals in social policy have . . .
lost authority because they are no longer doing much research," observed
Lawrence Mead in 1988. Leftist "authors have collected no fresh data about
the welfare problem, and in an age when most social policy analysis is highly
quantitative, that is disqualifying. A purely literary Left can no longer claim
the influence it once did on issues of social policy."[97]

While the left indulged in ideological hyperbole, the American public was
moving to the right, at least if public opinion polls were any indication. In 1976,
for example, most Americans opposed more spending for social welfare, regardless of age, education, gender, and political affiliation. Significantly, even
those earning less than $10,000 a year opposed additional funding for wel-
fare programs. Of all the subgroups sampled, only nonwhites approved of
welfare expenditures.[98] A subsequent poll conducted by the National Opinion Research Center revealed that while Americans favored aid to the poor,
respondents did not favor welfare as the proper conduit for assistance: while
64 percent thought too little was spent on the poor, 41 percent thought too
much was spent on welfare. "While *Americans favor government action to
help the poor,*" concluded Hugh Heclo, "*they generally dislike the subset of
government programs that are intended to be targeted on the poor.*"[99]

In 1988 Public Agenda, a nonprofit polling organization, considered social
problems with hypothetical costs attached:

> While a majority wants the government's role to be expanded in certain ways,
> there are definite limits to what people are willing to pay for expanding govern-

ment's role in social welfare. . . . Significantly, only a minority indicated a willingness to pay more than $25 per year for any of the proposals. This was true even for the most popular of them, the proposal to provide government assistance for long-term care.[100]

By the time Public Agenda revisited this subject in a 1996 survey of public opinion about welfare reform, public sentiment was clearer. Asked to consider several scenarios involving time limits, the public was increasingly impatient about indefinite receipt of public assistance. "Eight in ten (83%) would even place time limits on the benefits of an applicant sympathetically described as a woman with children who is abandoned by her husband of 15 years, who has never worked, and is running out of money," the study concluded. "The sole exception they make is for a welfare applicant described as a physically and mentally handicapped 25-year-old. Here, 80% say time limits are not appropriate."[101] By contrast, the public was less likely to cite structural causes of poverty; only 11 percent of whites and 15 percent of blacks attributed higher welfare rates among blacks to racism and discrimination.[102] This 1996 survey is particularly interesting because the sample was of sufficient size to include the responses of welfare recipients. As shown in table 2.1, the responses of beneficiaries of public assistance tend to follow those of the general public.

Thus, in 1996 on the eve of welfare reform, the American left had lost touch not only with minorities, but with the poor as well. Given the widening disparities in income between rich and poor—traditionally, the *raison d'être* of left-wing ideology—this is hard to imagine, but the left had managed to marginalize itself in the policy debate. "When the Right proclaims that socialism has failed and that capitalism is the only alternative, the cultural Left has little to say in reply," lamented Richard Rorty. The left "prefers not to talk about money. Its principal enemy is a mind-set [sexism, racism, homophobia, and so on] rather than a set of economic arrangements."[103] Instead of offering "inspiring images of the country," the American left indulged in posturing vis-à-vis an increasingly narrow spectrum of the nation's population, while the economic circumstances of ever greater numbers of Americans deteriorated.[104]

Had the left paid attention to more mundane and practical issues, it would have been well positioned to "start proposing changes in the laws of a real country, inhabited by real people who are enduring unnecessary suffering"[105]—in other words, to present a compelling case for a post–welfare state social policy paradigm. That the welfare state was an archaic idea would have been evident upon examination of statements made by leading Democrats. As early as 1988, Ted Kennedy had distanced himself from the welfare state: "We now stand between two Americas, the one we have known and the one toward which we are heading," he told the Women's National Democratic

Table 2.1   Problems with the Welfare System

Percentages saying item is a "very serious" problem	General Public	Blacks	Whites	Welfare Recipients
People abuse the system by staying on too long and not trying hard enough to get off	73%	72%	72%	67%
It's financially better for people to stay on welfare than to get a job	70	68	69	71
Welfare is passed on from generation to generation, creating a permanent underclass	68	62	68	59
The system gives people benefits without requiring them to do work in return	66	60	66	60
People cheat and commit fraud to get welfare benefits	64	69	62	67
Welfare encourages teenagers to have kids out of wedlock	60	59	61	64
The system costs taxpayers too much	59	55	59	55
The system undermines the work ethic and encourages people to be lazy	57	60	57	62
The system does not give people the skills and help they need to get off welfare	55	66	53	53
The system traps recipients and makes them dependent	54	50	53	52
The system gives out benefits too easily, without making sure applicants deserve them	51	50	51	43
People are no longer embarrassed about getting welfare	41	48	40	32
The system encourages criminal behavior	39	38	37	45
The system makes getting benefits a humiliating experience	19	30	16	30
Welfare benefits are too low	13	26	11	29

Source: Steve Farkas and Jean Johnson, "The Values We Live By" (New York: Public Agenda, 1996), p. 40.

Club. "The New Deal will live in American history forever as a supreme example of government responsiveness to the times. But it is no answer to the problems of today."[106] In the shadow of the 1994 Republican electoral triumph, "new" Democrat Al From was more blunt: "The New Deal is over. It was a grand and glorious era for Democrats, but it is over. The nails are in the coffin of New Deal liberalism, and it is dead and buried. It was a great ideology while it lasted—it was the ideology that built the middle class of America—but the policies that built the middle class can no longer earn their support. And we have lost them."[107]

The absence of rigorous analysis of welfare during the decades of liberal hegemony following the New Deal meant that most liberals were caught off-guard by the conservative juggernaut that swept them aside in the 1980s. Despite ample warning—the Reagan administration introduced its anti-welfare initiatives as early as 1981 via the Omnibus Budget Reconciliation Act—liberals struggled to find some vehicle for thwarting conservative designs in social policy. Yet, if the Reagan/Bush administrations were punitive, President Clinton's signature to the Personal Responsibility and Work Opportunity Reconciliation Act of 1996 was nothing less than apostasy. Fundamental aspects of the legislation, including terminating open-ended funding, instituting time limits, and devolving operations to the states, were simply revolutionary. The legislation represented a stunning setback for liberals who had hoped that Clinton's instincts, as evident in his advocacy for increases in the minimum wage, health care reform, and urban aid, would also yield enhanced opportunities for poor families.

Endeavoring to track the states' implementation of welfare reform, a group of liberal scholars under the auspices of the Tufts University Center on Hunger and Poverty developed the "Tufts Scale," which incorporated seven variables: "benefit levels and eligibility, time limits for receipt of benefits, work requirements and related sanctions, assistance in obtaining work, income and asset enhancement, availability of subsidized child care, and special provisions for legal immigrant families."[108] Possible scores ranged from −38 to +22. State rankings are listed in table 2.2. "Overall, fourteen states created welfare programs demonstrating greater investment in the economic security of poor families, while two states maintained the status quo under prior law," concluded the researchers. "Thirty-five states (including DC) designed welfare programs that are likely to worsen the economic security of poor families."[109]

State retrenchment in welfare, as suggested by the Tufts Scale, could not revive allegiance to a program that had experienced massive defections, even among African American intellectuals. "Indeed, today the welfare state faces its own crisis," concluded Orlando Patterson, "partly due to its expense, but, more importantly, due to the fact that it has taken the collectivist approach to welfare too far, resulting in the generation of dependency among the poorest groups that it aims to protect."[110] Welfare had become a liability not only to its disproportionately minority beneficiaries but to the very welfare state project itself.

DENOUEMENT

A convergence of events would prove inauspicious for welfare in America. Having grafted the American welfare state to the European model, liberal welfare philosophers pronounced that, despite its glacial advancement, pov-

Table 2.2   Tufts Welfare Reform Scores with State Rankings

State	Rank	Score
Vermont	1	12.0
Oregon	2	7.5
Rhode Island	3	6.5
Pennsylvania	4	4.5
New Hampshire	4	4.5
Maine	4	4.5
California	4	4.5
Washington	8	4.0
Connecticut	8	4.0
Utah	10	2.5
Illinois	10	2.5
Minnesota	12	2.0
Massachusetts	12	2.0
Tennessee	14	1.5
New York	15	0.0
Nebraska	15	0.0
Virginia	17	−0.5
Texas	17	−0.5
Montana	19	−1.0
Delaware	20	−1.5
Nevada	21	−2.0
Hawaii	21	−2.0
Colorado	21	−2.0
Arkansas	21	−2.0
Alaska	25	−2.5
New Mexico	26	−3.0
North Dakota	26	−3.0
Michigan	28	−3.5
Maryland	28	−3.5
West Virginia	30	−4.0
Wisconsin	30	−4.0
South Carolina	30	−4.0
Arizona	30	−4.0
South Dakota	34	−5.0
Oklahoma	34	−5.0
Kentucky	34	−5.0
Indiana	34	−5.0
Ohio	38	−6.0
Florida	38	−6.0
North Carolina	40	−6.5
Louisiana	40	−6.5
Iowa	40	−6.5
New Jersey	43	−7.0
Missouri	44	−8.0
Mississippi	45	−9.0
Alabama	45	−9.0

continued

Table 2.2   *Continued*

State	Rank	Score
Georgia	47	−9.5
District of Columbia	48	−10.0
Kansas	49	−11.0
Wyoming	50	−12.0
Idaho	51	−15.5

Source: "Are States Improving the Lives of Poor Families?" (Medford, Mass.: Tufts University Center on Hunger and Poverty, 1998), p. 21.

erty programs in the United States would eventually parallel those of northern Europe and provide an adequate income as a right of citizenship. A full array of income and opportunity insurances was inevitable in America; a fully elaborated social welfare institution was an unavoidable product of industrialization. For social work, the profession that had assumed welfare as its institutional assignment during the Progressive era, this fantasy resulted in complacency. If historical determinism preordained a welfare state in America, why bother with generating theory and research about poverty? Indeed, as social work shelved its interest in poverty, public welfare was no longer deemed worthy of academic scrutiny. Reflecting the left's preoccupation with issues other than economic stratification, social work stopped focusing on poverty altogether and turned to issues of race, gender, and other priorities of cultural politics.

Ideologically forsaken and academically forgotten, welfare would not go unnoticed by the public. Opinion polls as far back as the late 1970s showed that the public's primary attitude toward poverty policy was one of disenchantment, and this sense intensified during the 1980s. Rather than assume the task of re-envisaging poverty policy, liberals assumed that the welfare bureaucracy would lumber along indefinitely until a more propitious moment when equality could be advanced once again, as had been the case in the 1930s and 1960s, while the left abrogated any responsibility for reforming welfare and contented itself with sniping at the right. While liberals and the left diddled, conservatives had been doing their homework on the welfare state, going so far as to address the problem of poverty. By the early 1990s, this would pay off handsomely: welfare was ripe for the picking.

3

The New Paternalism

Cradling an antsy 18-month-old in her arms, Christian reflects on her decade of receiving public assistance.[1] While she has received Food Stamps and Medicaid all along, intermittent jobs have limited her receipt of cash benefits to three or four years. Her assessment of welfare? "They've made their mistakes," she says, recalling a bureaucratic foul-up that left her without child support for five years. "But, for me, it's been a blessing to get the help. You just gotta go by the rules."

Initially, Christian sought aid for herself and her son, then two. Getting on welfare was not easy, and the family spent a few months living in shelters or sleeping in her car. She recalls waking up to frost on the windshield. Drawing on her own reserves, the young mother located an apartment in public housing and worked at a variety of minimum-wage service jobs, eventually finding a job as a secretary for an auto mechanic shop. The job was part-time, but the $5.00 an hour wage meant the end of her welfare check. Because of sexual harassment by one of the mechanics and her interest in returning to college, Christian quit the job after three years and applied for a college grant. She now supports her family with a Pell Grant, Food Stamps, Medicaid, and thrift: "I could write a book on how to pinch pennies," she says. Asked how she manages, she points around the apartment; the sofa is used, her daughter's clothes are hand-me-downs, her own clothes are a gift from her mother. "I save money, that's how I survive," she elaborates, noting that because she lives in public housing her rent is zero, and she pays only for the utilities.

Welfare, she suggests, is not about money; it's a state of mind. For her, the solution has been God, who has provided her with everything she has needed. Referring to other mothers in the apartment complex who are on welfare, she observes that "a lot of these women are down on themselves; they kick back and expect welfare. But the money isn't the issue; they need help with the underlying problem. . . . If their mind was different, they could do so much with the money they have. A lot of it is responsibility and sacrifice, and saying 'no' to things you don't need."

Her solution would be programs focusing on sexual and physical abuse, as well as counseling. "Set up things that help their hearts more than their wallets, because once you get the heart and the mind right, they can do all right. They realize, I *am* somebody, I *can* do this."

In Christian's mind, "the goal of welfare is to get the dirt poor into the working class. But it's a big gap. There's got to be steps to help people." She is doubtful about time limits on welfare: "Time limits will only force [welfare mothers] to be more dependent on men, or other activities such as prostitution and drugs." As it is, "too many women are looking for a man to take care of them."

With two years left before she completes her undergraduate degree, Christian plans for a job in law enforcement that will pay at least 10 dollars an hour. Reminded that such a wage might leave her family with an annual income of only $15,000, she is undaunted: "I'd make it work, some kinda way." Much of her confidence is a result of her faith in God. As for marriage, she knows that "if God sends someone, it will be someone stable." Someday she will have a house, she says, and she will set aside a room "for someone who's needy, so I can be in a position to bless somebody."

In emphasizing her faith, thrift, and optimism, Christian echoes the conservative welfare reform refrain. As she understands poverty, providing cash misses the real problem: a defeated frame of mind and the behavior that results.

CONTROLLING THE MEANS OF ANALYSIS

Given the considerable reversals that liberals experienced during the 1980s, it is not surprising that they blamed the conservatives who occupied the White House, but cracks were evident in the foundation of the American welfare state well before then. The first nominally liberal critic of unbridled welfare spending was Daniel Patrick Moynihan, who would become an advisor to President Nixon and a senator from New York. Moynihan's 1965 report, "The Negro Family: The Case for National Action," followed in 1969 by *Maximum Feasible Misunderstanding*, contended that subverting traditional political and economic structures—the family and mayors, respectively—would eventually be counterproductive.[2] Late in the 1970s, Henry Aaron, a senior fellow at the Brookings Institution, was expressing reservations about the social programs consuming increasingly larger portions of the nation's economic bounty.[3]

Quite irrespective of the ideological infidelity of some liberal intellectuals, conservatives were already well on their way to overturning the liberal hegemony in domestic affairs. During the early 1970s, the conservative political scientist and editor Irving Kristol had made a shrewd observation in response to the unhappiness business executives had expressed about the liberal direction of public policy. Kristol noted that much of the intellectual groundwork for social policy was done at liberal policy institutes, like the Brookings Institution and the Urban Institute. "Why," he asked rhetorically, "if you don't like what's coming out of the liberal think tanks, don't you set up your own?"[4] Chief executive officers of America's major corporations responded with a vengeance, writing checks or channeling funds through foundations for a new intellectual infrastructure of right-wing policy institutes.[5] Over two decades Richard Mellon Scaife alone contributed $340 million to enhance the conservative ideological infrastructure.[6]

Conservative think tanks thrived. Once corporate executives recognized that "waging the war of ideas . . . required the development of a vast and interconnected institutional apparatus,"[7] revenues flowed freely to conservative policy projects. For their part, liberal intellectuals were so aloof from public discourse that a conservative intellectual infrastructure had evolved largely under their very noses in the nation's capital and achieved many of its initial triumphs before its supply lines could be identified. Between 1992 and 1994 a dozen foundations made grants totaling $210 million to conservative policy organizations. Of this, $88.9 million went to scholarships and programs designed to train the next generation of ideologues, and $79.2 million to think tanks and advocacy groups; of this, $64 million was targeted at domestic policy.[8] Of primary concern within the domestic policy sphere was public welfare, so conservatives drafted an outline for reform that resonated with conservative foundations. "If we are to address violent crime, rising illegitimacy, and declining values, we must revitalize civil society: families, neighborhoods, churches, schools and other private institutions," recited Jeremiah Milbank, Jr., in the 1995 annual report of the JM Foundation. "Since the public sector has played a key role in fostering dependency, entitlement, and victimization, we should also reduce the size and scope of government."[9] The assault on public welfare, a novel idea for conservatives of a generation before, involved the construction of a theoretical base, the application of relevant data, and its packaging to policymakers. Three think tanks choreographed this campaign: the American Enterprise Institute, the Heritage Foundation, and the Hoover Institution.

THE AMERICAN ENTERPRISE INSTITUTE

The first major beneficiary of conservative philanthropy was the American Enterprise Institute for Public Policy Research (AEI). In 1970, AEI was a small Chamber of Commerce clone with a budget of $800,000. By 1978, its budget had swollen to $5.0 million; it would expand to $11.7 million in 1982.

Shortly after the inauguration of Ronald Reagan, AEI's president William Baroody, Jr., stated the institute's ambitious objective:

> The public philosophy that has guided American policy for decades is undergoing change. For more than four decades, the philosophy of Franklin Delano Roosevelt's New Deal prevailed, in essence calling upon government to do whatever individual men and women could not do for themselves.
>
> Today we see growing signs of a new public philosophy, one that still seeks to meet fundamental human needs, but to meet them through a better balance between the public and private sectors of society.
>
> The American Enterprise Institute has been at the forefront of this change. Many of today's policy initiatives are building on intellectual foundations partly laid down by the Institute.[10]

By the time the 1980 presidential campaign was heating up, AEI had 30 scholars and fellows in residence (earning $30,000 to $50,000 per year), 77 adjunct scholars, and 250 professors associated with the institute nationwide. AEI's senior staff and board members represented a *Who's Who* of the nation's conservative and political elite.

In domestic affairs, AEI focused its considerable resources and talent on two projects. The "mediating structures project" enlisted the services of Peter Berger, a sociologist, and Richard John Neuhaus, a theologian. In the project's major publication, *To Empower People,* Berger and Neuhaus stated that the fundamental problem of our times was the growth of megastructures—big government, big business, big labor, and professional bureaucracies—and a corresponding decline in the importance of individuals. The route to empowering people, then, was to revitalize "mediating structures": the neighborhood, family, church, and voluntary associations.[11] *To Empower People* was a readable and lucid work that served AEI well. The apparent impartiality of the mediating structures project, however, was little more than a veneer—Berger's hostility toward liberals would surface in later works.[12] The project's implicit critique of government programs was clearly enunciated in a modest study of the Meals on Wheels program by AEI's Michael Balzano. In *Federalizing Meals on Wheels,* Balzano argued that the Older Americans Act diminished the voluntary impulses of church and community groups (mediating structures) by subsidizing nutrition programs for the elderly. "In most cases, common sense and the desire to help one's neighbor are all that are necessary," Balzano concluded. "One does not need a masters degree in social work or gerontology to dish out chow at a nutrition center."[13]

The second project, on democratic capitalism, endeavored to elevate the role of the corporation in public life. This necessitated a bit of theoretical hanky-panky, since the Berger-Neuhaus project had portrayed big business as a megastructure and therefore inimical to the vitality of mediating structures. The contradiction was disposed of deftly by Michael Novak, a theologian and the project director. In *Toward a Theology of the Corporation*, Novak used a single footnote to transfer big business from its designation as megastructure to that of a mediator, leaving big government and its allies—big labor and professional associations—as institutions of cultural and economic oppression against a corporate sector that contributed to the genius of the American experience.[14] Under Novak's direction, the project on democratic capitalism intended to transform public philosophy by portraying the corporation as a promoter of cultural enlightenment, as opposed to a perpetrator of vulgar capitalism. "The social instrument invented by democratic capitalism to achieve social goals is the private corporation," he proselytized. "The corporation . . . is not merely an economic institution. It is also a moral and a political institution. It depends on and generates certain moral-cultural virtues; it depends upon and generates new political forms. . . . Beyond its economic effects, the corporation changes the ethos and the cultural forms of society."[15] At the same time, Novak took careful aim at the public sector: "I advise intelligent, ambitious, and morally serious young Christians and Jews to awaken to the growing dangers of statism. They will better serve their souls and serve the Kingdom of God all around the world by restoring liberty and power of the private sector than by working for the state."[16]

Through the 1980s, AEI's mediating structures project provided a theoretical framework for criticizing government social programs that had been inspired by liberals. At the same time, the glorification of the corporation helped AEI attract a stellar cast of business leaders to serve on its board and contribute to its projects. Success, at least in part, was to prove AEI's undoing, however. During the latter part of the decade, AEI moved toward the ideological center under the direction of Christopher DeMuth, who had worked in the Office of Management and Budget and directed the Kennedy School of Government's program on deregulation.[17] Meanwhile, the conservative ideological vector accelerated, and the brash Heritage Foundation assumed leadership in the right's public policy crusade.

THE HERITAGE FOUNDATION

Started in 1973 with a $250,000 grant from the Coors family, the Heritage Foundation would have a budget equal to that of AEI within a decade. By the time the Reagan administration was in place, Heritage had placed more than 35 staff members in upper-level positions in the executive branch. Espousing a militant conservative ideology, Heritage proposed radical alternatives to established programs and molded its work to the more traditional tastes of the religious right. By breaking new ground while building mass support for policy initiatives, Heritage complemented the less partisan analysis of AEI. Heritage social policy initiatives emphasized privatization, reforming social welfare by transferring activities from government to business. The foundations's antagonism toward government intrusion in social affairs was unqualified. Government programs were blamed for a breakdown in the mutual obligations between groups, the lack of attention to efficiencies and incentives in the way programs were operated and benefits awarded, the induced dependency of program beneficiaries, and the growth of the welfare industry and related special interest groups, particularly professional associations.[18] Robert Rector provided trenchant quips to the media; Stuart Butler introduced urban enterprise zones into discussions of urban policy; and Peter Ferrara suggested privatizing Social Security.[19] The policy coup of the decade, however, was Heritage's fielding of Charles Murray.

In 1982 a pamphlet Murray had written for Heritage, "Safety Nets and the Truly Needy," came to the attention of William Hammett, the president of the Manhattan Institute, a conservative New York think tank. Murray's suggestion that welfare actually contributed to dependency appealed to Hammett, who offered $125,000 to support a book-length treatise on the idea. Traded by Heritage to Manhattan, Murray elaborated his thesis that Great Society programs had actually worsened the conditions of the poor. Murray's wrecking-ball thesis advocated a "zero-transfer system," which "consisted of scrapping the entire federal welfare and income-support structure for working-aged persons."[20] Remembering his earlier sponsor, Murray returned to Heritage on December 12, 1984, to promote his book to a standing-room-only audience as part of a symposium entitled "What's Wrong with Welfare." The Heritage appearance was one piece of a well-orchestrated public speaking blitz that placed Murray on major news programs and his book in dozens of editorials across the nation.[21] Instantly, *Losing Ground* became a social policy phenomenon that would define the welfare debate for a decade.

THE HOOVER INSTITUTION

Meanwhile, on the West Coast, Stanford University's Hoover Institution was taking a different tack. According to Hoover's Martin Anderson, liberal social programs were simply no longer necessary. "The war on poverty has been won, except for perhaps a few mopping-up operations," he wrote on the eve of the Reagan presidency. "The combination of strong economic growth and a dramatic increase in government spending on welfare and income transfer programs for more than a decade has virtually wiped out poverty in the United States."[22] Like so many promising conservative intellectuals, Anderson was to have a chance to see his platform for social reform put into action when he became policy advisor to the Reagan administration. For his move to Washington, Anderson packed a short list of welfare reform goals:

1. Reaffirm the need-only philosophical approach to welfare, and state it as explicit national policy.
2. Increase efforts to eliminate fraud.
3. Establish a fair, clear work requirement.
4. Remove inappropriate beneficiaries from the welfare roles.
5. Enforce support of dependents by those who have the responsibility and are shirking it.
6. Improve the efficiency and effectiveness of welfare administration.
7. Shift more responsibility for welfare from the federal government to state and local governments and to private institutions.[23]

THE MEANS OF ANALYSIS

It is sobering to see how much of the conservative agenda has come to pass—the transformation of public philosophy, the creation of urban enterprise ("empowerment") zones, the devolution of welfare, and serious discussions about the privatization of Social Security, to name a few items—particularly considering how radical these proposals were in the early 1980s. This establishment of conservatism as American public philosophy was orchestrated in large measure by the conservative policy institutes; they learned how to control the means of analysis. Irving Horowitz placed the context in the information age:

> The nineteenth century was largely defined by the struggle for control of the means of production; the twentieth is being defined as a struggle over the means of communication and information. The new technology forces us to come to terms with the social content of ideas; who controls the hardware, software, and marketing, or information about the information, may ultimately control the information itself.[24]

Exploiting information technology, conservative policy institutes prepared op-eds and crafted them for newspapers serving the largest American cities, to which they were sent routinely at no charge, taped video conferences on contemporary issues and distributed them free to television stations serving the largest media markets, and customized succinct monographs on important issues that were then distributed to members of Congress. The rule for policy overviews was that they had to be brief enough to be read during the cab ride from National (Reagan) Airport to Capitol Hill. Over the years, the strategy paid off. "Scholarly detachment lost ground to partisan marketing of ideas," noted one journalist. "The distinction between public policy research and propaganda mills is becoming increasingly blurred."[25] Curiously, the profundity of the development eluded most observers; conservatives were understandably reluctant to trumpet their victories, while liberals, in their more reserved policy institutes, waited complacently for the conservative moment to blow over. The journalist Cregg Easterbrook recognized that the rise of conservative public philosophy had less to do with the ascendance of Ronald Reagan than with the increased sophistication of policy institutes on the ideological right. "While the political ascent of conservatism has taken place in full public view, the intellectual transformation has for the most part occurred behind the scenes, in a network of [conservative] think tanks."[26]

The methods of the conservative policy institutes were decidedly entrepreneurial, in marked contrast to the more staid liberal think tanks. A student of policy institutes, James Smith, noted the differing styles: "[Conservative think tanks] were argumentative, more certain about their policy convictions. Their publications were shorter, more likely to take the form of a briefing paper, and always more quickly produced and disseminated. Their reports seemed to resonate with the press and within wider political constituencies." Meanwhile, "at Brookings and other mainstream institutions, we still thought in terms of scholarly books, hoping and praying that a few journalists might attend our occasional press conferences; we still conceived of an audience that was limited mostly to Washington policymakers and university-based policy scholars." The audience of the liberal policy institutes consisted largely of the intellectual elite that had managed social legislation since the New Deal, a group that the conservatives maneuvered around by crafting a populist message and dispatching it persistently through the media. "[Conservatives] built new institutional bastions; recruited, trained and equipped their intellectual warriors; forged new weapons as cable television, the Internet, and other communications technologies evolved; and threw their full resources into policy and political battles."[27]

The result was a rout, or perhaps more apropos, a revolution.[28] Conservatives commanded the print and electronic media, saturating a public whose appetite for social affairs had been ignored by liberal intellectuals comfortably tenured in their ivory towers. In an ebullient moment, Heritage's Burton Pines acknowledged the pivotal role of think tanks in the rapid evolution of conservatism in the United States: "Together, Hoover, AEI and Heritage can today deploy formidable armies on the battlefield of ideas—forces which traditionalist movements previously lacked."[29] A decade later, investigative reporters from the *Washington Post* concurred: the policy institutes established by wealthy conservatives "constitute a conservative intellectual infrastructure that provided ideas and human talent that helped Ronald Reagan initiate a new Republican era in 1980, and helped Newt Gingrich initiate another one in 1994. Conservative ideas once dismissed as flaky or extreme moved into the mainstream."[30]

It was almost two *decades* after conservatives had laid the foundation for this intellectual infrastructure that liberals became aware of the right's strategy. "Conservative think tanks outspend liberal organizations (loosely defined) by at least four to one," observed Karen Paget. "On many of the most important measures backed by conservative funders, left-liberal organizations simply aren't in the game. Meanwhile, over the past ten years the conservative right has excelled in changing the rules of the game by devising big, bold initiatives that tilt the system to their advantage."[31] Reflecting their mastery of the means of analysis, Paget noted, "conservative funders pay meticulous attention to the entire 'knowledge production' process. They think of it in terms of 'a conveyer belt' that stretches from academic research to marketing and mobilization, from scholars to activists." The result? "We've largely won the battle of ideas," boasted Kate O'Beirne, formerly of the Heritage Foundation. "We are in the implementation stage now."[32]

The conservative critique of welfare, elaborated and revised at AEI, Heritage, and Hoover, spread throughout the intellectual world of the ideological right. William Schambra, formerly of AEI, cycled through the Department of Health and Human Services as a speechwriter during the Bush presidency and eventually assumed a position with the Bradley Foundation in Milwaukee, headed by Michael Joyce. In collaboration with Joyce, Schambra redefined "citizenship" to refer to the civic activities of individuals in neighborhoods and communities, whose efforts were often thwarted by liberal social programs justified by the perverse notion that the nation was one giant community. Rather than binding together a nation of diverse groups, the "national community" assumption that undergirded the welfare state served to rob localities of their capacity for self-sufficiency. What was worse, Schambra and Joyce complained, was that the liberals' national community model was elitist, suggesting that only policy experts in Washington had the capacity to determine matters of domestic concern; local residents were, by implication, ignorant rubes. Community-based problem solving would be much more effective, *not* with the assistance of the federal government, but *only* if Washington got out of the way.[33] The conservative critique of social policy thus contained not only a powerful critique of federal programs but also a direct appeal to local control. What differentiated this conservative populism from earlier forms was its link to a technology that rapidly disseminated it to the hinterlands. Control of the means of analysis allowed conservatives to script an antiliberal tract on social programs at the same time that it cultivated a constituency outside Washington that would eventually elect representatives to reverse the alleged damage caused by "welfare."

Thus, through AEI, Hoover, Heritage, and other think tanks of the right, conservative intellectuals controlled the means of analysis in order to promulgate a persuasive critique of federal social programs and aggressively hustle it to the public. The welfare state was hazardous for several reasons, they maintained. First, social programs were funded through revenue derived from taxes that, if not so diverted, could be used for further capitalization of the private sector. Second, social programs invariably granted the state the right to intrude into areas that should be held private, such as the family. Third, social programs were administered through an unresponsive and expensive public bureaucracy. The surest way to make social welfare more cost effective was through assigning its responsibilities to the private sector (i.e., privatization) or, short of that, by eliminating unnecessary red tape (i.e., deregulation). This critique complemented the more traditional complaints that welfare benefits eroded the work ethic and family solidarity. The demerits of welfare were so numerous that virtually every conservative policy institute eventually prepared and distributed to the media its program for welfare reform.

BEHAVIORAL POVERTY

As conservatives became more familiar with welfare, their analysis became more astute. This evolution was not without faux pas, such as the Reagan administration's effort to have catsup classified as a vegetable in order to reduce appropriations under the School Lunch Program. Nor was it without guile, as when Office of Management and Budget director David Stockman invented numbers during his congressional testimony prior to passage of the 1981 Omnibus Budget Reconciliation Act. Whether specific maneuvers were bungling or brazen, the conservative incursion into welfare policy would eventually pay off handsomely. The upward trajectory of their learning curve vis-à-vis welfare policy was matched by the plummeting credibility of liberal welfare programs.

The first substantive beachhead gained by conservatives during the welfare policy skirmishes of the 1980s involved the number of poor people in the United States. Conservatives alleged that liberals provided a false portrait of poverty by failing to include the "market value" of noncash benefits, such as Food Stamps. The cash value of such welfare benefits significantly reduces the number of poor, they argued by about one-third (table 3.1). While liberals had argued that statistics based on the poverty line underestimated the number of poor because the line itself was dated (formulated during the early 1960s), conservatives used the market value of benefits to argue that liberals had been consistently *overestimating* the extent of poverty in America.[34]

Table 3.1   Population below the U.S. Poverty Line, 1985

	Cash Income Only (millions)	After Noncash Benefits (millions)	Change (%)
Individuals			
Total	33.1	21.9	−34%
In families	25.7	17.1	−33
In families with children			
under 18	20.3	13.7	−33
Unrelated individuals	6.7	4.3	−36
Over 64	3.5	0.9	−74
Under 18	13.0	8.8	−32
Families			
Total	7.2	4.7	−35
Married-couple	3.4	2.4	−29
Single-headed	3.8	2.3	−39

Source: Adapted from Michael Novak, ed., *The New Consensus on Family and Welfare* (Washington, D.C.: American Enterprise Institute, 1987), p. 27.

Emboldened by this victory, conservatives pursued a new, even more profound argument: that variations in family characteristics suggested alternative strategies in poverty policy. In this respect, they showed that female-headed households were much more likely to be poor than traditional, husband-wife households (table 3.2). One theme that emerges from table 3.2 has become fundamental to the conservative understanding of poverty: female-headed households are about four times more likely to be poor than husband-wife households. This is a particularly important observation for black families, since more than half of black female-headed households are poor. As Novak and his collaborators concluded, "Husband-wife families present fewer problems for public policy while the growing number of female-headed households involves higher public expenditures."[35]

From their preliminary explorations of poverty, conservatives learned a handful of lessons that would serve them well. "It is not entirely a mystery how many climb out of poverty. Some specific behaviors empower them," wrote Novak. "The probabilities of remaining involuntarily in poverty are remarkably low for those who:

• complete high school
• once an adult, get married and stay married (even if not on the first try)
• stay employed, even if at a wage and under conditions below their ultimate aims."[36]

This suggested that there was more to poverty than simple absence of income: the poor had low incomes in part because of their behavior. Implicated in this "behavioral poverty" was welfare. "Existing welfare policy [i]s toxic," Novak suggested. "Even if welfare policy has not *caused* the wide-

Table 3.2   Family Structure and Poverty, 1985

	Number of Families	Poor Families (millions)		Poverty Rate (%)	
		Cash Income Only	After Noncash Benefits	Cash Income Only	After Noncash Benefits
All families	63.6	7.2	4.7	11%	8%
Husband–wife	50.9	3.4	2.4	7	5
Female-headed	10.2	3.5	2.1	34	20
White families					
Husband–wife	45.9	2.8	2.1	6	4
Female-headed	7.1	2.0	1.2	27	17
Black families					
Husband–wife	3.7	0.4	0.3	12	8
Female-headed	2.9	1.5	0.9	51	30
Hispanic families					
Husband–wife	3.0	0.5	0.4	17	12
Female-headed	1.0	0.5	0.3	53	29

Source: Michael Novak, ed., *The New Consensus on Family and Welfare* (Washington, D.C.: American Enterprise Institute, 1987), p. 44.

spread behavioral dependency that has now become so highly visible, at the very least existing public policies have done little to remedy the situation."[37]

While the introduction of behavioral poverty represented increasing sophistication on the conservatives' part, it remained problematic. Behavioral poverty was highly correlated with variations in who was defined as low-income, so conservative investigators had a data base to substantiate and track its evolution. On the other hand, some of the "behaviors" were mutable, while others were contentious, especially for conservatives. For example, requiring school attendance was not so troublesome (virtually all communities had laws against truancy), but instituting a social policy encouraging marriage was a blatant intrusion into family life. As conservatives sorted through responses to behavioral poverty, a consensus emerged. The welfare-poor could be required to engage in one behavior that significantly elevated them from poverty—work; other behaviors would be at the option of state government.

From a conservative point of view, public policy can institute a de facto work requirement simply by eliminating social program supports for the able-bodied. This is what George Gilder meant when he wrote that what the poor needed most was not more government welfare assistance, but "the spur of their own poverty."[38] In *Losing Ground*, Charles Murray echoed that refrain by suggesting the elimination of all benefits for working-aged persons. In the political climate of the 1980s, with liberals railing about the destructive consequences of conservative social policy, this was perceived as too malevolent, and a middle ground was sought. Lawrence Mead offered a more plausible suggestion: receipt of welfare should be conditional—that is, available depending on adherence to specific behavioral standards. Most important, Mead proposed that AFDC recipients could be expected to work in exchange for benefits.[39]

THE NEW PATERNALISM

The idea that social program benefits should be predicated on specific behaviors is not new. Enduring principles of welfare policy have evolved with regard to the suitability of persons to receive benefits. The "principle of less eligibility," introduced through the Elizabethan Poor Laws of the seventeenth century, mandated that relief benefits be below the lowest prevailing wage in order to avoid subverting the work ethic. During the nineteenth century, the distinction between the worthy and unworthy poor revolved around their capacity to work. The worthy could receive "indoor relief" in their own homes; the unworthy poor, who were presumed to be able-bodied, would be consigned to "outdoor relief" in the workhouse.[40] Under a distinction structured into the American welfare state by the Social Security Act, social insurance provided more adequate benefits on the assumption that its recipients were male workers, while the beneficiaries of public assistance— welfare—were presumed to be female dependents and not in the labor market.[41] Thus, the value of work had been introduced into the American welfare state well before the advent of conservatism during the 1980s. What differentiated the New Paternalism from these preceding forms was its attention to detail.

Fundamentally, the New Paternalism was a prescription for alleviating behavioral poverty. If the poor suffered from poverty for reasons other than absence of cash, and this was attributed to volition, then a logical policy outcome would be to dissuade the poor from counterproductive acts. As Joel Handler has observed, there is nothing novel about the moral hazards of poverty:

> The "unworthy" poor have always been associated with sin, vice, disease, and crime. Adults who can work but do not are deviant. They fail as role models, jeopardizing the appropriate socialization of their children. In addition, today's welfare mothers do not marry but have children out-of-wedlock and engage in other forms of antisocial behavior, including drugs and crime. The result is that welfare children grow up in poverty; they suffer from bad environments, do poorly in school, and often follow the paths of their parents in dependency or worse.[42]

For conservatives, it was precisely because the welfare-poor tended to replicate poverty generationally that a new orientation toward the poor was justified. Mead, who coined the expression "the New Paternalism," described the new context of welfare policy:

> Government is moving away from freedom and toward authority as its basic tool in social policy. Opportunity is no longer enough to overcome low income, given the dysfunctional character of serious poverty today. The ghetto has become to a great extent self-perpetuating, and, for many residents, there remains no alternative to society attempting to redirect behavior. A tutelary regime is emerging in which dependents receive support of several kinds on condition of restrictions on their lives.[43]

Discreetly applied, the New Paternalism could redirect the poor away from destructive behavior. In so doing, it would create a constructive dynamic in social policy, promoting civic virtue.

Behavioral standards would apply to all recipients of welfare, though only the most dependent would be the real object. In this respect, the New Paternalism focused on the underclass, but as mediated by public opinion. "From the public's perspective," noted Mead, "the key aim of welfare employment is to change lifestyle—simply to have the welfare adults do more to help themselves. Actually working or leaving aid may be the final goal, but to show effort in that direction is also an end in itself." The ultimate object of the New Paternalism would be the poorest of the welfare-poor: "the long-term recipients [who] remain dependent largely because they do not work regularly and often have children out of wedlock." Given the severe and extenuating dysfunctional behavior of the poor, the New Paternalism invited interventions along a number of fronts, including work, procreation, education, health, and family life. By addressing all of these, Mead contended, the New Paternalism would stop the disabling behavior of the poor and in so doing integrate them into the social mainstream.[44]

Rarely has a novel idea been so quickly enacted as social policy. Mead's suggestion of reciprocity as a condition of welfare receipt coincided perfectly with the conservative concern about behavioral poverty. Within two years of the appearance of Mead's *Beyond Entitlement* in 1986, the Family Support Act was passed, mandating work, education, or training in exchange for benefits.

Not all conservatives subscribed to the New Paternalism. AEI's Douglas Besharov, for example, cautioned against large-scale "social engineering." "Many of the proposals now being made could end up hurting the poor, not helping them, and might taint more reasonable efforts to alter dysfunctional behavior," he testified before a congressional committee.[45] But Besharov's concerns were already swamped by state intentions in the name of welfare reform. As noted in table 3.3, the experiments in welfare reform encouraged by the Family Support Act addressed behavioral poverty directly via a number of penalties and benefits. As the Reagan administration proceeded to grant states waivers for welfare experiments, what had once been a national network of benefits for the poor overseen by the federal government was deconstructed state by state. As the states assumed greater control over welfare, momentum built for welfare reform that would make devolution federal policy.

THE FAMILY SUPPORT ACT

Enacted at the end of the Reagan presidency, the Family Support Act (FSA) of 1988 would prove as auspicious for conservatives as it was inauspicious for liberals. After the punishing welfare cuts of the 1981 Omnibus Budget Reconciliation Act and the doomed 1988 Catastrophic Health Insurance Act, which would be repealed in 1989, liberals perceived the FSA as imposing on poor mothers expectations that were utterly unrealistic. After all, the 1967 Work Incentive Program (WIN) had encouraged welfare mothers to engage in work or education, and compliance had been minimal; now FSA required such activity, or mothers would lose benefits. At the opposite end of the ideological spectrum, conservatives applauded the implementation of a work requirement with real sanctions, and waivers for state experiments were a boon to Republican governors who had their own designs on the poor. Indeed, Republican governors used welfare reform as their benchmark for "an experiment in activist, conservative, governance" that would prove to be "extraordinarily popular at home."[46]

In putting the New Paternalism to the test, FSA would presage truly radical reform in 1996. FSA incorporated work-related incentives and penalties for AFDC mothers. The carrot consisted of the Job Opportunities and Basic Skills (JOBS) program, which provided job training and "transitional benefits": the continuation of childcare, Medicaid, and transportation for one year after securing a job. The stick was the termination of benefits for a mother who refused to participate in "welfare-to-work" and did not have an exempting excuse, such as a pre-school-aged child. The act was budgeted at a Reaganesque $3.34 billion over five years. During this period, states were encouraged to develop innovative programs to wean poor mothers from AFDC and make them economically self-sufficient.

Actually quite modest in intention, FSA soon yielded surprises for liberals and conservatives alike. Liberals had long contended that welfare-to-work merely badgered poor women into dead-end jobs, exacerbating their hopelessness. Much to the liberals' chagrin, the majority of AFDC mothers re-

Table 3.3   The New Paternalism: Programs and Proposals

Behavior	Program/Proposal	Rule	Penalty/Benefit
Employment	California Welfare Reform Proposal	Able-bodied adults who remain on AFDC for 6 months without getting a job would receive lower benefits.	15% reduction in AFDC grant after 6 months for any family headed by an able-bodied adult
	New Jersey Welfare Reform	AFDC mothers who work can keep more earnings while retaining benefits.	Earned income disregard, increasing to an amount up to 25% of monthly AFDC grant
	Teenage Parenthood Demonstration (Ill., N.J.)	Unemployed teenage mothers must participate in education and employment services.	Reduction in AFDC benefits if recipient fails to participate in education and job training
School attendance	California Welfare Reform Proposal	Teen parents must attend school regularly.	$50 monthly reduction or increase contingent on school attendance
	Drivers' License (Ark., Fla., Ky., La., Miss., Tenn., Tex., Va., W.Va.)	Students aged 16–18 must remain in school to keep their drivers' licenses.	Loss of drivers' license if school attendance requirements are not met
	LEAP (Ohio)	Teen parents and pregnant teens on AFDC must stay in school.	$62 monthly reduction or increase contingent on school attendance
	Learnfare (Wis.)	All 13–19-year-olds on AFDC must stay in school.	Reduction in AFDC benefits until attendance requirements are met
	Maryland Welfare Reform Proposal	Children on AFDC must stay in school.	Reduction in AFDC benefits until attendance requirements are met
Teenage living arrangements	California Welfare Reform Proposal	Teen mothers must live with a parent or guardian to get AFDC.	Loss of AFDC benefits
Preventive health care	Maryland Medicaid Program	Parents must have a family doctor to get medical care.	Referral by family doctor required for Medicaid recipients to be hospitalized or see a specialist
	Maryland Welfare Reform Proposal	Parents must obtain preventive care for their children.	Reductions in welfare grants unless recipients provide proof of health care visits
	WIC Demonstration (Chicago and New York)	Mothers on WIC are rewarded for getting immunizations for their children.	3 months of vouchers issued at one time with proof of immunization

continued

Table 3.3   *Continued*

Behavior	Program/Proposal	Rule	Penalty/Benefit
Fertility	California Welfare Reform Proposal	Welfare grants for additional children are eliminated.	Elimination of AFDC grants for additional children
	New Jersey Welfare Reform	Welfare grants for additional children are eliminated.	Elimination of AFDC grants for additional children
	Parental and Family Responsibility Proposal (Wis.)	Welfare grants for additional children are reduced.	Reduction of AFDC grants for second children, elimination of aid for additional children
	Planned Parenthood "Dollar A Day" Program (Denver)	Teens at risk of becoming pregnant are encouraged to use contraception or practice abstinence.	$7 bonus for each week in which girls are not pregnant
Marriage	New Jersey Welfare Reform	Marriage is promoted among welfare recipients.	Increase in total AFDC benefits available to married couples
	Parental and Family Responsibility Initiative ("Wedfare") (Wis.)	Marriage of young couples is promoted.	Married young couples allowed to retain $200 or more of their income while receiving welfare

Source: Douglas Besharov, "Statement before the Select Committee on Hunger," U.S. House of Representatives, Washington, D.C., 21 May 1992, pp. 11–13.

sponded to their welfare-to-work requirement with interest, if not enthusiasm. Evidently, the prospect of education, job training, and employment was preferable to sitting at home with the kids. Furthermore, JOBS offered the promise of upward mobility for those AFDC mothers who took advantage of the earned-income disregard. Contrary to leftist predictions, AFDC mothers did not refuse en masse to participate in welfare-to-work programs—in effect, striking against welfare.

Conservatives got the real surprise, however. FSA was the first welfare reform clearly bearing a conservative imprimatur. It was traditional in its expectations: AFDC mothers with older children would have to work or participate in a training program. It was fiscally frugal, budgeted at less than $1 billion per year. It encouraged states to experiment with other ways to make welfare beneficiaries more conventional in their behavior. What was more, unanticipated developments propelled the conservative cause. States became increasingly ingenious in placing conditions on receipt of AFDC: Wisconsin required children on AFDC to attend school regularly; New Jersey refused to provide more assistance for additional children born to a parent on AFDC; Maryland required school-aged children to be vaccinated against communicable diseases.[47] Having found the front of the wave, conservatives discovered that it was breaking in ways they could not have imagined. Even poor, disproportionately minority women were showing a genuine interest in improving their financial circumstances. Nearing the end of the 1980s, conservatives celebrated a rather substantial accomplishment. In less than a decade, they had taken what had been perceived to be a dependency-inducing, liberal social welfare entitlement and converted AFDC to a conditional benefit that rewarded traditional values—particularly self-sufficiency.

Fortunately—considering the ideological baggage associated with welfare—the primary studies of welfare-to-work initiatives were conducted by a highly respected organization widely regarded as nonpartisan, the Manpower Demonstration Research Corporation (MDRC). The MDRC welfare-to-work studies conducted during the 1980s were a remarkable achievement in and of themselves. Instead of shrinking from the prospect of studying a new program (JOBS) appended to an unpopular welfare program (AFDC) that varied enormously from state to state, the MDRC saw this as an opportunity to conduct field experiments under varying conditions. Among the earlier findings, MDRC researchers concluded that welfare-to-work produced desirable benefits in communities where jobs were plentiful, as opposed to communities in which the unemployment rate was high. Interestingly, the benefits of welfare-to-work programs were greatest when targeted at AFDC recipients who had been most dependent on welfare, as opposed to those who had participated more in the labor market.[48] Such findings were less than unqualified endorsements of welfare-to-work, however. Toward the end of the 1980s, Harvard's David Ellwood summarized the early findings of relevant research: "Most work-welfare programs look like decent investments, but no carefully evaluated work-welfare programs have done more than put a tiny dent in the welfare caseloads, even though they have been received with enthusiasm." Ellwood calculated that the increased earnings attributed to an AFDC mother's participation in welfare-to-work programs ranged from $250 to $750 *per year,* hardly enough to make many women independent of welfare.[49]

In 1991 MDRC published a summary of welfare-to-work field experiments that had been conducted in 13 communities throughout the United States. Four of these are fairly representative and are summarized in table 3.4. Two elaborations will aid in interpreting the table. First, the Arkansas WORK Program and the San Diego Saturation Work Initiative Model (SWIM) were mandatory and, as a result, served a broad range of AFDC recipients. By contrast, the New Jersey On-the-Job Training (OJT) Program and the AFDC Homemaker-Home Health Aide Demonstrations were vol-

Table 3.4   AFDC Welfare-to-Work Programs

Program	Type	Cost per Experimental Participant	Outcome	Experimental/ Control Difference
Arkansas WORK Program	Mandatory	$118	Earnings:	
			Year 1	$167
			Year 2	223
			Year 3	337
			AFDC payments:	
			Year 1	−$145
			Year 2	−190
			Year 3	−168
San Diego Saturation Work Initiative Model (SWIM)	Mandatory	$919	Earnings:	
			Year 1	$352
			Year 2	$658
			AFDC payments:	
			Year 1	−$407
			Year 2	−553
New Jersey On-the-Job Training (OJT) Program	Voluntary	$787	Earnings:	
			Year 1	n/a
			Year 2	$591
			AFDC payments:	
			Year 1	−$190
			Year 2	−238
AFDC Homemaker– Home Health Aide Demonstrations	Voluntary	$9,505	Earnings:	
			Year 1	$2,026
			Year 2	1,347
			Year 3	1,121
			AFDC and Food Stamp benefits:	
			Year 1	−$696
			Year 2	−858
			Year 3	−343

Source: Adapted from Judith Gueron and Edward Pauly, From Welfare to Work (New York: Russell Sage Foundation, 1991), table 1.1.

untary and, as a result, more selective. Second, benefits of welfare-to-work programs are essentially twofold. A successful program would elevate participants' earnings as well as decrease AFDC program costs. Finally, because welfare-to-work programs entail startup and maintenance costs independent of the normal operation of AFDC, these administrative costs should be offset by AFDC program savings attributable to welfare-to-work. In the best of all welfare-to-work worlds, earnings would be up, program expenses would be down, and the cost per participant would be low.

The good news was that welfare-to-work programs increased earnings and lowered program costs, but not a lot. Only one of the programs increased earnings more than one thousand dollars for each year after a participant had graduated. As Ellwood had observed, earnings remained too low to vault the typical AFDC mother off welfare. While welfare-to-work did lower AFDC program costs, these savings were also modest; none of the programs realized savings of one thousand dollars for each year after graduation. The bad news was that the cost per participant was not recovered until well after a participant had graduated from the program and been in the labor market for some time. Only Arkansas's WORK Program recovered its investment per participant in the first year after completion of the program. In most of the programs, welfare-to-work investments were not recouped until a few years later. Thus, from an administrative standpoint, the welfare-to-work payoff is not immediate but long-term.

MDRC data did not indicate that welfare-to-work had failed; rather, they reflected the incredible inertia that impedes upward mobility for poor families on AFDC. In order to generate earnings sufficient to ensure economic independence from AFDC, a huge investment would be necessary—on a par with the AFDC Homemaker-Home Health Aide Demonstration's cost per participant of $9,505, as noted in table 3. 4. It was unlikely that the federal government would accept this high an investment to make AFDC families self-sufficient. Most programs cost less than this to mount, of course, and their returns were correspondingly modest. Regardless of outcome variable, the returns on getting AFDC mothers to work were small. For pragmatically minded conservatives who had butted heads with bleeding-heart liberals throughout the 1980s, the MDRC results had to be disappointing. Subsequent research by the General Accounting Office (GAO) would be no more encouraging. In late 1994 the GAO noted that no JOBS program had moved a majority of AFDC recipients off welfare; between 1991 and 1993 only 11 percent of AFDC beneficiaries had participated in JOBS. Ominously, only 24 percent of pregnant teens on AFDC had enrolled in JOBS.[50] Having implicated AFDC in inducing dependency on government and the rise of the underclass, the conservative prescription for welfare reform was not producing the desired results. Welfare-to-work was a wash.

"THE END OF WELFARE AS WE KNOW IT"

Among the welfare-to-work field demonstrations, the Arkansas WORK Program was among the most successful. Although earnings of AFDC recipients increased only modestly, participant costs were recovered soon after graduation from WORK. Even if AFDC mothers were not leaving the program in droves, at least the state of Arkansas was saving money. This doubtless fueled then-Governor Clinton's enthusiasm for welfare reform as part of the Democratic platform during his campaign for the presidency. Other developments served to highlight welfare reform during that campaign. Preoccupied with foreign affairs, particularly the Persian Gulf War, President Bush had paid scant attention to social policy, hoping that "a thousand points of light" would sufficiently illuminate domestic concerns. The American middle class struggled against stagnating incomes to maintain a standard of living. As more working-class families lost health benefits, a paradox became unavoidable: working stiffs were unable to get health insurance, while unemployed welfare recipients received Medicaid. Resentment of welfare increased.

Despite passage of the FSA only a few years before, Democrats suspected that welfare reform remained a viable issue. Writers of the Progressive Policy Institute, the think tank appended to the Democratic Leadership Council (chaired by Governor Clinton), endorsed a two-year time limit for receipt of welfare.[51] An aggressive welfare-to-work program would provide training and education for two years, after which an AFDC recipient would have to obtain employment in the private sector or accept a government-created job. Limiting AFDC to two years was a relatively safe bet for campaign rhetoric, since a study conducted prior to implementation of the welfare-to-work provisions of the 1988 FSA indicated that half of AFDC recipients were on the program less than two years anyway.[52] With a more adequate JOBS program in place, coupled with the exemption of mothers with disabilities or very young children, the number of AFDC mothers facing a cutoff of benefits after two years would be manageable—at least for presidential campaign purposes.[53]

After the election, President Clinton moved expeditiously to reform AFDC once again. Wary of the influence that would be brought to bear on the two-year time limit by liberal interests (89 liberal advocacy groups had transmitted their objection to time-limited welfare), Clinton adopted a strategy of empanelling a relatively small group of 30 experts, all of whom held positions within the new administration. The charge to the Working Group on Welfare Reform was fourfold:

- *Make Work Pay*—families with full-time workers should get adequate income supports so that they would not have to resort to welfare.
- *Dramatically Improve Child Support Enforcement*—government should be more aggressive in extracting child support from absent parents.
- *Provide Education, Training, and Other Services to Help People Get Off and Stay Off Welfare*—redoubling JOBS provisions of the Family Support Act would make self-sufficiency more feasible for AFDC mothers.
- *Two-Year Time Limit*—AFDC would become a two-year transitional program if the first three provisions were in place.[54]

So constituted and charged, the Working Group on Welfare Reform promptly bogged down. Of the primary objectives, three were relatively incontrovertible. With regard to the working-poor, steady increases in the Earned Income Tax Credit (EITC), accelerated during the Reagan presidency, offered a substantial rebate from the Internal Revenue Service to low-income workers. Much of this objective would be accomplished when the president's economic program was enacted, since it contained a $28 billion increase in the EITC. Subsequent increases in the minimum wage paralleled EITC enhancement, further reinforcing the value of work. Improvements in child support enforcement would be tacked onto Title IVD of the Social Security Act, which had been in place since the amendments of 1975. Education, training, and other services would be reinforced by investing more in the JOBS provisions of FSA. Clearly, the sticking point was the two-year time limit.

To take the edge off liberal criticism that his two-year limit was too harsh, candidate Clinton had promised a public sector job when welfare to work graduates could not find one in the private sector. While this mollified liberals during the campaign, the postelection implications of government-created jobs were enormous. To be consistent with the first principle of welfare reform—Make Work Pay—such a job would have to bring a family above the poverty level. For the number of AFDC families who might require public employment, the costs appeared plausible. Yet it would be blasphemous to assure AFDC welfare-to-work graduates an income above the poverty line when people laboring for the minimum wage fell far below it. To be fair, the assurance of a public sector job would have to be extended to them, too, and the fiscal implications of that were on the order of $43 to $59 billion, an amount that would have taxpayers gagging.[55] This exceeded what the president was prepared to present to Congress as welfare reform.

Other issues dogged the president's welfare reform panel. If welfare-to-work were pursued more vigorously, there would be about 3 million more AFDC mothers seeking training and employment, imposing an enormous demand for child daycare. Financing such an expansion of daycare could cripple welfare reform, particularly if AFDC children were to be assured professional-quality care.[56] Panel deliberations on financing welfare reform considered solutions ranging from a new tax on gambling to drawing on savings attained by eliminating welfare benefits for noncitizens.[57] The ultimate snag, however, remained the two-year time limit. "What happens if a woman is not disabled and has a three-year-old kid who is not disabled, but she does not show up to work?" complained Congressman Robert Matsui (D. Calif.). "Do we take the child away from her and let her wander the streets?"[58]

While the Working Group on Welfare Reform dithered, states forged ahead with their own versions of welfare reform. More than a dozen states

Table 3.5   Common Welfare Reform Waivers

A. Earnings and assets
    1. Allowed workers to keep more of their earnings under the earned income disregard
    2. Allowed beneficiaries to retain a higher value of assets
B. Child support enforcement
    3. Immediately garnisheed any payments in arrears
    4. Aggressively determined paternity in hospitals upon birth of a child
    5. Required absent parents in arrears to participate in JOBS
C. Electronic benefit transfer
    6. Dispersed AFDC and Food Stamps benefits via plastic cards with magnetic strips
    7. Used "smart cards" as a generic means of access to benefits of various programs
D. Supporting intact families
    8. Allowed both parents to live with a family receiving AFDC
    9 Eliminated the requirement for unemployed wage-earners to stay at home
    10. Eliminated the 100-hour work limit for working parents
E. Transitional benefits
    11. Extended Medicaid and childcare benefits beyond six months
    12. Adopted a sliding scale to reduce transitional benefits
F. Job creation
    13. Used benefits to augment wages of private sector employment
    14. Developed microenterprise funds to incubate independent businesses
G. School attendance and completion
    15. Instituted bonuses and penalties related to attendance and graduation
    16. Provided intensive case management for pregnant teens
H. Time limits
    17. Established strict time limits for receipt of benefits, such as two years or 30 months
    18. Individualized contracts with beneficiaries that include stiff penalties for noncompliance
I. Alternative benefit payment
    19. Encouraged working families to replace AFDC with the 100 percent federally financed EITC
    20. Allowed families to receive lump-sum benefit payments, up to three times the normal grant, on a one-time basis.

Source: Based on Julie Strawn, Sheila Dacey, and Linda McCart, *Final Report, The National Governors' Association Survey of State Welfare Reforms* (Washington, D.C.: National Governors' Association, 1994).

had already received federal waivers to experiment with welfare reform by early 1994. Typical welfare reform waivers are subclassified in table 3.5. Among these dozen states, four proposed reducing or terminating AFDC after two years.[59] Florida proposed putting in place a two-year time limit for AFDC in two counties, a plan similar to Clinton's campaign promise.[60]

As enthusiasm for welfare reform spread among Republican governors, requests for federal waivers to mount welfare experiments escalated.[61] By the mid-1990s, with some 40 states seeking or having received waivers for welfare reform demonstrations, the administration was suddenly behind the policy curve in welfare reform.[62] Spying an opening, congressional Republicans patched together a 150-page welfare reform proposal of their own. Included in House Resolution 3500 were Republican suggestions to convert AFDC to a block grant, require teen mothers to live with their parents in order to receive AFDC, eliminate welfare benefits to aliens, and impose random drug tests on SSI recipients (a positive test would immediately terminate benefits).[63] With the president's promised welfare reform proposal already overdue, competing plans were attracting media attention.

The stalemate within the Working Group on Welfare Reform was finally broken by a suggestion from Paul Offner, an aide to Senator Moynihan. Not a member of the panel, Offner effectively used the print media to disseminate a brilliant example of policy incrementalism. The president's welfare reform group had reached an impasse: in order to avoid a punitive two-year limit on AFDC, welfare-to-work provisions would have to be so extensive that the costs of welfare reform would become impractical. Offner's solution was to target generous JOBS benefits coupled with a two-year time limit specifically to young mothers who were new to AFDC. "Teen-age mothers would have to live with their families to receive AFDC (they could not move out and get their own apartments), and they would have to stay in school until graduation or until they reached the age of 20," Offner proposed. "After receiving their degrees, or reaching the age of 20, they would be offered work, but not welfare." The cost of selective application of welfare reform, he speculated, would be no more than $500 million—a manageable amount, a shrewd investment of public funds, since it addressed the teenagers who were most likely to become dependent on welfare.[64]

On June 14, 1994, President Clinton announced his welfare reform proposal in a Kansas City bank that had hired former AFDC mothers. The proposal emphasized education and training benefits for recipients born after 1971, as Offner had suggested. For these prospective beneficiaries, AFDC would be limited to a single two-year benefit over a lifetime. Following training, AFDC recipients would have to find private sector employment or accept a community service job paying the minimum wage. Failure to comply would be grounds for terminating benefits. In order to dissuade teens from becoming pregnant, the proposal called for a nationwide campaign to reduce teenage pregnancy. Other features of the president's proposal included more aggressive child support enforcement, a national information clearinghouse to reduce welfare fraud, and limits on welfare benefits for legal immigrants. Clinton budgeted the plan at $9.3 billion over five years.

Public response was swift. Judith Gueron, president of MDRC, suggested that the president's proposal was "a step toward ending the current welfare system," though she suspected that it was inadequately funded.[65] Predictably, Will Marshall, president of the Progressive Policy Institute and an early enthusiast for time-limited welfare, characterized the plan as "radical, yet constructive change." If women's rights groups saw the proposal as punitive toward women, they reserved comment. Conservatives, on the other hand, were fuming. "A joke, a half fraud," remarked Reagan administration Secretary of Education and conservative lightning-rod William Bennett, "marginal tinkering."[66] "Tinkering," echoed Wisconsin governor Tommy Thompson, whose state had pioneered some of the features Clinton had pirated for his reform plan.[67] The public, however, was clearly behind Clinton. An April *Los Angeles Times* public opinion poll registered that 90 percent of Americans endorsed a two-year limit to welfare coupled with a job requirement. Moving tactically, editors of the *New Republic* used their editorial column to remind Clinton of the poll and goad him to propose "two-years-and-work" welfare reform the very week that Clinton made the announcement.[68]

More seasoned welfare reform observers were less sanguine about the Clinton proposal, however. Reserving the time limit to beneficiaries born after 1971 meant that two-thirds of AFDC recipients would remain virtually unaffected. By the year 2000, between 7 and 14 percent of AFDC recipients would be in job training or would have left the program.[69] Such modest expectations led one policy pundit to brand welfare reform à la Clinton as an extension of the Reagan reforms of the 1988 FSA—"much more incremental change in the welfare system than the sweeping reforms [Presidents] Nixon and Carter offered."[70]

RADICALLY CONSERVATIVE WELFARE REFORM

The Clinton welfare reform initiative foundered on White House ineptitude; once the administration expended all its momentum on the ill-fated Health Security Act, there was insufficient time for the 103rd Congress to act on welfare reform. The results of the 1994 midterm congressional elections fundamentally changed the context of any discussion of social policy, let alone welfare reform. Instead of a truculent Democratic Congress, Clinton was suddenly confronted with the first Republican Congress in 40 years. Moreover, the new Speaker of the House, Newt Gingrich, had made it patently clear through the "Contract with America" that radical change in social policy was in the offing. After much stumbling, President Clinton righted himself; by the end of his first term, he would be conceding to Republican principles of welfare reform. His pre-reelection conservative conversion on welfare reform prompted the resignation in protest of three high-level appointees—Mary Jo Bane, Peter Edelman, and Wendell Primus. Not only had any liberal aspect of welfare reform been defeated, but fundamental change in welfare policy would be implemented. Reversing the incremental nature of social policy change that marked the half-century following the Social Security Act, the 1996 welfare reform was radically conservative.

The framework of conservative welfare reform was a prominent part of the Contract with America, a campaign gimmick that Gingrich fabricated in order to build Republican unity prior to the 1994 congressional elections. Gingrich had long been disillusioned with federal social programs—at one point he suggested that the American welfare state should "be blown up to be replaced"[71]—and he wanted to replace the welfare state with the "opportunity society," at the same time transferring power from the federal government to the states. "We wanted," he remembered later, "to set out with the governors to create block grants; to begin to reduce the Washington bureaucracy; to cut out the red tape; to get power back home."[72] The Contract with America attributed behavioral poverty to the War on Poverty and was determined to correct it:

> The Great Society has had the unintended consequence of snaring millions of Americans into the welfare trap. Government programs designed to give a helping hand to the neediest Americans have instead bred illegitimacy, crime, illiteracy, and more poverty. Our Contract with America will change this destructive social behavior by requiring welfare recipients to take personal responsibility for the decisions they make. Our Contract will achieve what some thirty years of massive welfare spending has not been able to accomplish: reduce illegitimacy, require work, and save taxpayers money.[73]

Immediately after the 1994 Republican congressional election triumph, the welfare reform components of the Contract with America were incorporated in the Personal Responsibility Act (PRA), the conservative template for overhauling public assistance. Twice Congress presented PRA to the president, and twice Clinton vetoed it.[74] With the presidential campaign heating up, however, Clinton capitulated the third time that PRA passed. In order to salvage social programs depleted by Congress as well as preempt Republican presidential candidate Bob Dole from exploiting any reneging on his campaign promise to "end welfare as we know it," Clinton signed the Republican welfare reform plan.

The Personal Responsibility and Work Opportunity Reconciliation Act (PRWORA) was truly revolutionary. It not only terminated AFDC, a 60-year-old entitlement, but included virtually every component of the Contract with America. Through PRWORA:

- AFDC was replaced by Temporary Assistance for Needy Families (TANF), a block grant that would be devolved to the states.
- TANF appropriations would be for fixed amounts, the total amount representing a $55 billion reduction in federal payments to the poor over six years.

- Receipt of TANF benefits would be limited to five years over a lifetime, with the option for states to institute shorter time limits.
- Recipients of TANF would be required to work, and states would be held accountable for increasing labor force participation from 25 percent of recipients working in 1997 to 50 percent in 2002, although states could exempt 20 percent of cases from working.
- Child support enforcement was strengthened by requiring TANF recipients to identify paternity for children on assistance and assign child support collection to the states as well as take prompt action denying license renewals to parents in arrears.
- States were required to prepare plans to diminish the "illegitimacy ratio" from 1996 through 2005, with the five best-performing states eligible for $20 million bonuses.
- All TANF and Food Stamp benefits would be permanently denied to persons convicted of felony drug possession, use, or distribution unless the states pass legislation to the contrary.
- All newly arriving immigrants would be denied all federally funded, means-tested benefits for the first five years they are in the United States.

Liberals were crestfallen; after all, the Congressional Budget Office, whose director had been chosen by the Republican leadership, had projected that "between 2.5 million and 3.5 million children could be affected by the bill's five-year time limit when it is implemented, even after the 20 percent hardship exemption is taken into account."[75] And this was only one of several damaging provisions of PRWORA. The liberal columnist Bob Herbert evoked a metaphor that was enjoying increasing use by the left—the "war" being waged on the poor—when he chastised Clinton: "He may have avoided the draft as a young man, but history will remember him as a more than competent general in the war against the poor."[76]

Whatever else the federal welfare reform of 1996 would do, it erased any illusion that Bill Clinton was a latent liberal. The veteran Washington journalist Elizabeth Drew placed Clinton's apostasy in signing the welfare reform bill in perspective: "Thus, Clinton colluded with Newt Gingrich in removing a cornerstone of the New Deal, or what Gingrich called 'the welfare state.' This had been Gingrich's highest goal."[77] In signing PRWORA, in other words, Clinton moved farther to the right than most Democrats would have thought conceivable.[78] Clinton had not only slid past moderate Republicans on the ideological continuum but had done what few of even the most ardent conservatives could have imagined possible: he had out-Reaganed Reagan.

4

Welfare Behaviorism

Over the muted tones of a television talk show (*Sally*—the program is "Stop Me from Killing My Child"), Sheila Mayes explains how she has become a childcare provider as an alternative to welfare. Although she has received Medicaid and Food Stamps for several years, she received a welfare check for only 18 months or so. For nine years, she and her 16 year-old daughter have lived in a two-bedroom apartment in public housing, an arrangement that limits her rent to $10 a month. After several excursions into the labor market, she found minimum-wage service sector jobs that paid enough to cancel her welfare check but not enough to support her family without Medicaid and Food Stamps.

Income from childcare is proving more dependable than her welfare check had been. She is the only private provider in the apartment complex, where childcare is in constant demand, and she can negotiate flexible terms with working mothers who live nearby. Today, she is caring for three children of a neighbor who used to be on welfare; while we talk, another mother stops by to drop off her child for a few hours. At $50 a week for each child, her rates are low, but she is unwilling to overcharge the poor mothers who are her neighbors. Once she becomes a certified childcare provider, she figures she could care for five to seven children, a number that seems high for the confines of her apartment, especially since her second-floor unit makes it impossible to allow older children outside while keeping an eye on toddlers inside. But in all likelihood this is a temporary arrangement; the apartment complex is constructing a child development center where she hopes to work soon as a salaried employee.

Sheila's experience with welfare has made her sympathetic to the circumstances of her neighbors. Quoting HUD Secretary Andrew Cuomo, she says, "All of us are just one paycheck away from being on welfare." But she has mixed feelings about welfare reform. When asked if welfare reform is making mothers more self-sufficient, she responds, "I think it is, I think it is. Mothers go to work and come home tired, but it's a good feeling." She is reminded of her childhood: "When I grew up, I saw my father come home from work; we were all taught to be self-sufficient. It's the way we were raised."

But she is also concerned about the "scare tactics" that have been used by welfare reformers. "Everybody needs a net," she says. Referring to many of the younger mothers in the complex, she observes, "Most of them are between 18 and 25 years old and were brought up different. Those who never had a work history need training and childcare." How long? "Maybe five or six months."

Sheila is optimistic about her future. So long as she continues to receive Medicaid for her health problems, she can manage financially. "I'm pretty confident about the future," she says. "I can take my childcare certificate and my housing voucher and move anywhere."

Because she is generating income through childcare, Sheila is ineligible for cash assistance, but she is aware that most of the welfare mothers in the complex make creative use of resources—welfare, work, boyfriends, hustling—when they become available, disregarding the welfare reporting requirements. Getting by on welfare requires creativity, as Sheila appreciates.

THE CONSERVATIVE TRIUMPH IN WELFARE REFORM

On August 22, 1996, President Clinton signed the Personal Responsibility and Work Opportunity Reconciliation Act, ending the welfare entitlement to poor families through AFDC and devolving responsibility to the states in the form of a block grant.[1] Congressional Republicans had been eager to call the president's bluff with a welfare reform proposal that he could not veto without risk of voters' disapproval. Conveniently, the most punitive part of the plan—the five-year lifetime limit on welfare receipt—would not take effect until Clinton left the White House.

Yet as an attempt to reprogram the behavior of the poor, Republican-inspired welfare reform seemed a mixed blessing. In the first place, conservatives celebrated an astonishing drop in the welfare caseload—30 percent between January 1994 and September 1997.[2] Less often cited was the evidence accumulating from the multitude of state welfare demonstrations that imposing conditions for welfare yielded modest results at best; at worst, the consequences were downright perverse. Despite data demonstrating the marginal economic benefits of making welfare conditional, conservatives effectively leveraged a moral argument that public policy should change the behavior of the welfare-poor. In so doing, welfare behaviorism represented a change in the way that conservatives had come to understand poverty.

Sheila Mayes

THE NEW CONSENSUS ON BEHAVIORAL POVERTY

On the eve of passage of the 1988 Family Support Act (FSA), conservative theorists had arrived at a "new consensus" on poverty: although the liberally inspired public assistance programs, such as AFDC, may have once been appropriate for the "cash poor," they were counterproductive for the "behaviorally poor."[3] Rather than alleviating the problems of the behaviorally poor, public welfare exacerbated the "culture of poverty." As poverty programs expanded, conservatives contended, the social dysfunctions of the behaviorally poor metastasized: beginning as teen mothers, women dominated family life, ultimately becoming generationally dependent on welfare; young men dropped out of school, failed to pursue legitimate employment, and resorted to sexual escapades and repetitive crime to demonstrate prowess; children, lacking adult role models of effective parents at home and capable workers on the job, promised to further populate the underclass.

Conservatives, however, had differed on how to respond to behavioral poverty. In *Losing Ground,* Charles Murray suggested "scrapping the entire federal welfare and income support structure for working-aged persons."[4] Not long thereafter, Lawrence Mead offered a less draconian measure in *Beyond Entitlement:* make receipt of public aid contingent on conventional behaviors, particularly work.[5] Eventually, both prescriptions were to be incorporated in welfare policy. Mead's admonition was reflected in the prescriptions of the New Paternalism (see table 3.3); some states sought waivers to implement Murray's recommendation that public assistance be terminated for the able-bodied. As momentum for welfare reform increased, the time-limiting of welfare benefits was incorporated into congressional proposals. Thus, the welfare reform plan Clinton signed allowed states to limit AFDC to less than two years for any stretch on aid, and to no more than five years over a lifetime.

Symbolically, PRWORA is a radical departure in American social welfare, and the political fallout has been extensive. Die-hard conservatives justified termination of welfare, frequently quoting George Gilder's endorsement of "the spur of their own poverty,"[6] while "bleeding heart" conservatives found a rationale in "tough love."[7] Either way, welfare reformers conceded that terminating benefits would probably worsen deprivation, but that was necessary too. If making welfare conditional worsened poverty, that was the price of combating the underclass. As a manifestation of public policy, welfare behaviorism might not be pretty, but it was essential to restore social order.

Liberals were aghast. Following Marian Wright Edelman's demand that the president veto the welfare reform program crafted by the 104th Congress,[8] the *Washington Post* weighed in with an editorial declaring that signing the welfare reform plan would be "the low point of his presidency."[9]

Citing conservative analysts, such as James Q. Wilson, Lawrence Mead, John DiIulio, and William Bennett, who had trepidations about the welfare reform plan, Senator Moynihan castigated Clinton for endorsing a bill whose premise was "that the behavior of certain adults can be changed by making the lives of their children as miserable as possible."[10] Liberal advocacy groups scrambled to persuade the president to veto the legislation, but they failed. Cleverly, Clinton had preempted their condemnation by announcing his intention to sign the plan before the conference proposal was voted on by either chamber of Congress. But heat from liberal activists intensified, leading Clinton to promise ameliorative action on the most controversial features of the welfare reform plan—elimination of benefits for the handicapped and legal immigrants—through the incoming 105th Congress. That the president would seek to reclaim such major concessions drew the fire of the usually even-tempered *Washington Post* columnist David Broder, who likened Clinton's expectation to Jack the Ripper's fancying a scholarship to medical school.

If the rhetoric of welfare reform was hyperbolic, the research on various welfare waivers scarcely mattered. By mid-1996 evaluation research revealed that the results of state welfare demonstrations were mixed and often problematic. Yet regardless of what both liberal and conservative policy analysts were coming to conclude about making welfare receipt contingent on specific behaviors, the momentum behind welfare reform seemed to accelerate. Indeed, the contradictory evidence may well have fueled the urgency that propelled welfare reform through the 104th Congress and on to the White House. Accumulating research on a range of welfare reform experiments—welfare-to-work, learnfare, teen pregnancy, paternity, and time limits—suggested caution in proceeding with major changes in public assistance programs. But data be damned, Congress and the White House were intent on reforming welfare in anticipation of the upcoming election.

WELFARE-TO-WORK

By the early 1990s, the Manpower Demonstration Research Corporation (MDRC) had amassed considerable evidence about the performance of state welfare-to-work programs, and the results appeared to fall short of what conservatives had promised. In the best of all welfare worlds, state welfare-to-work programs would show positive outcomes in three ways: welfare participants' earnings would improve, optimally allowing them to become economically self-sufficient; AFDC expenditures would decrease; and states would recover the costs of putting welfare-to-work programs in place. Of 13 welfare-to-work programs evaluated in 1991, most boosted participants' earnings little more than $700 per year. Most programs also experienced reductions in AFDC payments, but these too were modest, typically less than $400 per year. Significantly, in only two programs were AFDC payment reductions greater than the cost per welfare-to-work participant. In other words, in 11 of 13 welfare-to-work programs, the cost of mounting the program was not recovered initially in welfare savings.[11]

As in most field research, these findings are accompanied by important caveats. First, the welfare-to-work program that met all three requirements most efficiently was Arkansas's; for the first year of the program, earnings increased on average $167, and AFDC payments were reduced $145, enough to recover the additional cost of the state's WORK program, $118 per participant. This helps to explain Clinton's enthusiasm about "ending welfare as we know it." Second, two programs were notable for significantly higher annual earnings (over $2,000) as well as welfare savings (more than $700); but in both cases the cost per participant was also high (over $5,000). Thus, independence from welfare carries with it an acute case of sticker shock.

Yet such modest accomplishments did not dampen the fervor of welfare-to-work zealots. Quickly, they pointed to the GAIN program of Riverside County, California, as an exemplar.[12] Culminating an eight-year investigation of California's GAIN program, the nation's largest welfare-to-work effort, Judith Gueron, head of MDRC, chronicled Riverside County's achievements: an increase in AFDC parents working of 26 percent, an average earnings increase of 49 percent, and a saving in welfare payments of 15 percent. Over three years, Riverside County GAIN participants' incomes increased $3,113; welfare savings for the same period were $1,983. In Gueron's words, these were "the most impressive [outcomes] measured to date anywhere."[13] On an annual basis, of course, such figures diminish in significance. Earnings increases on the order of $1,000 a year are unlikely to vault the typical AFDC family off the program; nor do welfare savings of little more than $600 a year raise the specter of cashiering the welfare bureaucracy. Indeed, the Riverside experience led Randall Eberts of the Upjohn Institute for Employment Research to observe that only 23 percent of participants were still employed and off AFDC three years after beginning GAIN.[14] Riverside County's vibrant economy probably accounted for much of this superior performance, raising the question of how representative it is of other American communities. To welfare reform researchers, the welfare-to-work bandwagon was less than the star-spangled apparatus that its proponents had made it out to be.

But perhaps the modest returns from welfare-to-work programs would be amplified over a longer period, welfare reform proponents averred. If many AFDC recipients have been out of the labor force for a long time, they suggested, a two- or three-year assessment of a welfare-to-work program's performance might not reveal more substantial, longer-term benefits. A five-year assessment of welfare-to-work programs in Virginia, Arkansas, Baltimore, and San Diego examined this possibility. At the end of five years, Virginia and Arkansas participants increased earnings a little more than $1,000, while those in Baltimore and San Diego experienced an earnings increase of a little more than $2,000. Welfare savings, on the other hand, varied widely; Baltimore reduced welfare costs $62, while San Diego reported the greatest savings, $1,930. Net program costs varied as well, from $118 per participant in Arkansas to $953 per participant in Baltimore. Once annualized, these figures confirm the shorter-term experience of welfare-to-work programs in other locales. Again, earnings increases are modest; welfare program savings somewhat less so; and the recovery of setup costs iffy.

The long-term study of welfare-to-work provides additional insight that had not been available in previous research, however. Participants' earnings do not necessarily continue to increase with each additional year; rather, earnings tend to peak during the second or third year, then fall back toward the range prior to enrollment in welfare to work. The only place in which earnings did not fall was in Baltimore, whose program had the highest cost per participant. By definition, higher per participant cost is inconsistent with welfare savings; hence, a tradeoff appears. The objectives of increasing earnings in order to make families independent of welfare and reducing government welfare payments are contradictory.

If welfare reform means modest work opportunities for AFDC recipients, it has come to mean something else for welfare program managers, however. Confronted with static, if not declining, revenues, welfare officials—both elected officials and appointed department heads—have come under increasing pressure to reform the system, by whatever means. Exactly how this has come about is revealed in the five-year study noted above. From the perspective of welfare administrators, there are three ways to reduce welfare costs: trim monthly benefits to AFDC recipients who have found work (but are not earning enough to escape reliance on welfare completely), sanction families who are not complying with work or other conditions attached to receipt of benefits, or simply terminate cases. Regarding these options, researchers found that reducing benefits in relation to earnings accounted for no more than 2 percent of savings, while sanctioning noncompliant recipients produced only a "very small *direct* effect." Most of the savings in welfare costs were generated by terminating cases as soon as possible. In Arkansas case closings reduced AFDC receipt three months on average; in San Diego, almost four months. Yet case closings did not alter recidivism (frequent cycling on and off welfare). Even those AFDC recipients who had found work and were terminated from public assistance were soon back on welfare. What is going on here?

The likely answer can be found in the way welfare programs are administered. Welfare programs like AFDC require a significant amount of paperwork to establish and maintain eligibility.[15] Yet welfare departments are rarely staffed adequately to process the mountains of paperwork that program management dictates. The resultant quagmire is familiar to anyone who has spent time in a welfare department: applicants for assistance spend hours waiting to be seen by eligibility workers, often only to be sent off in search of additional documentation to support an application. Until the application is complete, no aid will be forthcoming. Facing a lobby full of anxious and resentful applicants, eligibility workers exercise latitude in making decisions about the fate of those applying for benefits, occasionally expediting the application of someone in dire straits, often impeding the application of the more troublesome ("bureaucratic disentitlement," to use Lipsky's term). The prevalence of outright denial of benefits to those who are entitled is unknown, but probably approaches one in four cases in some welfare offices. Given that administrative caprice is routine in public assistance, it requires little imagination for the ambitious welfare administrator to use welfare reform as an opportunity to accelerate the denial of benefits, thereby achieving significant savings. Given the difficulty in reestablishing eligibility, any case termination realizes a three- to four-month dividend in benefit reductions simply because it takes that long for a recipient to reactivate a claim. In New York City, for example, the number of applicants receiving Food Stamps was halved—from 53 percent to 25 percent—after welfare procedures were changed, denying receipt of benefits on the same day and requiring a return to the welfare office.[16] Texas has employed a more oblique method of dissuasion, offering awards "to welfare offices that discourage the largest number of people from applying for welfare and food stamps."[17]

The role of administrative discretion in welfare reform has been examined by Bradley Schiller, using state AFDC caseload data from 1990 to 1996. Schiller distinguished "hard" state-level reforms—time limits, a family cap, and firm exemption criteria for participation in JOBS—from other, "soft" reforms. States with two of the three "tough" exemptions were differentiated from the others, and statistical analysis was employed to test hypothesized relationships with caseload reductions. "Tough welfare-reform provisions account for most of the caseload reduction attributed to [welfare caseload changes]," Schiller concluded. "These results confirm that reform provisions that limit accessibility to welfare do have their intended caseload effect."[18] Thus, purging and churning the AFDC caseload generates savings, but not necessarily for the reasons claimed by proponents of welfare reform.[19]

JOBS VERSUS EDUCATION

As states assumed direct control of AFDC through federal waivers, many opted to place welfare recipients in jobs immediately rather than invest in education and training. This was consistent with the goal of optimizing state savings on welfare expenditures, as welfare mothers who went directly into the labor market stood a greater chance of obtaining sufficient income to be ineligible for public assistance or at least to have their benefits reduced. Critics of the strategy, on the other hand, argued that immediate job placement only assured a welfare recipient an inferior job at lousy wages, and might actually impair her participation in an education or training experience that would ensure employment adequate to allow her family eventually to escape poverty. Proponents of prompt employment argued that the most important factor in successful labor market participation was getting a first step on the ladder, after which decisions on training and education would be more prudent. To assess the virtues of these divergent strategies, the Department of Health and Human Services (DHHS) and the Department of Education (DOE) contracted with MDRC to produce the "National Evaluation of Welfare-to-Work Strategies."

MDRC chose seven sites for evaluation but prepared its first assessment (covering two years) on three of them: Atlanta, Georgia; Grand Rapids, Michigan; and Riverside, California. In each site participants were randomly assigned to one of three groups: a cohort that received services emphasizing prompt labor force attachment (LFA), a group that featured education/training or human capital development (HCD), or a control group that received neither of these. Unless a welfare mother was exempt from JOBS, participation was mandatory. Finally, the programs had different reputations. Atlanta's caseworkers had emphasized HCD, encouraging welfare mothers to take full advantage of counseling and support benefits, such as transportation and childcare, while imposing sanctions on program laggards only reluctantly; the priority of the Grand Rapids staff was immediate employment, and they regularly imposed stiff sanctions to ensure compliance. Riverside's focus on LFA had made it a national leader in welfare reform, and its HCD services were reserved for welfare mothers who lacked a high school diploma or GED.[20]

Researchers who prepared the two-year report noted that welfare mothers did indeed have different experiences through the LFA, HCD, and control groups. The program outcomes also differed:

• HCD cost almost twice as much as LFA.
• Both HCD and LFA increased participants' employment and earnings, though HCD increases were smaller.

- Both HCD and LFA reduced welfare outlays, largely as a result of imposed sanctions.
- Both HCD and LFA reduced the proportion of recipients who had been continuously on welfare.
- Both HCD and LFA generated increased earnings and lower welfare outlays for mothers with pre-school-age children at home.

Inauspiciously, the researchers noted that although the programs evaluated were not operated under the new welfare reform legislation, none of the sites evaluated met the enrollment requirements of PRWORA.[21]

The National Evaluation of Welfare-to-Work Strategies presented the most detailed assessment of various welfare reform initiatives since the 1991 MDRC study (see Chapter 3). As noted in table 4.1, the results are not dissimilar. As before, the central questions of welfare reform are: (1) do earnings increase enough to make a family economically self-sufficient, and (2) are reductions in welfare costs significant, at least adequate to offset the cost of establishing a welfare-to-work program? Increased earnings through LFA were reported from all three sites, slightly over $1,000 over two years. Given a 2,000-hour workyear, this comes to about $0.25 per hour, an amount unlikely to leverage most families off public assistance. In two of the sites, LFA earnings in the second year were lower than in the first, suggesting an earnings plateau. As might be expected, HCD earnings increases were smaller, reflecting participants' enrollment in education/training and delayed entry into the labor market. All three sites also reported reductions in AFDC payments, though only two—Grand Rapids and Riverside—claimed sufficient LFA-attributed savings above the cost per experimental participant, thus recovering the cost of mounting the program, and then only after the second year. HCD welfare savings were smaller and failed to exceed the cost per experimental participant in each site; only the Riverside HCD group—limited to participants without high school diplomas or GEDs—came close to recovering the cost per participant, and then only after two years. Thus, for these general features of welfare reform, the National Evaluation of Welfare-to-Work Strategies reflects the modest benefits reported earlier.

Nevertheless, the study does demonstrate important efficiencies associated with different strategies of welfare reform. In all three sites, LFA benefits exceed those of HCD.[22] At best these differences are modest—on an annual basis between $200 and $250 per case. Multiplied by a large caseload, however, the benefits balloon accordingly. Thus, a pattern emerges from the data on welfare-to-work as a strategy of welfare reform: while earnings are unlikely to remove participants from public assistance (let alone poverty), for administrators of large public assistance programs, welfare savings are justifiable (they exceed the cost of deploying a welfare-to-work program),

Table 4.1   Two-Year Outcomes of Welfare-to-Work Strategies

Program	Net Cost per Experimental Participant		LFA Impact (LFA − control)		HCD Impact (HCD − control)		LFA − HCD Difference
Atlanta	Direct:	$1,587	Earnings:		Earnings:		
	Support:	691	Year 1:	$347	Year 1:	$184	
	Total:	2,278	Year 2:	753	Year 2:	396	
			Total:	1,100	Total:	580	$520
			AFDC payments:		AFDC payments:		
			Year 1:	−130	Year 1:	−127	
			Year 2:	−238	Year 2:	−206	
			Total:	−368	Total:	−333	35
Grand Rapids	Direct:	922	Earnings:		Earnings:		
	Support:	186	Year 1:	543	Year 1:	136	
	Total:	1,108	Year 2:	475	Year 2:	450	
			Total:	1,019	Total:	586	433
			AFDC payments:		AFDC payments:		
			Year 1:	−688	Year 1:	−311	
			Year 2:	−650	Year 2:	−514	
			Total:	−1,338	Total:	−826	512
Riverside	Direct:	1,156	Earnings:		Earnings:[a]		n/a
	Support:	107	Year 1:	651	Year 1:	148	
	Total:	1,263	Year 2:	561	Year 2:	39	
			Total:	1,212	Total:	188	
			AFDC payments:		AFDC payments:[a]		
			Year 1:	−581	Year 1:	−532	
			Year 2:	−686	Year 2:	−602	
			Total:	−1,267	Total:	−1,134	n/a

[a] Participants without a high school diploma or GED only.
Source: Gayle Hamilton et al., *National Evaluation of Welfare-to-Work Strategies* (Washington, D.C.: Department of Health and Human Services, 1997), tables 9.2–4, 10.2–3, 10.8.

and they can be substantial (when extrapolated over an entire caseload), particularly when immediate job placement is emphasized.[23] Of course, this generalization is somewhat preliminary, especially since the long-term benefits of education and training are unlikely to be registered in either earnings or lower AFDC payments in only two years.

Subsequently, DHHS, DOE, and MDRC released a more encouraging analysis of welfare-to-work in Portland, Oregon. There 5,547 single adults were randomly assigned to either a program group or a control group that received typical JOBS services. Members of the program group received flexible case management services that customized immediate job placement or education and training, depending on client needs, in order to obtain optimal employment as determined by higher wages and job benefits. At the end of two years, 11 percent more program group participants than controls were employed, and they were earning $1,800 ($0.86/hour) more than the comparison group. Approximately 10 percent more program group workers than controls obtained employer-provided health benefits. At the end of two years, MDRC researchers noted that the program group experienced reduced AFDC benefits ($1,200 less), and a 12 percent reduction in caseload.[24]

While the positive impacts of the Portland demonstration eclipsed the early enthusiasm generated by Riverside's work-first approach, the Oregon results required some qualification. Although the program group experienced greater savings compared with the control group, the net cost per program group member was $2,017; thus, the demonstration failed to recover its implementation costs in welfare savings, at least within the first two years of operation. Moreover, program benefits remained modest. "Despite the positive effects of the program," researchers concluded, "about two-fifths of program group members *were* receiving AFDC at the end of the two-year period; moreover, about one-quarter were both receiving AFDC benefits and not working."[25] Such participation rates are below the requirements established by PRWORA, a sobering realization considering that the Portland welfare-to-work program is an exemplar. If Portland was unable to attain PRWORA objectives under the most desirable conditions—low unemployment, cooperation from community organizations, and the like—what would be the experience of welfare-to-work programs in less beneficial settings?

LEARNFARE

Insofar as the underclass was the result of the isolation of the poor from the mainstream, conservatives ranked two social institutions as pivotal for social reintegration: employment, addressed in welfare-to-work, and education, reinforced through "learnfare." As introduced in Wisconsin in the fall of 1988, Learnfare targeted teenagers who had more than two unexcused absences from school. Under Learnfare "sanctions," the family's AFDC benefits for a dependent teen were reduced $77 a month; for an independent teen with a child, the penalty was $190 a month. Wisconsin officials contended that such sanctions would result in the return of 80 percent of teens on AFDC who had dropped out of school. But subsequent evaluation of the Milwaukee demonstration, conducted by an independent agency, "did not show improvement in student attendance that could be attributed to the Learnfare requirement." Undeterred, state officials wrote to the evaluators demanding that they suppress parts of the study that detailed the failure of Learnfare to enhance teen school attendance. When the researchers refused, Wisconsin officials canceled the contract, in the process impugning the evaluators' professionalism.[26]

Meanwhile, Ohio promised teens a $62-a-month carrot for good school attendance, coupled with a $62-a-month stick for truancy through LEAP (Learning, Earning, and Parenting). Three years after the program's inception, an interim assessment caused LEAP to be heralded in the media as a major victory in the battle against teen profligacy. Pundits like William Raspberry trumpeted LEAP's 20 percent increase in teens' high school completion rate and 40 percent increase in employment. Alas, on closer examination the LEAP evaluation was less sanguine. The glowing results were reported only for those teens currently enrolled in school and excluded those who had dropped out, even though both groups were part of the study's population. If one includes dropouts, LEAP's outcomes plummet: the proportion completing high school was not 20.0 percent, but 6.5 percent; the proportion employed was not 40.0 percent, but 20.0. By comparative measures, LEAP *did* improve teen behavior, but only modestly. And if LEAP generated outcomes that were positive, it also produced negative ones. For teens who had already dropped out of school—arguably, those most likely to join the underclass—LEAP produced no *discernible* effect. However, because the benefit reduction sanction was levied against all truant teens, a significant number of all mothers in the study reported "diminished spending on essentials for their families, especially clothing and food." In their concluding observations, evaluators conceded that changing adolescent behavior is difficult and admitted that LEAP produced some "perverse effects."[27]

A more recent assessment of LEAP revealed that the program "prevented 1 in 5 enrolled teens who otherwise would have dropped out from leaving school during their first year in the program," and that LEAP accounted for a 13 percent increase in dropouts' returning to school.[28] Beyond these modest accomplishments, questions about the program's impact persist. The researchers noted that "even among LEAP incentives and penalties, more than half the dropouts did not resume their education during the follow-up period."[29] Moreover, dropouts tended to respond to LEAP by enrolling not in regular high school, but in GED classes, possibly as a way to dodge LEAP school enrollment requirements.[30] Ominously, the researchers noted that a followup survey revealed that "many of the teens have had additional children since the [advent of the program]."[31] The final MDRC evaluation of LEAP addressed the ultimate outcome questions regarding graduation rates as well as employment and earnings. Significantly, LEAP did not produce an increase in high school completion rates and showed an increase in GED completion only for those participants who were not dropouts. Increased earnings were similarly lackluster: the only statistically significant earnings increases were reported by those who were enrolled in high school at the beginning of the study, and these were only $544 above control group earnings over the entire four years of the demonstration. Among LEAP participants who had dropped out, the only significant outcome was their continued school attendance, presumably to avoid having their benefits sanctioned. Although the data were not statistically significant, the LEAP control group of dropouts actually outperformed the program group with respect to several variables: high school completion, receipt of the GED, and total earnings over four years.[32] Among the report's more interesting conclusions, however, were those relating to the distribution of the expense of mounting LEAP. LEAP cost $1,388 per participant, an amount that MDRC reported was recovered in reduced AFDC, Food Stamp, and Medicaid benefits at a rate of 99 cents on each dollar invested. This cost was unevenly distributed, however. Taxpayers recovered 75 cents on every dollar invested in LEAP, but LEAP participants experienced a loss of $1,110 over four years, primarily due to the failure of earning increases to make up for lost public assistance benefits.[33] Thus, one of the most heralded teen intervention programs ultimately enhanced school attendance, though not graduation rates, and increased earnings marginally, all at modest expense, most of which was borne by the participants themselves.

TEEN PARENTHOOD

As Learnfare and LEAP demonstrated the difficulty of altering the behavior of the poor, interest focused on teen mothers. Research had identified a number of welfare-related problems correlated with single parenthood; among the most welfare-dependent were women who had come onto AFDC as teenagers. This led conservatives to attribute underclass status largely to teen parenthood. More than 30 percent of never-married adolescent mothers aged 15 to 19 receive welfare, and their average length of time on public assistance is over nine years. Teen parenthood was claimed to cost taxpayers almost $40 billion in 1989. Clearly, substantial welfare savings could be achieved by dissuading teenage girls from becoming pregnant. Furthermore, since children who had been on welfare were more than twice as likely to be welfare-reliant themselves, reducing teen motherhood would lower the likelihood of future welfare dependence.

The first evaluation of a teen pregnancy prevention program involved Project Redirection. From 1980 to 1982, 805 AFDC-eligible mothers who were 17 or younger received intensive services to optimize educational, employment, and life-management skills. Evaluation of Project Redirection mothers at one-, three-, and five-year intervals was mixed. Of the five outcomes—education, employment, welfare dependence, childbearing, and parenting/child development—participants showed significant improvement over the control group only in the last. Project Redirection teens fared no better than the control group in obtaining a high school diploma or GED certificate. They were more likely to be employed one year after exiting the program; however, their weekly earnings five years later were only $23 more than those of the control group. Five years later, the weekly household income of the control group exceeded that of the Project Redirection group by $19. The effect on welfare dependence was also ambiguous. Two years after participation, 7 percent fewer Project Redirection teens than control group members were on welfare; five years later, however, 10 percent fewer controls than project group members were on welfare. As for childbearing, Project Redirection teens reported fewer pregnancies in the first and second years after the program, yet they exceeded the control group in the number of pregnancies, as well as the number of live births, five years after that. Researchers noted that many of the improvements shown by Project Redirection teens had disappeared after two years, leading "the evaluators to conclude that the program impacts were largely transitory."[34]

Transitory benefits via Project Redirection were to prove superior to those generated by a larger project mounted a few years later. Between 1987 and 1991, DHHS mounted the Teenage Parenthood Demonstration (TPD) in Newark and Camden, New Jersey, and southern Chicago. Some 5,297 first-time teen mothers were randomly assigned to a control group or a program group whose members were required to participate in employment and education/training programs facilitated by case managers who coordinated childcare, transportation aid, and parenting workshops. The results of TPD were perplexing, to say the least. In Camden, a member of the experimental group was more likely to receive a high school diploma, while in Newark the control group performed better—in both cases at statistically significant levels.[35] Experimental participants' reading levels sometimes improved more than controls' but just as often did not. The employment and earnings of TPD participants lagged behind those of controls. TPD students in the experimental group exceeded controls' earnings by $79, but among TPD graduates, controls surpassed experimentals by $84. With respect to AFDC costs, TPD dropouts in the experimental group showed a statistically significant reduction in benefits of $16 a month compared with controls.[36] Finally, there was no discernible difference between TPD participants and controls with respect to procreative behavior, except that experimentals in Chicago were more likely (at a statistically significant level) to have abortions. [37] In a moment of candor, the researchers observed, "It is hard to find much good news in such data, especially when they are coupled with data showing a low level of intentionality and a low level of contraceptive use."[38]

Efforts to dissuade teen mothers from repeat pregnancy were also thwarted in the New Chance demonstration. From 1989 to 1992 researchers randomly assigned 2,322 poor young mothers, aged 16 to 22, either to New Chance, a program through which they received health, education, and welfare assistance coordinated by a case manager, or to a control group that received no special services. At the 18-month followup, the experimental group was faring worse than the control group in two important respects. First, New Chance mothers were less likely to be using contraception, were more likely to become pregnant, and were more likely to abort their pregnancies than the control group. Second, New Chance mothers were less likely to be working after entering the program, were earning less, and during the fourth to the sixth months more likely to be on AFDC. To compound matters, the interim report found that New Chance cost $5,073 per participant, excluding childcare; if childcare was included, $7,646 was spent on each New Chance mother.

The final MDRC report on New Chance was a testament to the persistence of social researchers in the midst of a project that was becoming increasingly cloudy despite state-of-the-art program design. Summing up, researchers concluded that

> experimental group members did *not* advance further than control group members in most respects. New Chance did boost participants' levels of GED receipt above those of the control group. The added services provided by the program, however, did not help participants secure skills training credentials, get and maintain employment, or reduce their rates of welfare receipt or subsequent childbearing relative to outcomes for control group members. The program did not improve their children's preschool readiness scores, and it had an unexpected small but negative effect on participants' emotional well-being and their ratings of their children's behavior.[39]

As the interim evaluation suggested, teen mothers were a tough bunch to socialize formally. Not only did the majority of New Chance participants fail to use the volume of services the program planners had anticipated; they also failed to move to the second phase of the program, which emphasized employment. Compounding the unpredictability of the experimental group, it later appeared that many mothers in the control group were able to access somewhat comparable services in the community, negating the intervention designed for program participants.[40] This complication notwithstanding, New Chance failed to provide compelling alternatives to pregnancy for teen mothers:

> about three quarters of the young mothers in both groups had another pregnancy during the follow-up period, and just over half had another baby. New Chance did not reduce the rate of pregnancies or childbearing. Indeed, women

in the experimental group were more likely than women in the control group to be pregnant during 9 of the 24 months after [the study began].[41]

The New Chance mothers' inconsistent performance on child behavior— their scores on the Behavior Problems Index were slightly higher than those of the control group, although they scored slightly worse than controls on the Positive Behavior Scale—caused the researchers to project an ominous future: "The fact that children of New Chance sample members had pre-school readiness scores placing them at only the 15th percentile nationwide suggests that, without intervention, these children may be prime candidates for poor academic performance, school dropout, premature parenthood, and unemployment."[42]

The disillusioning outcomes of New Chance were not without cost, of course. The final report on New Chance placed the net program cost at $9,000 per participant; if program design expenses were backed out, the net cost ranged from $6,197 to $7,445 per participant.[43] Such outcomes are disheartening, to say the least. Indeed, if social research attempts to define patterns within the often chaotic human condition, New Chance seemed to be breaking new ground—instead of improving the circumstances of poor young mothers, New Chance contrived to worsen their situation, and did so at significant expense.

Findings from research on programs designed to divert young people from welfare are, at best, vexing. When Learnfare seemed to be a wash, Wisconsin officials attempted to suppress research findings. In response to LEAP, proponents have exaggerated benefits, gleaning for public dissemination the positive results for participants remaining in high school but omitting the negligible impact on dropouts, the most likely candidates for the underclass. Those conservatives who, conceding the modest benefits of welfare-to-work and other ventures in welfare behaviorism, decided to target teens could not have chosen a more troublesome scapegoat. With respect to conservatives' key concerns—education, employment, welfare dependence, and childbearing—the outcomes of Project Redirection are often contradictory. It must be a relief to proponents of welfare behaviorism that TPD and New Chance, programs that have produced results that are utterly perverse in relation to their social objectives, remain virtually ignored.

FAMILY CAP

Arguably the most moralistic expression of welfare behaviorism is the family cap, which denies welfare for children born 10 months after an adult has become eligible for aid. New Jersey was the first state to institute the family cap as part of the Family Development Program (FDP), a multifaceted initiative to reinforce two-parent working families. Beginning in 1992, New Jersey instituted the family cap at the same time it allowed working families to keep up to 50 percent of their income without losing cash benefits, retained Medicaid eligibility for two years after leaving aid for employment, and removed penalties that disadvantaged two-parent welfare households. By 1996 these provisions were believed to have contributed to marked changes in procreative behavior on the part of FDP families: a reduction of 14,057 in the number of births, an increase in abortions of 1,429, and over 7,000 encounters with family planning agencies.[44]

The New Jersey experience with the family cap has been controversial, but 22 other states would eventually adopt it. Despite suits by the American Civil Liberties Union and the National Organization for Women claiming that the policy was injurious to children who otherwise would be entitled to benefits, and, moreover, virtually mandated family planning, if not abortions, New Jersey's governor, Christine Todd Whitman, was unapologetic: "The decrease in birth rates demonstrates that many welfare mothers have appropriately made the choice not to have additional children while on welfare because of their financial condition. The message of personal responsibility is working."[45]

PATERNITY

Within the current context, child support enforcement (CSE) is the penultimate strategy for welfare reform: each dollar paid in child support is a dollar saved in welfare expenditures. Conservatives understood correctly that much of the AFDC program would simply be unnecessary if absent parents conscientiously paid child support. Whenever welfare behaviorism flagged, welfare reformers knew that they could go to voters and assert that the least absent fathers could do was to support their offspring, and that the public would heartily agree. As has been the case with making receipt of AFDC conditional on various virtues, CSE has yielded diminishing dividends on investment.

Having been incorporated into AFDC in 1975, CSE is the oldest of contemporary welfare reform initiatives. For 1996, $12.0 billion was collected through CSE, but it cost the government $3.1 billion to do so. Obtaining payments from 2.9 million AFDC families removed 294,000 families, or about 10 percent, from AFDC; 15.5 percent of AFDC payments for that year were retrieved through CSE. As a welfare prevention strategy, CSE is available to the nonpoor as well as those on welfare, a feature that obscures the limited effectiveness of the program as a welfare reform measure. Thus, of the $12.0 billion collected under CSE, most—$9.2 billion—went to families not on AFDC; only $2.9 billion was collected for AFDC families. While CSE is a strong performer in overall collections, it actually loses money with respect to the welfare population, collecting only $0.93 for every dollar in program costs.[46] In its total impact on public revenues, CSE is a net loser, in 1995 reporting a $853 million *loss;* so much of the cost was borne by the federal government—$1.3 billion—that the states received a benefit of $421 million.[47]

During the two decades since its inception, several changes have been introduced to CSE to make it more effective, such as requiring establishment of paternity in order to receive AFDC and garnishing wages for absent parents whose payments are in arrears. These have improved CSE, but modestly. For example, from 1978 to 1993, the proportion of families with a child support order increased 2 percent; the proportion of families receiving some payment increased 6 percent; and the proportion of families receiving full child support payments also increased 6 percent.[48] The efficiency of enforcement, however, has been declining. For 1996 the ratio of child support collections to dollars spent on administration was 3.93, a level that was last reported in 1988.[49] Why are CSE benefits so limited?

Much of the variation in child support payments can be attributed to social class: wealthier absent parents pay more than poorer parents. Researchers from the Urban Institute found that in 1990 "60 percent of noncustodial fathers in the highest income quartile paid child support for that year," while "only 27 percent of noncustodial fathers in the lowest income quartile paid." Beyond that generalization, the profile of the "deadbeat dad" reflects family life—or the lack of it—in the underclass. Absent fathers who are dropouts, who are African American, who fathered children out of wedlock, and who have a new family with children are less likely to pay child support. On the other hand, the formality of family life is an indicator of child support payment. Noncustodial fathers who were married longer, who recently left a family, and who have a child support court order are more likely to pay support. Absent fathers who move out of state are *more* likely to pay support, presumably because they relocate in pursuit of job opportunities.[50]

These data sketch the limits of CSE for welfare reform. Essentially reformist rhetoric collides with the reality of poverty. Between 1970 and 1994, the wages of male high school graduates fell 33 percent, while those of men with less than four years of high school fell 47 percent. If the declining wages of poorly educated men meant that they were less able to pay child support, the fate of their female counterparts was little better: during the same period, wages of women high school graduates dropped 12 percent, while dropouts saw their wages plunge 31 percent.[51] Illicit activities and welfare fill the void. Confronted with stiff paternity requirements, AFDC mothers do whatever is necessary to get and keep welfare, at the same time managing the relationship with an absent father as best they can.

Kathryn Edin reported that more than half of AFDC mothers meet paternity requirements by fudging information, a practice she labeled "covert noncompliance." In her study of 214 families in four cities, she discovered that 57 percent of mothers "either lied about the identity of the father of one of their children or had hidden crucial identifying information (Social Security number, address, or current employer) from the enforcement agency." Another 41 percent received "regular financial support" from their children's fathers under the table, an average of $190 per month.[52] By contrast, the federal government reports that only 39 percent of welfare mothers have child support orders and only 24 percent actually receive payments.[53] Thus, much of what welfare administrators claim as progress in making welfare mothers more responsible about childbearing is actually indicative of the ignorance of the former and the inventiveness of the latter.

The most ambitious initiative to enhance child support payments to poor families has been Parents' Fair Share (PFS), a pilot project operated from 1992 through 1993. PFS attempted to increase the child support payments of some 4,000 noncustodial parents (97 percent of whom were male) who had support orders for families on AFDC. Attributes of the noncustodial parents recruited for PFS suggested poor candidacy for full and regular payment of child support: nearly two-thirds reported working three months or less during the previous year; almost three-fourths stated that their most recent wage was less than $7.00 an hour; almost 40 percent stated that they had gone hungry during the previous three months; nearly one-third had trouble paying rent during the past quarter; and three-fourths reported having been arrested at least once since their sixteenth birthday. Typically, the noncustodial parent was $4,252 in arrears for child support.

PFS was a comprehensive program including employment and training services, peer support groups, enhanced support payment activities, and conflict mediation. *Preliminary* analysis indicated that the average monthly child support payment for noncustodial parents decreased from $22.95 for the four months before referral to PFS to $22.62 four months afterward. When those PFS participants who had made no previous support payments were excluded, the amount decreased from $63.80 to $62.89.[54] *Final* analysis was more positive, yet troubling at the same time. Eventually, 7 percent of PFS participants were more likely than members of the control group to make support payments, though these payment increases averaged only $10.00 per month. PFS services were not positively associated with enhanced employment or earnings of participants.[55] Note that the modest PFS outcomes do not incorporate the costs of mounting the program; had they done so, the results might well have been negative.

TIME LIMITS

The ultimate in welfare behaviorism is time-limiting AFDC. The Urban Institute's LaDonna Pavetti was the first to elucidate this strategy. Using a computer simulation, Pavetti programmed a number of scenarios constructed from the primary features of welfare reform proposals before Congress. Both two- and five-year time limits were simulated; in addition, a series of exemptions were incorporated, including having a child under 18 months of age, having a disabled child, and already having a job. Pavetti then projected the consequences for families who were newly eligible for AFDC as well as those who were long-term dependents on public assistance. As might be expected, many permutations were generated by this complex analysis; however, the major findings were as follows:

- In the long run, 58 percent of families receive AFDC for more than two years; more than one-third for more than five years.
- Because the welfare rolls are populated by families who have been on AFDC for a long period, at any given time about 70 percent have *already* received AFDC for more than two years, and 48 percent for more than five.
- Exempting a recipient because of a very young child at home reduces the number of families hitting a two-year time limit from 37 percent to 10 percent.
- Exempting a recipient who has a young or disabled child, or who is already working, reduces the number of families reaching a two-year time limit to 5 percent.

Time limits without exemptions would cut a swath through AFDC. Given the number of AFDC recipients in 1993, a prospective two-year time limit would dump 2.07 million families out of the safety net into the underclass; a five-year limit, 1.42 million families. The two-year scenario would delete 3.07 million children from AFDC; the five-year scenario, 2.11 million. If exemptions were granted for young children under Pavetti's scenarios, a two-year time limit would eliminate 207,000 families, including 307,000 children. A two-year time limit granting multiple exemptions would halve that figure. Pavetti's calculations paralleled those of the Congressional Budget Office, which estimated that between 2.5 million and 3.5 million children could be affected by the federal five-year lifetime limit on aid, despite the 20 percent hardship exemption.[56] A subsequent analysis indicated that from 10 to 15 percent of all children, or 40 percent of those receiving public assistance, would have been denied welfare benefits under a five-year limit.[57] Logically, more troubled families are more likely to run afoul of time limits, a prospect investigated by researchers who constructed a "risk index" consisting of "young age, never married, and low education"; 57 percent of such mothers would encounter a five-year limit.[58]

In the absence of data from states with welfare waivers that included time limits, researchers relied on reductions in General Assistance (GA) as a proxy. GA was not an ideal mirror of AFDC, since most GA recipients are male and most AFDC heads-of-households are female, but it was better than computer simulations, researchers contended. Since GA uses no federal revenues, states were free to alter the program in any way consistent with their constitutions; accordingly, between 1991 and 1992 some 22 states reduced or eliminated GA benefits. Research from three of those states—Pennsylvania, Michigan, and Ohio—revealed that considerable hardship followed reductions in GA. Tony Halter concluded that "over 80 percent of the GA population did not find work."[59] The GA experience was thus inauspicious, particularly in light of the PRWORA requirements that substantial majorities of welfare recipients find work or the states would risk fiscal penalties from the federal government.

By 1997 states with waivers that incorporated time limits began to report on their experience. In Virginia a preliminary review of records of the first 40 families who had had benefits terminated under a two-year time limit found that 35 members were employed, most in service industries. Of these, half earned less than $6.00 per hour; only two earned more than $7.00 per hour; and only seven had found jobs that included health insurance benefits. When welfare was terminated, these families also lost the benefit of a generous earned income disregard that allowed them to retain welfare benefits and earnings up to the poverty level. But once welfare was stopped, families remained poor. Only one of the 35 families reported earnings above the poverty level, which was $13,000 for a family of three. Of those terminated from welfare, over a third reported incomes below 50 percent of the poverty level; on average, income for terminated families was only 16 percent of the median family income in their respective communities.[60]

A more extensive evaluation that attracted media attention was the Family Transition Program (FTP) of Escambia County, a midsized Florida jurisdiction. In collaboration with MDRC, local welfare officials agreed to randomly assign 2,800 welfare families to an experimental group that received FTP services or a control group that continued receipt of AFDC. The FTP group received individual attention from case managers who were authorized to help them engage in education/training or find employment; FTP participants were also entitled to an increased earned income disregard that allowed them to keep the first $200 and 50 percent of earnings thereafter as well as more assets. While the AFDC group did not receive special job-related assistance, they were nonetheless expected to comply with the FSA requirement to participate in a work-related activity. In addition to the support offered to the FTP group, its members were exposed to a two-year time limit that could be extended for an additional year only under exceptional circumstances. By June 1997, 102 welfare families had been terminated from welfare, their experience then permitting a comparison with the control group that remained on AFDC. Two years into the study, 52 percent of the FTP group was employed, compared with 44 percent of AFDC controls; by various measures of participation, FTP was a statistically significant success. During the two years of FTP, its participants increased their earnings ($902 on average), and showed a reduction in AFDC and Food Stamps valued at $490, amounts that were not atypical for welfare-to-work programs.[61]

Of particular interest was the experience of FTP families just prior to the two-year time limit: knowing that the end of cash assistance was imminent, would they behave in ways that would radically enhance their self-sufficiency? During the last quarter of the second year, the earnings of FTP families eclipsed those of AFDC families by a statistically significant $207.00, and their receipt of AFDC and Food Stamps decreased $169.00. On the other hand, the wages claimed by FTP participants were comparable to those of the AFDC control group, just over $6.00 per hour.[62] Six months after termination from welfare, 16 of 25 family heads interviewed were working, although their monthly income had fallen from $913.20 to $756.20.[63] "Despite the modest overall income loss," researchers concluded, "[FTP] sample members were no more likely to be experiencing serious material hardship at the six-month point than during their last months on welfare."[64] Since the preliminary report on FTP contained no data on program cost, there is no basis for assessing return on investment.

WISCONSIN

If initiatives to reverse behavioral poverty generated ambiguous outcomes when instituted separately, there remained the possibility that their integration in a full frontal assault on welfare dependency would prove effective. Many states had requested multiple waivers for welfare demonstrations, of course, but none pursued them more systematically than Wisconsin. Under its Republican governor Tommy G. Thompson, Wisconsin had become a leader in experiments in welfare reform, in the process becoming the poster child of poverty policy.[65]

Few would deny that Wisconsin's performance with respect to welfare reform was exceptional. Between 1987 and 1994, when the national welfare caseload increased by 29 percent, Wisconsin's welfare caseload had plummeted 23 percent—more than twice as far as the state with the second-largest drop, Mississippi at 9 percent.[66] Much of the credit for the drop was claimed by Thompson, who as minority leader in the state legislature had championed welfare reform. Upon his election to the governorship, Thompson moved swiftly and imaginatively to restructure welfare as an employment-focused program. In 1987, Wisconsin received federal waivers to mount several innovations:

- Learnfare was instituted, through which truancy would result in loss of benefits.
- Welfare mothers with preschool children would participate in JOBS at least 20 hours per week.
- Employed recipients would receive lower benefits for the first four months after getting a job, but higher benefits for the subsequent eight months.
- Medicaid would be continued for 12 months after a mother left welfare for a job.
- The federal prohibition on working more than 100 hours per month was waived so long as a family remained eligible for welfare.[67]

At the same time Thompson sought to reduce state welfare payments. The legislature offered to reduce public assistance benefits by 1 percent, from 85.0 percent to 84.04 percent of the state's standard of need, but Thompson wanted further cuts. Ingeniously, he used his line-item veto authority to eliminate the 4's and the decimal in the legislature's budget, transforming 84.04 to 8//0/, or 80 percent of need, a 6 percent reduction in benefits.[68] Consolidating his leadership in state welfare reform, Thompson sought an additional set of waivers, establishing "bridefare" (allowing mothers to retain benefits while cohabiting with their partners in order to avert family dissolution) and increasing asset limits on the value of automobiles as well as special resources accounts for education and training.[69] But these would prove merely incremental compared with Thompson's next set of reforms.

On August 3, 1995, Thompson announced "Wisconsin Works" (cleverly, "W-2"), the most radical state welfare reform to date. As the social policy critic Mickey Kaus enthused, "To the vast majority of families seeking aid, [W-2] doesn't offer *any* period of cash assistance. The time limit, in effect, is zero."[70] Immediately upon becoming eligible for assistance, a mother would be matched with a private sector employer or be assigned a community service job. The disabled who do not qualify for SSI and mothers of

110

infants would be eligible for transitional aid, but aid to mothers would be limited to 12 weeks, and the disabled would be required to work in a sheltered workshop. If W-2 waved a large stick, it also featured a carrot of unprecedented size. Thompson offered to make workfare available to every poor head-of-household in the state and subsidize childcare as well as health insurance.[71] By instituting a graduated schedule of employment ranging from (1) private sector jobs, through (2) subsidized employment, to (3) community service, and concluding with (4) mandatory treatment and rehabilitation for addicts and the disabled, W-2 effectively repealed welfare as it was known in Wisconsin. Costs were expected to escalate accordingly: prior to W-2 the state spent $9,700 for each welfare case; after W-2, the cost was projected to increase to $15,700.[72] Nonetheless, caseloads continued to fall—by 26 percent between December 1994 and October 1996.[73]

Perhaps the boldest of Thompson's welfare reform initiatives has been New Hope, a multiyear demonstration begun in two high-poverty areas of Milwaukee. Unlike W-2, which is targeted at welfare recipients, New Hope provides a range of health and human services to anyone working at least 30 hours per week: (1) job search help is available to the unemployed and those seeking another position, (2) wages are supplemented to guarantee full-time workers an income above the poverty level, (3) health insurance is available on a sliding fee scale, and (4) childcare is made affordable according to family income. To coordinate programs, "all New Hope services are available in one place from a personal project representative."[74]

An outcome study of the 1,357 participants in New Hope revealed that "a package of earnings supplements, health and child care benefits, and full-time job opportunities can substantially increase the work effort, earnings, and income of those who are willing to work full time, but need assistance to do so."[75] Of New Hope program supports, 78.0 percent of participants used wage supplements (increasing their incomes above those of the control group by $1,165 over the two-year span of the program); 47.6 percent elected health insurance; 27.9 percent sought help with childcare; and 32.0 percent needed Community Service Jobs because of an inability to locate private sector jobs.[76] The earnings increases of New Hope participants were modest, paralleling those of welfare-to-work projects, as were welfare savings. Interestingly, the work participation of New Hope volunteers was slightly lower, suggesting a modest reduction of job effort, but researchers dismissively attributed this to a reduction in the number of jobs that had been held by participants. In addition, a slight enhancement in family life, suggested by a modest improvement in parent-child relations, may have been a result of fewer hours at work. Perhaps most significantly, children of New Hope participants, primarily boys, showed enhanced school performance compared with children of families in the control group. As in other welfare demonstrations, however, the cost of supporting low-income workers was not cheap; New Hope cost $7,200 per participant.[77]

Explanations for Wisconsin's imploding welfare caseload—down 60 percent since Thompson's election a decade ago—are varied. Liberals, such as Michael Wiseman of the University of Wisconsin Institute for Research on Poverty, attribute the drop to a vibrant economy; a thriving industrial sector continues to generate demand for skilled jobs, so that unemployment is low.[78] "A tight job market generates many openings even for people without skills or a work history," concurred Lawrence Mead. "It also enables fathers of welfare families to get jobs good enough to pay their child support judgments."[79] Regression analysis confirmed that "higher levels of adjudication and sanctions—clients with grants reduced for noncooperation—means faster caseload fall, because these are among the processes that enforce participation," Mead observed. "Over time, a tough program that sanctions a lot may drive more people off the rolls or divert more from welfare by that means."[80] Thus, Mead concluded that an essential complement to a tight labor market is an efficient administrative structure that imposes effective penalties swiftly. These twin strategies, Mead noted, reflect liberal and conservative impulses in social policy: liberals prefer lower unemployment through macroeconomic policy, while conservatives have shown a preference for administrative sanctions. Mead, of course, had introduced this two-part mantra a decade before, prior to the advent of the 1988 Family Support Act.

> Polls show that the voters want a welfare system that is simultaneous and demanding. Most people want to help families in need, but they also demand that the adults in those families do more to help themselves, particularly by working. Hence, if reformers wish to be politic, they cannot just aid the needy to prevent hardship, nor refuse to aid them to promote self-reliance. They must somehow do both. That requires enforcing work in and through the welfare system.[81]

Rhetoric aside, Mead's regression data proved "inconclusive" as an explanation for caseload changes: something was happening that induced a precipitous drop in the welfare caseload, and that something could not be accounted for by the modest outcomes demonstrated by conventional statistical analysis. Clearly, other factors must be involved in the imploding caseload.

DIVERSION

The most likely explanation is that a tough welfare-to-work program brings to light what many welfare mothers had been doing all along: trying to make ends meet by relying on the resources at hand. Kathryn Edin and Laura Lein

112

documented that virtually all welfare mothers depend on a variety of income sources—surreptitious child support, nonreported earnings, as well as gifts from family, friends, and paramours—survival strategies dictated by the meagerness of welfare benefits.[82] Although such activity was disallowed by welfare regulations, welfare officials were unprepared to root it out. As we have seen (Chapter 2), state lawmakers standardized benefits in response to the welfare rights movement, and then allowed them to deteriorate in relation to inflation; so long as their official error rate was not so elevated that federal funding was jeopardized, welfare mothers could do whatever was necessary to get by. Once the reforms of the New Paternalism were overlain on the programmatic anarchy that had come to typify public welfare, significant efficiencies suddenly emerged. Rigorous case management on the part of welfare workers announced to current and future applicants the rules of the new regime: work would be enforced, and there would be certain sanctions for noncompliance. As might be expected, a significant number of what Mead would call "smoke outs" were generated, as mothers who were already working but off the books realized that inadequate welfare benefits were not worth the extra hassle and simply left public assistance. Another subgroup was diverted from welfare: anticipating the new rules, they simply opted not to apply. Thus, diversion is a likely reason for the steep caseload drop.[83]

Poor families can be prevented from becoming dependent on welfare in several ways. Three strategies figure prominently among *formal* diversion initiatives. First, lump sum payments, often comparable to several months of cash welfare, are paid in order to resolve a specific crisis, such as an eviction threat or a car in need of repair, that might lead to welfare eligibility. In Virginia such diversion tactics accounted for 455 payments over three years, the average award being $1,005.[84] In 1998, 23 states made such diversionary payments. A second form of diversion is an aggressive form of "Work First"—requiring applicants for welfare to engage in a job search first, the failure for compliance being the denial of aid. In 1998, only three states used this form of diversion. The third formal diversionary tactic is the exploration of other resources. The 16 states that employed this strategy in 1998 emphasized the use of alternative sources of support from families and communities to avoid the provision of welfare.[85]

Given some of the welfare department practices described in Chapter 2, it is easy to envision instances in which *formal* diversion shades over into *informal* diversion—the subtle, but no less effective, denial of aid to those who would otherwise be eligible. "While many poor families have moved off public assistance and into jobs, many others simply have never gone on the rolls," noted two *Washington Post* reporters, "raising questions among policy analysts whether they have found jobs on their own, never truly needed them in the first place, or have been scared off or intimidated from applying for help that their children genuinely require."[86] Diversion analysts suggest that this is most likely to occur when "Work First" is pressed: "If programs provide minimal support and require relatively stringent job search activities that are unrealistic in terms of the abilities of most potential TANF applicants, mandatory applicant job search programs may result in substantial, and possibly undesirable, informal diversion."[87] Noting that the casualties of informal diversion are not tracked by the states—indeed, there are incentives *not* to account for such families—the *Washington Post* editors were concise about the implications: "The states have been given not merely permission but what amounts to a standing invitation to cut the rolls."[88]

EXCURSUS

That welfare behaviorism as an instrument of social policy would generate welfare savings far greater than conservatives expected is an irony of spectacular proportions. As late as 1995, liberals had held out the hope that Clinton's vetoes of conservative welfare reform would result in indefinite delay, if not compromise, in the draconian deconstruction of AFDC.[89] Only three years later, states were benefiting from a welfare windfall as caseloads continued to drop. Despite the modest outcome data on various conditions attached to receipt of welfare, poor mothers were abandoning public assistance in unprecedented numbers. The social policy consequences were equally paradoxical. Liberals had prophesied that Republican welfare reform would generate massive dysfunction on the part of the poor, requiring additional federal revenues. The welfare block grant "surplus"—the difference between block grant allocations predicated on the caseload levels of the early 1990s and the spending required by the new reduced caseloads—stood this on its head. Not only were states rolling in excess revenue from the block grant surplus, but the amounts were so large that many questioned the need to participate in the Welfare-to-Work Grants appended to TANF in the 1997 Balanced Budget Act.

Budgeted at $3.0 billion over two years, the Welfare-to-Work Grants were designed to encourage the states to serve the most welfare dependent heads-of-households through Private Industry Councils.[90] However, the Welfare-to-Work Grants required state matching funds as well as reports on their use, conditions that many states found objectionable.[91] Why invest further in welfare reform for even the most unemployable welfare mothers when current initiatives were generating surpluses far exceeding existing program obligations?

Welfare reform, liberals were chagrined to discover, was working far better than even conservatives could have hoped. In cashiering AFDC for a work-oriented initiative, conservatives had tapped into a dynamic that liberals had failed to acknowledge: deteriorating welfare benefits were already requiring poor mothers to be creative, and work was among a few options upon which they were increasingly reliant to balance fragile family finances. When conservatives launched welfare reform in the form of welfare behaviorism and required poor mothers to work for their benefits, many welfare mothers responded affirmatively. An unknown but probably large number of them were already engaged in unreported work of one kind or another. The big question for them was not whether or not they should work, but how adequate wages and benefits would be. Now the central issue of welfare reform revolved around the experience of welfare mothers in the labor market.

5

The Dynamics of Welfare and Work

Tammy Emerson was clearly fed up with welfare. "It's the worst feeling in the world, being on welfare," she says. Referring to her most recent caseworker, who had accused her of fraud on four different occasions, Tammy's voice rises: "They're so controlling; you can't even breathe; it's like suffocating!" She continues, "If they penalize you every time you get a raise, it's gonna drive you nuts; you feel like you're being punished. It's like an abusive relationship; you're trapped, and the only way to get free is to walk away from it." So she did. Tammy received her last welfare check six months ago.

As is true for many welfare mothers, Tammy's story is convoluted, a maze of false starts, dashed hopes, and diminishing expectations. All told, she was on public assistance, on and off, for five years. She first applied when her salary as a waitress, originally $400 a week, deteriorated to $97 a week when the business moved. By that time she had already left her husband because of his failure to support the family, so it was not particularly difficult to leave the boyfriend with whom she had been living—he drank and was unemployed—even though they lived in a rural community. Without a car, her options were limited: "It was a 45-minute walk to the nearest store, and the closest place to work was a chicken farm beyond that." So she walked to her job at the chicken farm for two months. Over the next few years she changed jobs almost annually. When her car broke down, she found herself on public assistance.

By the time welfare reform was introduced, Tammy was a work-study student at a community college and working half-time at another job. The new welfare reform rules required her to submit 30 applications a month for full-time work, however, and her caseworker was unwilling to bend the requirement and take into consideration Tammy's work-study status and part-time job. When she was offered a full-time job at a convenience store/gas station, Tammy was told she had to take it or lose her welfare benefits. She signed on to work from 3 P.M. to 11 P.M. That meant that she was getting up at 6 A.M. or 7 A.M. and, except for running home in the afternoon to pop dinner for her two children into the microwave, not returning home until midnight.

116

Tammy Emerson

At best, she saw her kids an hour or two each day, even on weekends, when she worked full-time. Her grades dropped a notch. When the car broke down again, she quit the gas station job but, fearing that the welfare department would find out, quickly took a job at McDonalds. When her welfare worker questioned her bank passbook, evidently mistaking withdrawals for deposits, Tammy had had enough. She moved her kids to her mother's house and began looking for other ways to get by. Currently, she is making it on $39 a week in child support, the generosity of her mother, and two businesses she is cultivating: yard sale consignments and selling grocery coupon books.

Tammy is frustrated by her experience, particularly when she recalls the welfare mothers who have been her neighbors. "Over half of the welfare mothers here are living with men who are also working full-time—the fathers of their kids!—and they're getting welfare. That's not just welfare fraud, it's Section 8 fraud," she complains. She suspects that "90 percent of the welfare mothers suffer from the Cinderella syndrome," looking for a man to take care of them.

For herself, Tammy knows that she has 20 months of eligibility left, having used only four of the 24 months allowed by the newly instituted time limit. "If something really drastic happens, it's there," she observes ruefully. "It's a pretty nice feeling, even though it's a pain in the ass."

In moving to her mother's house, Tammy will be returning to the rural community from which she came, leaving behind not only welfare, but also the community college in which she had enrolled. Her experience with welfare has been negative. "It's only by the grace of God that I've been able to do as well as I have," she says.

WELFARE DEPENDENCY

Welfare caseloads plunged beyond the parameters predicted by research on welfare-to-work programs because poor mothers were a much more dynamic population than stereotype had indicated. Traditionally, the optimal routes off public assistance have been marriage/remarriage or work; less ideally, some mothers exit welfare when their children become too old to receive benefits, leaving the mothers ineligible for further aid. Prior to the 1988 Family Support Act (FSA), most mothers—34.6 percent—left Aid to Families with Dependent Children (AFDC) because of (re)marriage; only 21.3 percent became ineligible for welfare because of increased earnings.[1] Once the work requirements of FSA had taken effect, however, these exit options were reversed. By the early 1990s, 45.9 percent of mothers had left AFDC because of earnings, while 11.4 percent were ineligible as a result of (re)marriage.[2]

Regardless of how mothers left welfare, large numbers remained on the program, suggesting variations in dependency; mothers may rely on welfare in the short term in order to regain social and economic security, or they may become intransigently dependent in the long term (table 5.1). Two important distinctions emerge from the data. The first is the difference between poor mothers who rely on welfare at any given time and those who return to public assistance after leaving. Logically, returnees are more likely

Table 5.1 Distribution of Length of Time on AFDC (percent)

| Expected time on AFDC | Single-Spell Analysis | | Multiple-Spell Analysis | |
	Persons Beginning a Spell	Persons on AFDC at a Point in Time	Persons Beginning a Spell	Persons on AFDC at a Point in Time
1–2 years	48%	14%	30%	7%
3–4 years	14	10	20	11
5–7 years	20	25	19	17
8+ years	17	50	30	65
All	99%	99%	99%	100%

Note: Columns may not add up to 100 percent because of rounding.
Source: Committee on Ways and Means, House of Representatives, *Overview of Entitlement Programs* (Washington, D.C.: GPO, 1996), p. 505.

to become long-term dependents of welfare simply because their exit options, such as (re)marriage and work, have failed. There is also a difference, at a cross-section of time, between those mothers who have just become eligible for welfare and those who have been on the program. At least half of mothers who are eligible for the first time are off the program within four years. At the same time, a cross-sectional analysis reveals that at least half of welfare mothers are on aid for eight years or more. These apparently contradictory data are a result of different perspectives on the problem. Because of the rapid turnover of short-timers who are just entering welfare, an analysis at the end of the year will show that most are no longer eligible. But the families on the program for longer periods will tend to show up more often if the analysis is cross-sectional at a given point in time. Thus, the data show considerable heterogeneity among welfare families: one subgroup consisting of short-timers who are on and off the program as soon as possible, the other consisting of long-term recipients. The latter subgroup is of most concern because it consumes half of welfare expenditures.[3]

With the passage of the Personal Responsibility and Work Opportunity Reconciliation Act (PRWORA) of 1996, two indicators of dependency—the five-year receipt that represents the federal lifetime limit and the shorter two-year period chosen as the cutoff point by several states—became central to welfare policy analysis. LaDonna Pavetti computed that 57.8 percent of new entrants will use welfare beyond two years, and 34.8 percent beyond five years; that 90.6 percent of current recipients exceed a two-year time limit, and 76.2 percent exceed a five-year limit; and that, perhaps most significantly, 71.7 percent of current AFDC recipients have *already* exceeded two years, and 47.8 percent are beyond five years. These time limit differences vary according to features of specific subgroups, such as education, work experience, and children in the family (table 5.2). Not surprisingly, younger, never-married minority mothers with less education and work experience but with larger families stand a good chance of long-term receipt of welfare,[4] thus increasing their likelihood of violating two-year time limits as well as the five-year lifetime limit. On the other hand, of all new welfare mothers, more than 40 percent will likely avoid a two-year time limit, and more than 60 percent will probably be off welfare before five years. If, as plummeting caseloads suggest, welfare mothers are more employable than had been previously thought, the percentage who are welfare-dependent may be significantly smaller than indicated by the figures above.

In addition to length of time on public assistance, generational receipt of welfare has been investigated as an aspect of dependency. As is the case with length-of-time studies, results for generational dependency vary with methodology. Regardless of methodology, however, a young woman's family's receipt of welfare significantly increases the likelihood that she also will re-

Table 5.2   Time on Welfare and Selected Variables for New Entrants (percent)

Characteristics at beginning of first AFDC spell	All first-time recipients	Expected to spend >2 years on AFDC	Expected to spend >5 years on AFDC
All recipients	100.0%	57.8%	34.8%
Education:			
<9 years	13.0	75.3	63.4
9–11 years	34.0	66.2	40.0
12+ years	53.0	48.2	24.3
Work experience:			
No recent	38.7	67.1	44.9
Recent	61.3	52.0	28.3
Age:			
Under 24	52.7	64.5	41.9
25–30	24.9	51.9	25.6
31–40	19.3	48.4	28.3
Over 40	3.1	51.1	25.2
Race:			
White/other	55.6	50.9	26.7
Black	28.4	66.4	41.4
Hispanic	16.0	66.9	50.7
Marital status:			
Never married	58.2	65.5	43.1
Ever married	41.8	47.2	23.0
Age of youngest child:			
<12 months	52.1	64.8	39.2
13–36 months	16.6	55.5	37.9
37–60 months	10.9	54.3	29.5
61–120 months	11.2	49.7	29.9
121+ months	9.3	37.1	15.2
Number of children:			
1	57.2	57.0	35.8
2	33.2	58.2	31.9
3	7.5	58.7	35.9
4+	2.2	71.0	43.1

Source: Committee on Ways and Means, House of Representatives, *Overview of Entitlement Programs* (Washington, D.C.: GPO, 1996), p. 507.

ceive public assistance. One study found that 58 percent of daughters from welfare families eventually obtained assistance, compared with 27 percent of daughters from nonwelfare families. In another, 55.8 percent of women from welfare families received welfare, compared with 32.9 percent of non-welfare families.[5] Thus, in addition to the socioeconomic risk factors typically associated with welfare—race, education, income—a behavioral variable is introduced: pregnancies of young women who are on public assistance.

BARRIERS TO EMPLOYMENT

The expectation that many poor mothers would run afoul of time limits pre-occupied liberal policy analysts. After the GOP won control of Congress in 1994, the prospect of *radical* welfare reform dictated by conservatives pushed liberals to reconsider the unemployability of welfare mothers.

The relationship between employment and welfare has been an ongoing issue in social policy. The problem tends to be understood rather simply in terms of individual features that make workers poor candidates for employment or structural aspects of the social economy that impair their employment. When poor individuals are disabled, they are not expected to work; traditionally, this group has constituted the "worthy" poor. When prospective workers are impeded in their search for employment by circumstances beyond their control—employers' discrimination, remote employment, a lousy job market—remedies have been sought to make work more accessible. Once welfare is added to the equation, however, moral considerations tend to dictate the program options. While the disabled have been excused from work, those contending with structural problems are expected to continue to seek it. Thus, the time limit on receipt of Unemployment Compensation, designed to encourage the able-bodied unemployed to redouble their search for employment, was replicated in the 1996 welfare reforms as a signal to able-bodied women that they are expected to participate in the labor market.

INDIVIDUAL FACTORS

In 1974 the old disability programs—Old Age Assistance, Aid to the Blind, and Aid to the Disabled—were consolidated into Supplemental Security Income (SSI), and the federal government assumed full fiscal responsibility for the program, although states were free to augment federal benefits. The change in funding and the more generous benefits offered under SSI, coupled to the higher benefits of Social Security Disability Insurance (DI), gave the states an incentive to shift the welfare burden to the federal government. Having AFDC recipients certified as eligible for SSI and DI eliminated the states' 50 percent funding obligation while giving recipients a significant increase, since SSI and DI benefits (for the "worthy" poor) customarily exceeded AFDC benefits (for the "unworthy," employable poor). State fiscal crises and deteriorating welfare benefits were powerful reasons to transfer poor mothers from AFDC to SSI and DI, until the Reagan administration put on the brakes. During the first Reagan administration, tens of thousands of beneficiaries were reevaluated and terminated from DI, and even though many of these terminations were later reversed, the message was clear: the federal government's disability programs would no longer be a dumping ground for the states' welfare problems. To the surprise of many liberals, the Clinton administration continued this strict-constructionist interpretation, following the lead of a Republican Congress that jettisoned tens of thousands of poor children from SSI on the pretext that the marginally disabled were abusing the more generous SSI benefits.[6]

Although the Clinton presidency adhered to a firm distinction between AFDC and SSI, the 1996 federal welfare reform legislation included an important concession to liberals: states were allowed to exempt 20 percent of recipients from time limits. In light of the draconian nature of conservative federal reform, the liberal response to this arbitrary 20 percent exemption was an audible sigh of relief. The downside was that the historical record on welfare usage, as Pavetti's research demonstrated, suggested that a much higher percentage of families were unemployable. If welfare beneficiaries were technically not disabled, liberal analysts reasoned that they might still encounter enough "barriers" to employment to make them functionally unemployable. If welfare mothers were sufficiently impaired, a case could be built for an expansion of the 20 percent exemption or a loosening of the disability criteria.

To determine the extent of disability among poor mothers, Pamela Loprest and Gregory Acs examined three sets of national data from the early 1990s and extracted information on "functional limitations, impairments, or conditions that would most likely reduce the ability of a woman to work or care for basic needs." Included in their definition of disability were problems such as "mental or emotional disorders, including substance abuse, that impair an individual's ability to carry out his or her regular activities."[7] When the data on mothers and children were merged, it appeared that between 18 and 30 percent of families evinced a serious impairment or disability.[8] Subsequently, a more detailed analysis of the relationship between disability, welfare, and work revealed that disability, variously defined, affects about one in five AFDC recipients (table 5.3). Predictably, disabled welfare recipients were more dependent on aid because it was more difficult for them to work. Regardless of the way in which disability was defined, approximately 90 percent of disabled recipients were unlikely to exit AFDC.[9] Nonetheless, the disabled did manage to leave AFDC, though those with more severe disabilities were about three times less likely to exit the program than AFDC recipients reporting no disability. Disabled AFDC recipients who did leave the program did so via work only about one-third of the time.[10] Finally, 12.3 percent of AFDC adults reported a disabled child at home, though paradoxically this had virtually no effect on a family's exiting welfare because of work.[11]

In related research, Krista Olson and LaDonna Pavetti investigated "barriers" to employment experienced by welfare mothers. For Olson and Pavetti,

Table 5.3   Disability among Women Receiving AFDC

Disability Measure	Percent
Some functional limitation	20.1
Degree of difficulty with functional limitations	
Needs help/unable to perform	8.4
Some difficulty	11.7
Number of functional limitations	
Needs help/unable to perform	
1 activity	4.5
2+ activities	3.9
Some difficulty	
1 activity	7.4
2+ activities	4.3
Type of functional limitations	
One or more ADLs[a]	
1 activity	7.3
2+ activities	3.3
One or more IADLs[b]	
1 activity	4.8
2+ activities	4.6

[a]Activities of Daily Living (ADLs) include dressing, eating, etc.
[b]Instrumental ADLs include doing light housework, walking, using the phone, spending money, etc.
Source: Pamela Loprest and Gregory Acs, "Profile of Disability among Families on AFDC" (Washington, D.C.: Urban Institute, 1995), pp. 6–7.

barriers included the impairment/disability components as well as social factors like domestic violence, involvement with the child welfare department, inadequate housing, and low skills and learning disabilities. The prevalence of these problems varies (table 5.4), but given the multiplicity of problems evident in welfare families, "barriers" easily eclipse instances of "disability/impairment":

> Just over 30 percent of the AFDC caseload report a serious barrier to employment and two-thirds report either a serious or modest barrier, excluding low basic skills. When one takes into account extremely low or very low skills, the percentage of the caseload with a moderate or severe barrier increases to 89 percent.[12]

Olson and Pavetti concluded "conservatively" that "25 percent of the caseload is likely to experience difficulties entering the labor force," but when time limits are introduced the number increases dramatically to 51 percent.[13] Thus, research on welfare dependency as well as functional impairments and barriers to employment took a somber view of the employment prospects of welfare mothers.[14]

Table 5.4   Potential Barriers to Employment among AFDC Recipients—Range of Estimates

Barrier to Employment	Low Estimate	High Estimate
Serious disability—household head	6.1%	13.6%
Any health limitation	16.6	28.5
Mental health problem	2.0	28.4
Child with some level of disability	11.1	21.1
Substance abuse	4.9	37.0
Domestic violence	6.1	80.0
Child welfare involvement	3.2	20.0
Homelessness or housing instability	9.3	48.0
Low skills (grade school education)	10.0	30.0

Source: Krista Olson and LaDonna Pavetti, *Personal and Family Challenges to the Successful Transition from Welfare to Work* (Washington, D.C.: Urban Institute, 1997), p. 21.

STRUCTURAL FACTORS

Individual factors alone fail to account for all of the difficulties people experience with employment; a host of larger circumstances—high unemployment, plant closings, inferior schools, discriminatory hiring practices—cast shadows over the labor market. This focus on structural problems that constrain social and economic participation has, of course, been the province of liberal ideology. According to the liberal economic critique, capitalism is a huge engine that generates wealth but does so at the expense of the poor and to the benefit of the affluent. In the best of times, capitalism offers opportunities that "'trickle-down' to low-paid production and service workers," in so doing exacerbating inequality.[15] Because capitalism is dynamic, only government is capable of correcting its flaws. Thus, Randy Albelda and Chris Tilly posit structural remedies to poverty as *authentic* welfare reform:

(1) Create an income-maintenance system that realizes the need for full-time childcare.
(2) Create jobs that don't assume you have a "wife" at home to perform limitless unpaid work.
(3) Close the gender gap in pay, and boost wages to a living level.
(4) Tame the family budget busters—housing and health care.
(5) Expand the safety net.
(6) Make education and training affordable and available for all.
(7) Promote community-based economic development.
(8) Secure funding with a fair tax structure.[16]

The laissez-faire response to this, as we have seen, has been to impugn the behaviors of the poor.[17]

Insofar as employment problems are rooted in macroeconomic phenomena, individuals are all but irrelevant to resolving problems relating to the job market. At the same time, structural factors impeding employment are, by their very nature, particularly stubborn. Sheldon Danziger, Robert Haveman, and Robert Plotnick speak to the scale and complexity of the task:

> Securing full participation of the poor in economic life requires a long-run effort and involves improving their employability and expanding educational opportunities for their children, changes in labor markets, the provision of social and job-related services, the provision of transitional income, employment, and in-kind support, and a growing economy. No simple formula—no isolated policy measure or approach—is likely to make a substantial dent in the problem.[18]

According to many analysts, poverty has become more intractable as a result of the dynamics of global capitalism. "The primary source of increased economic hardship has been a set of structural changes in the labor market. Less-educated workers have found it harder to secure employment, and those who are hired tend to receive low wages," concluded Sheldon Danziger and Jeffrey Lehman. "There [has been] a decline in the demand for less-skilled workers, who were either displaced by . . . automated systems or had to compete with overseas workers producing . . . rising imports."[19]

A primary concern of macroeconomic analysts has been flagging family income despite the general prosperity that followed World War II. The Economic Policy Institute notes that median family income doubled between 1947 and 1979 but remained static from 1979 to 1995.[20] If income for all families has flat-lined, that of poorer families has actually declined. In order to correct for structural flaws in the labor market that contribute to poverty, various policies have evolved, such as the minimum wage and the Earned Income Tax Credit. The effectiveness of such national interventions can be significant; between 1989 and 1997, for example, raising the minimum wage and EITC has increased the average earnings of mothers with two children from $9,850 to $13,950 annually, or 42 percent.[21]

With respect to metropolitan labor markets, some analysts observe "mismatches" between unemployed workers and available jobs.[22] John Kasarda has documented "spatial" mismatch, when newer jobs are available in suburbs but poorer job-seekers reside in inner cities; William Julius Wilson has observed other disconnects that contribute to poverty, including the gaps between the skills necessary to secure service jobs in the information economy and the aptitude of poorly educated minority job applicants, between the plethora of single mothers in ghetto neighborhoods and the dearth of marriageable males as a result of encounters with the criminal justice system. In such instances, program interventions have been more specific. "Policies aimed at reducing spatial mismatch should therefore focus primarily on enabling inner-city workers to adjust more readily to suburbanizing labor demand," suggested Harry Holzer, "either through aiding residential relocations to the suburbs or through improved transportation and job placement services for

Table 5.5   Share of Workers Earning Poverty-Level Wages, by Race/Ethnicity and Gender (percent)

Males	1973	1979	1989	1995
White	10.7	11.4	17.6	18.7
Black	24.8	23.4	33.2	33.8
Hispanic	25.0	23.3	39.0	44.5
Females	1973	1979	1989	1995
White	12.5	6.3	16.9	16.6
Black	50.7	42.8	43.6	43.7
Hispanic	50.4	49.1	50.9	53.5

Note: In 1994 the hourly wage to lift a family of four above poverty was $7.28.
Source: Adapted from Lawrence Mishel, Jared Bernstein, and John Schmitt, *The State of Working America* (Washington, D.C.: Economic Policy Institute, 1997), p. 339.

those remaining in the inner cities."[23] Similarly, an analysis of regional labor markets revealed that "local area conditions do influence welfare exits."[24]

Despite national and regional interventions to alleviate poverty, race and gender continue to disadvantage workers significantly (table 5.5). In reality, of course, individual and structural factors interact, contributing to poverty and eligibility for welfare. As employment opportunities change, workers must adapt or settle for lower wages and possibly unemployment; social program benefits may be available, but historically these have been circumscribed so as to minimize interference with the labor market. Welfare has been the social program of last resort.

In response to the liberal-conservative polemic, the Pulitzer Prize-winning economist Robert Solow has proposed, modestly, that the relationship between the poor and the society be viewed interactively: social altruism in the form of social program benefits requires a measure of effort on the part of recipients, most clearly evident in self-reliance. "A modest work-welfare system, with an adequate supply of jobs, stands a chance of reinforcing both self-reliance and altruism," suggested Solow, "but such a system does not come cheap. There is no sign yet that the United States is willing to put the necessary money where its mouth is."[25] Having reviewed the welfare-to-work literature, Solow concluded correctly that the poor have no aversion to work; rather, the problem is arranging productive activity so that it respects the reality of poverty.

> A well-constructed substitution of work for welfare, provided it is applied humanely to those who are disabled or personally troubled, and provided it pays careful attention to the needs of children and the self-respect of adults, would be felt to be a step in the right direction by almost everyone, including those who would find their benefits replaced by a requirement to work.[26]

Solow's reciprocal interaction between work and altruism is reinforced by Richard Sennett's view of dependence. Rather than continue a rhetorical argument that pits dependence against self-sufficiency, Sennett proposed interdependence as a guide for managing social affairs. Moreover, a constructive understanding of the matter sees dependence as a *sine qua non* of a healthy society. The reverse, Sennett aptly noted, is also true: demonizing the welfare-poor abrades the civic fabric. "Shame about dependence has a practical consequence. It erodes mutual trust and commitment, and the lack of these social bonds threatens the workings of any collective enterprise."[27] The relevance of any welfare-to-work initiative thus rests, in large measure, on its being crafted in a way that facilitates meaningful employment for the welfare-poor. Obvious components of such an orientation could be derived from the experience of welfare adults who have successfully negotiated the transition.

AFTER AFDC

It follows that welfare mothers' likelihood of making a successful transition to the labor market is contingent on individual and structural factors relating to employment. Recent evidence suggests that the interface between welfare mothers and the labor market is more fluid than had been suspected; many welfare mothers not only left public assistance, but escaped poverty. To understand what happened to poor mothers after AFDC, Daniel Meyer and Maria Cancian examined a national data set that provided detailed economic data on the experience of 878 women who had exited welfare. Poor women who left welfare often returned—37 percent within one year, 50 percent within two. On the other hand, 40 percent of welfare mothers did not resort to AFDC five years after leaving, and 20 percent did not claim any public assistance benefits five years after exiting welfare. Significantly, almost 60 percent of mothers worked; their earnings were the largest source of income in each of the postwelfare years. Meyer and Cancian found that some mothers who had left welfare also eventually escaped poverty: "There was a trend toward improved economic status over time, with the percentage of poor dropping from 55 percent in the first year to about 40 percent in the fifth year and the proportion who had incomes over twice the poverty line increasing from 15 to 22 percent."[28] Upward mobility among poor mothers varies, however. Black welfare mothers are less likely to become independent of public assistance programs. While 48 percent of white women failed to secure incomes twice the poverty line within five years of exiting welfare, many more black women, 67 percent, were unable to escape poverty.[29]

Subsequently, Meyer and Cancian examined the postwelfare circumstances of 594 women. As before, some mothers had vaulted out of poverty within five years of exiting welfare. "There is a trend toward improved economic status over time," observed the researchers, "with the percentage poor dropping from 56 percent in the first year to 41 percent in the fifth year, and the proportion who have incomes over two times the poverty line increasing from 15 to 23 percent."[30] The experience of welfare mothers during those five years is one of trying numerous methods to provide more adequately for their children. While about two-thirds of women who exit are off AFDC during any one year, only 39 percent were able to stay off AFDC in all of the first five years. Only about one-fifth of the women exiting AFDC were able to stay off all means-tested programs over the five-year period, and more than one-fourth received public assistance during every year. Finally, while 22 percent of the women had family incomes above poverty every year, only 7 percent would have been above poverty in all years based on their own incomes alone.[31]

As before, the portrait of poor mothers who have exited welfare leaves the viewer frustrated; clearly discernible figures blur into one another, producing a fuzzy collage. At year five, more than half (54.6 percent) of mothers are independent of public assistance altogether, yet only one-third (35.8 percent) rise above the poverty line on the basis of their incomes alone.[32] Thus, marriage and family continue to play an important role in the prosperity of poor families who have been on welfare.

While extracting the postwelfare experience of poor mothers from national data sets is methodologically convenient, a more direct analysis could be conducted by directly tracking those who have left public assistance programs. That such data have not been systematically collected over the decades is but another indictment of public welfare administrators and social work academics, who might have monitored the experience of poor mothers vis-à-vis public welfare. In one of the first such studies, Cathy Born and her associates examined the fate of 1,600 Maryland welfare recipients who left the program between October 1996 and June 1997. Three- and six-month followup interviews revealed diverse reasons for exiting public welfare:

> The most common recorded reasons that study families' cash assistance cases have closed are: the family was receiving other income (19.6 percent); the payee did not appear for or complete the redetermination process (19.8 percent); the payee failed to provide agency-requested verification (13.9 percent); the client started work (12.3 percent); and residency (7.3 percent). Together these "top five" accounted for seven of every 10 case closures during the first nine months of welfare reform.[33]

These administrative explanations for case closings obscured the fact that many recipients who had left welfare in Maryland were participating in the labor market. Born and her associates found that 73.5 percent of payees had some paid employment during the two and one-half years preceding their departure from welfare. "About half (49.3 percent) were employed in the calender quarter in which their welfare case was closed; two of three (66.3 percent) were working in the quarter immediately after their exit from the welfare rolls."[34] The jobs most often reported for family heads who had been on AFDC were in the service industries. Average wages for those who had left welfare were $3,367 in 1995 and $4,818 in 1996.[35] Given such low earnings, the Maryland researchers were sensitive to the possibility that welfare reform would further destabilize poor families, eventually to the point that children who had been on public assistance would be placed in foster care. In their followup review of cases, only three children from one family were identified as having been placed in foster care after their grandmother left AFDC, though it was not possible to attribute foster care placement to changes in welfare rules.[36]

By the fall of 1997, a kind of vacuum had occurred in welfare policy. President Clinton announced the success of the 1996 federal welfare initiative, the welfare caseload continued to drop, and there was a dearth of evidence that radical, conservative welfare reform had generated the crisis among the welfare-poor that many liberals had anticipated. In response to work mandates reinforced by time limits, heads of welfare households entered the labor market and found jobs. For 1997, the DHHS reported that 28.1 percent of adults on welfare were working or about to, a figure well within the work requirements of the 1996 welfare reform act.[37] The extent of employment surprised many liberal policy analysts. Only two years earlier Sheldon Danziger and Jeffrey Lehman had recited the liberal line on the employability of welfare recipients: "It is simply not the case that most of today's welfare recipients could obtain stable employment that would lift them and their children out of poverty, if only they would try harder."[38] Yet despite the bleak employment prospects of poor mothers, legions of them were leaving welfare, often for jobs.

Accordingly, labor economists reconsidered the job market. "Given recent industry shifts (particularly the robust growth in low-wage services), there is the possibility that welfare recipients may not have as hard a time as is sometimes suggested finding work, though I want to be careful not to overinterpret these results," suggested Jared Bernstein tentatively. "We might be able to muddle through welfare reform, at least initially."[39] Although welfare recipients had found work, the jobs tended to pay low wages, about $5.50 an hour, and the earnings increases resulting from employment had not been sufficient to lift many out of poverty.[40] Caveats aside, Bernstein's reading of welfare reform represented a discernible shift in thinking at liberal EPI, where only two years earlier Lawrence Mishel and John Schmitt had concluded, "Even if the private sector could find work for a huge inflow of welfare recipients without displacing those currently in work, it can do so only at a wage that is considerably [11.9 percent] below the already depressed earnings levels prevailing in the low-wage labor market."[41]

The limited capacity of the low-wage labor market to absorb large numbers of welfare mothers was most thoroughly addressed by Harry Holzer, who conducted 800 employer interviews in each of four cities, Atlanta, Boston, Detroit, and Los Angeles, between 1992 and 1994. The employers provided surprising and heartening information about their hiring practices. For example, a large majority had no reservations about hiring welfare mothers: "80–85 percent of employers claim that they would hire welfare recipients or applicants with GED and/or government training."[42] Significantly, willingness to hire the welfare-poor was altered by two conditions: applicants with part-time or short-term experience were half as likely to be hired, and those with a criminal record were only one-third as likely to get a job.[43] Given the multiple problems that affect many welfare recipients, Holzer concluded that, despite the probability that the labor market could eventually absorb three million welfare mothers, their problems—poor skills, high dropout rates, low test scores, little work experience, minority status, welfare dependency, and the like—made this unlikely:

> It is highly likely that a fairly large fraction of current long-term AFDC recipients who will be required to enter the labor force will likely be unable to find work in the short term, especially if they receive no special training and in the absence of public job-creation efforts (such as subsidies for their employment in the private sector or direct public-sector employment).[44]

Holzer's research was unusual in that it included gender and race as variables in employer interviews. Employers preferred black female to black male applicants; moreover, they preferred Latinos over blacks even when the former have greater deficiencies. To some extent this may be due to the fact that black women were offered the lowest wages for any race and gender subgroup. Hourly wages paid to black women were $6.00 for manufacturing jobs and $6.49 for other employment, versus $7.61 for black men in manufacturing and $7.42 for black men doing other work.[45] Holzer's study suggested that black welfare mothers were more likely to be employed than had been previously thought, though their prospects diminished rapidly once employers learned of additional problems. Employers' preference for black women over black men suggests more intense competition between them for low-wage jobs.

As the job prospects of welfare mothers were examined more thoroughly, the pessimism about their employability gradually began to lift. "There is no empirical evidence to support the assumption that welfare recipients lack a work ethic," notes Vicki Lens. "To the contrary, studies conducted in the early 1970s indicate that welfare recipients possess a strong work ethic."[46]

The stereotype of welfare mothers as stay-at-home deadbeats was contradicted by research portraying women on welfare as reflecting mainstream norms and preferring work to staying at home. In an investigation of 357 welfare mothers enrolled in JOBS, Jan Hagen and Liane Davis found that "over half (54%) of the women believed that even a low-paying job was better than being on welfare." With respect to remaining at home, the responses were even clearer: "Relatively few (19%) of the women indicated a preference for being at home full-time caring for their children."[47]

Yet the conventional liberal wisdom remained unsure about the employability of welfare mothers. In a review of the evidence that had accumulated by the fall of 1997, Gary Burtless concluded that "while it is realistic to expect that most adult recipients can find and hold jobs, at least eventually, it is unrealistic to believe the job market will provide all of them with an adequate standard of living."[48] Although the evidence was fragmentary and less than definitive, many welfare mothers had found jobs despite low test scores, few job skills, and little employment experience. In 1996, for example, the Census Bureau reported that the median income for single black female heads-of-households had increased to $15,530, more than 21 percent more, in inflation-adjusted dollars, than it had been in 1993 ($12,765). For those with children, earnings were greater: $16,265 in 1996.[49] In the context of a vibrant economy and tight labor market, Burtless found the glass more full than empty: "It is not unreasonable to expect that at least three-quarters of current welfare recipients could contribute to their own support through wage earnings," he concluded.[50] Burtless's judgment was important in two respects. First, if we factor in the 20 percent exemption on employment included in the federal welfare reform law, Burtless's 75 percent employability figure came very close to covering the entire welfare population, essentially leaving only 5 percent who might be terminated from welfare without being able to find and keep a job. Second, if the vast majority of welfare mothers can reasonably be expected to work, the central question driving the welfare debate is no longer about their ability to work but about the adequacy of their wages and benefits over time—in other words, their upward mobility.

UPWARD MOBILITY

An important exception to researchers' insistence on the dismal prospects of welfare mothers in the labor market was research conducted under the auspices of the Institute for Women's Policy Research (IWPR). In addition to reproductive rights, comparable pay in the workplace has been a bedrock issue within the women's movement, and the fact that women earned less than men helped explain their disproportionate representation among the nation's poor. Gender analysis of welfare programs, moreover, indicated that AFDC for mothers functioned as Unemployment Compensation did for male workers, essentially tiding them over between jobs.[51] Once feminist researchers began to investigate the income dynamics of poor mothers, the interaction between low-wage work and public welfare became obvious. Thus, IWPR researchers showed that a sizable majority of mothers on AFDC had participated in, or were seeking entrance into, the labor force. They divided the AFDC population into six groups according to the way in which welfare mothers related to the labor market:

- 22.8 percent were *cyclers,* alternating between work and welfare as economic circumstances demanded.
- 20.1 percent were *combiners,* coupling welfare benefits with work that failed to pay enough to get them off public assistance.
- 23.4 percent were *job-seekers,* dependent on AFDC but actively looking for work.
- 7.4 percent were *looking for part-time* work but continued to depend on welfare.
- 19.7 percent were *out of the labor force,* and reliant on AFDC.
- 6.6 percent were *exempt* from work because of a disability and reliant on AFDC.[52]

IWPR research suggested that the AFDC population was heterogeneous with regard to candidacy for employment, and that only about one in four had no experience with, or could not reasonably be expected to, work.

IWPR findings were complemented by the research of Brad Schiller, an economist. The author of a standard text on poverty and discrimination that is in its seventh edition, Schiller has developed a reputation for concern about fairness and opportunity in economics.[53] Among his interests are the upward mobility of the poorest Americans and, in its absence, the intractability of the underclass. Using a national data set, Schiller examined the experience of youths earning the minimum wage and their subsequent earnings. He found that one-third of minimum-wage workers received a raise within a year, and that 60 percent were beyond the minimum wage within two years. Of those who entered the labor market in 1980, a recession year, only 15 percent continued earning the minimum wage after three years.[54] Furthermore,

> the available perceptions of minimum-wage youth seem to dispel the notion that minimum-wage jobs offer low wages and nothing more. Over 85 percent of the

minimum-wage entrants stated that they liked their jobs, and over 60 percent felt that they were learning skills that would be valuable in attaining better jobs. Only one out of eight minimum-wage youth perceived a total lack of on-the-job training—a condition compatible with the notion of "dead-end" jobs. Over half (56 percent) of the minimum-wage workers perceived opportunities for promotion with the same employer.[55]

Seven years after beginning a minimum-wage job, the average worker was earning $7.19 per hour, an increase of 154 percent, or about 15 percent per year. Although non-minimum-wage job entrants were earning $8.56 per hour by 1987, the minimum-wage entrants had closed the gap significantly. Notably, race did not appear to retard young people's wage increases. "The longitudinal experiences of minimum-wage youth . . . refute the notion of a 'minimum-wage trap,'" concluded Schiller. "Youth who started at the minimum wage in 1980 recorded impressive wage gains over the subsequent seven years both in absolute and relative terms."[56]

Subsequently, Schiller studied the work experience of teens (aged 16–19) and youths (aged 20–24), during their first 10 to 15 years in the labor market. All these young people were divided into twenty categories (ventiles), and their mobility was tracked over time. Again, mobility was pronounced: "Relative mobility is pervasive among younger workers. Eight out of ten teenagers with significant attachment to the workforce in 1978 were in a different relative earnings position ten years later," Schiller found. "Less than one-fourth of either cohort stayed in the same or adjacent rank of the earnings distribution during the observation period."[57] Because Schiller's analysis encompassed the universe of young workers, upward mobility, ipso facto, was accompanied by comparable downward mobility; however, a general increase in wages during the span of the analysis benefited both cohorts. "Youth who were initially on the lower rungs of the earnings distribution moved significantly up the ladder in subsequent years. Youth initially in the 15th ventile, for example, moved up the distribution an average of nearly five ventiles in the subsequent seven years."[58] With regard to race and gender, Schiller found that minority youths and young women were inclined to hold onto top rankings, while at the same time tending to remain in the bottom ventiles longer, compared with white males, suggesting a bifurcating dualism in the younger population of the labor market.[59]

Lower-wage workers' upward mobility weakens the case for rigid stratification of the labor market. This mobility probably accounts for much of the surprising surge of welfare mothers into the labor market. In an analysis of the decline of AFDC cases in Ohio, Schiller and an associate found that stringently enforced welfare-to-work rules reduce AFDC cases by 7 percent, but that the impact accelerates, eventually yielding reductions in the 20 percent range.[60] The interaction of latent upward mobility afforded by the labor market coupled with work benefits, such as Medicaid and childcare, results in significant numbers of poor mothers doing what they would have done had such supports been there before—they find jobs. The evidence of welfare mothers' willingness—if not eagerness—to work pervades the literature on welfare reform, spanning the range of job opportunities. Recalling the perceptions of welfare- and working-poor women who were referred to positions as nurse assistants in a nursing home, Frances Riemer observed that "the women at Church Hall, whether from welfare or not, were glad to be at work, and their initial reactions to Church Hall were all positive."[61] In a more extensive study of welfare mothers trained by Pennsylvania Blue Cross/Blue Shield to be claims processors, Felice Perlmutter noted that "the trainers at [the training sites] estimate that 90 to 95 percent of the women who participated in the program wanted to be there. They were highly motivated and were determined to succeed."[62] A summary of 235 welfare recipients who graduated from Eastern Washington University concluded that "most welfare graduates have demonstrated considerable success in earning sufficiently high wages to work their way out of AFDC dependency."[63]

If the aspirations of welfare mothers have been undervalued in research on welfare and work, their desires for themselves and their children must be appreciated in context. Too often, "the overriding experience of welfare recipients with employment is not only that it is difficult to get work, but the jobs they do get are often temporary or part-time; thus they are low-paying and without benefits."[64] As is often the case with social phenomena, however, perseverance endures under the most competitive and adverse circumstances. An intricate analysis of worker mobility in New York City between 1980 and 1990 is seminal in this respect. David Howell and Elizabeth Howell constructed a matrix of "job contours" consisting essentially of self-employment and white-collar, blue-collar, and low-wage jobs, and then analyzed the workers' mobility according to race, gender, and immigrant status. During a period of enormous compression in job opportunities because of an influx of immigrants, the researchers found that among workers who had worked at least 20 weeks in the previous year, "male and female African American and female new immigrant workers show[ed] substantial improvements in their employment distribution, shifting from the two 'worst' (secondary) job contours toward the two 'best' (independent primary) contours."[65]

Low-wage workers thus show upward mobility over time, as has been the case with the general population. Daniel McMurer and Isabel Sawhill note that upward mobility is more pronounced than data on a stagnating income distribution would suggest.

> Mobility in the United States is substantial, according to the evidence. Large portions of the population move into a new income quintile, with estimates rang-

ing from about 25 to 40 percent in a single year. As one would expect, the mobility rate is even higher over longer periods—about 45 percent over a 5-year period and about 60 percent over both 9-year and 17-year periods.[66]

Among the poor, mobility is also pronounced. Reporting on data from the mid-1990s, the Census Bureau found that while 30.3 percent of Americans lived below the poverty line for at least two months during a three-year span, only 5.3 percent were poor continuously for two years. On average, families were below the poverty line for four and a half months.[67] Welfare mothers' ability to take advantage of the dynamics of upward mobility depends, of course, on several factors. So long as more jobs are generated by a vibrant economy and welfare mothers gain education and employment experience, they will prosper along with the mainstream of Americans.

WELFARE MOTHERS AND WORK

The relationship between poor mothers and the labor market would have remained in a fog of disputed data had not a female graduate student begun getting to know low-income women in order to get a clearer idea of their actual circumstances. In 1988 Kathryn Edin began interviewing welfare mothers in Cook County (Chicago and environs) under the supervision of the policy researcher Christopher Jencks. Her work provided the first in-depth portrait of poor mothers, and the depiction was considerably more ambiguous than official statistical accounts of families in poverty. Edin reported that all of the welfare mothers with whom she had established confidence supplemented their welfare check in order to provide minimally for their children, and that none of the mothers reported all of their income to welfare caseworkers. Of all the mothers studied, only one came close to managing on her public assistance benefits alone, and her circumstances were so precarious that she risked losing custody of her children on grounds of neglect. "Only 58 percent of their income came from food stamps and AFDC," reported Edin and Jencks. "Of the remaining 42 percent, just over half came from absent fathers, boyfriends, parents, siblings, and student loans, while just under half came from unreported work of various kinds."[68] In the face of deteriorating welfare benefits, welfare mothers were much more enterprising than researchers might have suspected.

Recognizing the substantial limits imposed by the size of her original sample, Edin teamed up with Laura Lein and began getting to know low-income mothers in other cities. By the early 1990s, Edin and Lein had interviewed 214 welfare mothers and 165 low-wage mothers who lived in Chicago, Boston, San Antonio, and Charleston. Both groups made creative use of a range of options to balance their budgets (table 5.6), but with limited

Table 5.6   Monthly Income and Expenses of Welfare and Low-Wage Working Mothers

	Welfare Mothers	Low-Wage Working Mothers
Total Expenses	**$876**	**$1,243**
Housing costs	213	341
Food costs	262	249
Work-related costs		
Childcare	7	66
Medical	18	56
Clothing	69	95
Transportation	31	57
Car payments and insurance	30	71
Other costs	245	308
Total Income	**892**	**1,239**
Welfare and in-kind income		
AFDC	307	—
Food Stamps	222	57
SSI	36	3
Other contributions		
From family and friends	62	65
From boyfriends	56	60
From absent fathers	39	127
Other income	37	36
Earnings		
Main (reported) job	19	777
Second job	—	59
Overtime	—	27
Earned Income Tax Credit	3	25
Income from unreported job	90	—
Income from underground economy	19	2
Welfare (including SSI)		
Minus total expenses	−311	—
Minus housing and food	90	—
Regular earnings (including EITC)		
Minus total expenses	—	−441
Minus housing and food	—	212

Note: Columns may not add up to totals because of rounding.
Source: Kathryn Edin, "The Myths of Dependence and Self-Sufficiency," *Focus* 17 (Fall/Winter 1995), p. 2.

success. Clearly, if welfare was inadequate to raise a family, work was not much of a solution either. "The average mother who left welfare for full-time work would . . . experience at least a 33 percent gap between her expected earnings and her expenses."[69] Of the welfare mothers, 86 percent stated that they planned to leave public assistance for work; only 14 percent indicated interest in staying on aid. Yet the inadequacy of earnings from work made this a doubtful proposition; in Edin's words, "The future they were building through low-wage work was a house of cards."[70]

Various problems accounted for the inadequacy of those earnings to make ends meet. Most of the jobs were unskilled or semiskilled (clerks, cashiers, nurse's aides, or childcare workers); only a third were employed as secretaries, practical nurses, cooks, or teacher's aides—skilled positions that characteristically pay low wages. In some instances, mothers failed to exploit available resources; for example, only 28 percent reported receipt of the EITC, though virtually all would have been eligible.[71] A chronic feature of the low-wage jobs welfare mothers took was the inability to move upward and establish a career. For them "the labor market was not a ladder leading upward to better wages and opportunities but a carousel on which they went around and around in circles, with an occasional change of horses."[72] Because of such features, welfare mothers who had left welfare for work tended to return to public assistance. National data indicate that two-thirds of welfare mothers who had left public assistance for work returned within six years.[73] Despite its structural limits, however, poor women continued to go to work. The benefits of welfare were even lower than their earnings, and work contributed to a sense of pride, the antithesis of welfare.

The dynamic relationship between work and welfare has also been charted by the urban anthropologist Katherine Newman. After following the families of workers in Harlem's fast food industry, Newman concluded that welfare and work are "intertwined" in most of the families studied.[74] Her observations of one worker's circumstances are noteworthy:

> There is a steady income stream coming into Rey's home, because most of the adults are indeed working, often in the mostly unregulated economy of small-scale services and self-employment, including home-based seamstresses, food vendors, gypsy cab drivers, and carpenters. Most of this income never sees the tax man.[75]

Importantly, Newman notes that minimum-wage workers develop "moral armor" in order to persevere in low-wage, tedious labor in an environment that all too often rewards their peers for the con, the ripoff, and the quick fix, even at the expense of longevity.[76]

Thus, in-depth studies of welfare families reveal a considerable degree of microeconomic flux as they struggle financially. Significantly, Edin and Lein's research was conducted well after the work mandate of the 1988 FSA had taken effect, so welfare mothers and the welfare departments on which they depended had had ample time to make adjustments to the labor market. To provide for their children, many welfare mothers migrated back and forth between welfare and work, and much of the latter went unreported to welfare officials. Neither welfare nor work was sufficient, so mothers often overlapped them. This solution was illegal, of course, since welfare regulations required reporting all income; but mothers took the risk in their dealings with a discredited welfare program. The implications of their research provoked Edin and Lein to comment on the more stringent work requirements incorporated in the 1996 PRWORA:

> The real problem with the federal welfare system . . . was a labor-market problem. The mothers we interviewed had made repeated efforts to attain self-sufficiency through work, but the kind of jobs they could get paid too little, offered little security in the short term, and provided few opportunities over time. Meanwhile, mothers who chose to work were even worse off in material terms than their welfare counterparts. To "make it" while working, unskilled single mothers had to be extraordinarily lucky: they had to have a set of special circumstances that artificially lowered the cost of working, and they had to be able to employ a set of survival strategies that were consistent with work.[77]

In the absence of substantial supports and a reliable means of upward mobility, work would prove futile, regardless of the severity of the benefit sanctions imposed to prod welfare mothers into the labor market.

The tenuousness of employment among welfare mothers was examined more extensively through the Post Employment Services Demonstration (PESD), which enrolled almost 5,000 welfare beneficiaries in four cities—Chicago, Portland (Ore.), Riverside (Calif.), and San Antonio—during 1994 and 1995. Participants were randomly assigned to a treatment group, for whom case managers coordinated employment opportunities and could authorize special assistance to facilitate obtaining a job, or a control group that received standard services through JOBS for 90 days as well as limited assistance in securing employment. Jobs obtained by the treatment group were not unlike those reported in other studies: almost one-fourth were temporary, more than one-half included no benefits, the vast majority were in services or unskilled work, and the average wage was less than $6.00 per hour. The jobs often involved night or weekend hours and averaged 34 hours a week. Many switched jobs.[78] Of job changers, two-thirds experienced wage increases that averaged $1.62 per hour; one-quarter, however, found their wages an average of $1.58 an hour lower.[79]

PESD researchers identified several barriers to work: 15 percent of the women had health problems that interfered with work, sometimes boyfriends objected to their employment, and more than one-fourth reported transportation difficulties, but the overriding concern related to childcare. Despite these problems, mothers who were able to work regularly experienced upward mobility. "Those who were continuously employed were likely to continue to get off welfare during the year, and only a third were receiving welfare by the end of the year," the researchers concluded. "In contrast, those intermittently employed and those who held only one job that they exited had higher rates of welfare receipt. For instance, of the group that held only one job that they exited, over three-quarters were receiving welfare at the end of the follow-up year."[80] Beyond reiterating the value of perseverance, the PESD study revealed two significant findings. First, "human capital variables," such as education and previous job experience, have little relationship to the length of employment for welfare mothers who find work.[81] Second, although 80 percent of sample mothers were aware of the EITC, only 42 percent had received this benefit.[82] Once again, welfare mothers exhibited persistence in employment, despite myriad difficulties, and often without full knowledge of income supplements such as the EITC.

PERFECTING WELFARE-TO-WORK

The period following passage of PRWORA in 1996 was one of fine-tuning the work-oriented components of welfare-to-work programs. Despite the long-term dependency of many welfare mothers and the multiplicity of problems they faced, those who stuck with a job tended to get raises, and many eventually became independent of welfare. Some observers of poverty programs suspected that such initial returns of welfare-to-work were attributable to "creaming," the practice of preferentially selecting the most employable while neglecting multiproblem recipients. But welfare reformers made a compelling case that significant benefits could be realized by serving the *most* dependent cases simply because those were the ones that consumed the greatest volume of program resources over time. By way of illustration, once welfare-to-work was targeted at the "bottom third" of Oregon's caseload, an evaluator claimed that the state saved $5.60 in costs for every dollar invested in work-related social services.[83] In order to serve particularly difficult groups of welfare recipients, states contracted with nonprofit agencies, which introduced basic skills and socialization components, sometimes with a strong dose of attitude correction. A Massachusetts nonprofit called One With One, for example, claimed to have found jobs that paid decent wages for *all* of its program graduates, even if it charged the state $8,000 per trainee.[84] An assessment of job training programs for welfare mothers in New York City and Chicago revealed that "combining specific, short-term training with work experience can lead people to full-time jobs," even those considered welfare-dependent.[85] Thus, with varying degrees of success, even the most problematic of welfare recipients seemed to appreciate the promise of life after welfare if only they could find a good, dependable job.

The unexpected welfare caseload drop is often explained as a response to either a continually tight labor market or stringent welfare reform. Yet the research on welfare mothers who have taken jobs fails to account for the surprising success of welfare reform, at least as it is reflected in plummeting caseloads. Studies of welfare reform initiatives demonstrate that among the various attempts to change the behavior of welfare mothers, welfare-to-work is the most effective. Yet driving welfare recipients into the labor market yields only modest increases in their earnings and modest savings in averted welfare costs. *At best*, welfare reform demonstrations generate positive program outcomes on the order of 20 percent; however, welfare caseloads have dropped much more than that. The veteran poverty journalist Jason DeParle noted at the end of 1997 that caseloads had "fallen 27 percent and the pace continues to accelerate."[86]

Within the historical context of welfare and the low-wage labor market, a likely suspect emerges: welfare mothers themselves. As welfare benefits lost real value during the past two decades, poor mothers had little choice but to become more creative in managing their families' finances. The standardization of AFDC as a consequence of welfare rights litigation not only resulted in flat grants modified only by family size but also lessened oversight in the process of initial eligibility determinations and recertifications. As the oversight of benefits became less rigorous, welfare mothers resorted to an assortment of survival strategies. These strategies, as might be expected, varied with the circumstances of individual mothers, but three warrant special mention. First, sale of Food Stamps at a discount on the black market converted vouchers to cash during periods when family finances were particularly strained. Despite the occasional sting operation, the scale of Food Stamp fraud as an essential and routine way of augmenting of family income has yet to be adequately investigated. Second, mothers contrived with their children's fathers to bypass child support authorities in order to receive more than the niggardly $50 "pass through" allowed by the Child Support Enforcement program. That putative fathers would risk the penalties for failure to make formal child support payments, yet often made such payments to the mothers of their children under the table, may well be an unappreciated testament to their self-perception as fathers. Finally, welfare mothers worked. The employment may not have been formal, or legal for that matter, but it generated significant income for their children.

The extent of such activity might have been appreciated had social welfare scholars conducted field research on the actual experiences of welfare families. For most social welfare scholars, studying welfare families was an unnecessary distraction, since, as we have seen, public assistance programs were thought to represent a temporary interlude prior to the inevitable deployment of a European-style welfare state that would guarantee everyone an annual income. Such specialists in ideological nostalgia and leftist arcana never stooped to empirical investigations of the welfare-poor. The small number of poverty researchers were predominantly economists who, because of the intricacies of their art, had a specific methodological requirement: large data bases were necessary to draw inferences about the poor, just as data bases had been constructed around the middle class. Given their precarious individual circumstances, the likelihood is high that welfare mothers responded to interviewers who were assembling the large data bases in much the same way that they responded to the welfare caseworkers who were the gatekeepers for public assistance benefits—they hedged, contrived, and when necessary reworked reality to bring it into some approximation of what they had done to survive. The result may well have been closer to fiction than an empirical reflection of reality. For public officials, such behavior technically constituted welfare fraud, but to welfare mothers, it was but another concession needed, using the apt expression that Edin and Lein employ, "to make ends meet."

It is entirely possible, then, that welfare mothers' engagement in remunerative activity—working—had long been underreported.[97] With the inception of welfare reform that provided nominal supports, particularly health care and child daycare, mothers converted from the informal labor market to its formal counterpart, essentially declaring their availability for employment.[88] Proponents of welfare-to-work, such as Lawrence Mead (see Chapter 4), have conceded that an unknown number of "smoke outs" occurred as a consequence of welfare reform, largely because of the sanctions exacted from welfare mothers' benefits. It is also possible that many mothers went "legit" when it was in their interests to do so. When compliance with welfare reform generated more benefits than dodging punitive welfare rules and engaging in deviant behavior—recall "Merton's constant"—welfare mothers entered the labor market with enthusiasm, a significant minority of them eventually escaping poverty altogether.

The underreporting of welfare mothers' work experience has major consequences for the prospects of families on public assistance, for it has allowed proponents of *limited* welfare reform to claim that the rapid decline of welfare caseloads is a sufficient outcome in and of itself. As welfare mothers have become more transparent with respect to their microeconomic circumstances, more recent data indicate the myopia of this logic. Welfare reform that offers the welfare-poor an opportunity to become working-poor is no reform at all. The challenge that remains is to devise the mechanics that will further accelerate the incipient upward mobility of welfare families so that they too can partake in the American dream.

6

Bootstrap Capitalism

In a soft voice that belies her New York origins, Veena Allen explains that things are looking up for her. After moving from New York City into public housing in suburban Virginia with her seven-year-old daughter, she has found a job and is finally off welfare and Food Stamps. Convinced that her evangelical faith and religious work are being rewarded, Veena feels that her life is coming together. The only benefit she is continuing is Medicaid—her daughter has asthma.

Her road to financial independence was by no means smooth. In New York she could have gone to college while on welfare if it had not been for concerns about her daughter's education. Teachers' unwillingness to control unruly classes had impeded her own high school education, and she was not about to have that happen to her daughter as well. Coincidentally, a religious experience provoked her to reevaluate her life. After a day of smoking pot and drinking wine coolers, she heard a voice say, "You're done. Call a cab, and throw that stuff away!" Not long thereafter, she moved out of state to be near an uncle.

Living in a housing project helped keep the rent low; nonetheless, the gas was shut off during her first winter. Even though she might have been el-igible for public assistance at the time, she was "fed up" with welfare because of problems related to her employment at a temp agency. But that job pro-vided a badly needed paycheck. "The first check went to getting the gas on, and I cried like a baby," she recalls. At the temp agency she met a woman who made two essential referrals: one to her husband's church, the other to a delivery service. Upon joining the church, Veena found a community that would help with some of her needs, such as dependable childcare. From the delivery service, she secured a $5.50-an-hour job driving a truck at night. Initially, she worked 50 hours a week; between her first year's pay and an EITC refund, she had enough to buy a car. The job is not ideal, however: a promised raise to $6.05 has yet to materialize, and she has not been re-assigned to the day shift.

Veena puts welfare into perspective: "Welfare is a stepping stone when

Veena Allen

you use it for transition, but it's also a crutch. If you're not smart, you get stuck." Time-limited welfare is a particular hazard for younger mothers, she explains. "Welfare allows the woman to be dependent on social services; so they spend six or seven years doing nothing. You have no goals; for those mothers, you can't pull the rug out from under them." To correct any misperception, she quickly adds, "I think welfare reform is a good thing, but that it should be gradual . . . educate them . . . a lot of them haven't finished high school." She recalls the first time the welfare department van pulled up to take welfare mothers to an orientation on welfare reform: "They were frantic, like someone dropped the atom bomb in their living room."

Ordained by her church as an evangelist and certified by the state as a drug counselor, Veena spends much of the week advising wayward neighbors, encouraging them to reject their sinful ways, accept the Lord, and often, to marry the men with whom they live. The neighbors' response? She laughs heartily. "They call me 'the crazy lady.'" But she has made inroads as well as friends along the way.

Veena would like to return to college to complete her studies in special education. It is unlikely that she will be able to do that in the foreseeable future as a single mother, but the future is not an immediate concern. "I'm just knitting my life together," she says quietly, "just keeping it together."

STRATEGIES OF WELFARE REFORM

What can fairly be called "the conservative triumph in welfare reform" has caused a reappraisal not only of poverty policy but of social policy in general in the United States, and among other Western nations.[1] In the United States, two streams of poverty policy have become discernible during the past decade. The first, instituted through the 1988 Family Support Act (FSA), mandated that welfare mothers participate in the labor market through welfare-to-work initiatives. The second, welfare behaviorism, evolved with the proliferation of state "experiments" that made receipt of welfare contingent on specific standards of conduct. Both streams are evident in the 1996 Personal Responsibility and Work Opportunity Reconciliation Act (PRWORA).

To be sure, the cashiering of AFDC has not been without controversy, and the various experiments in welfare behaviorism—Learnfare, the family cap, child support enforcement, teen pregnancy reduction, and time limits—have been anything but uniformly successful. Indeed, Rebecca Blank raises fundamental questions about behavioral programs targeted at the poor, noting that *they cost more per participant, require greater effort and skill to manage and operate effectively, and may have less overall effect on economic poverty than more broad-based transfer programs.*[2] Yet there is no evidence of public sentiment in favor of scrapping Temporary Assistance for Needy Families (TANF) and reviving AFDC. If many human service professionals expected the imposition of time limits to ignite public revulsion against the PRWORA, this has not happened. "Looking back," Judith Havemann and Barbara Vobejda noted, "experts say they did not anticipate the combined effect of a robust economy and the reaction the new rules sparked in welfare families, many of whom responded by finding jobs or supporting themselves in other ways."[3] Whether a plummeting caseload is attributed to a vigorous economy or rigorous welfare reform, there is little doubt that public perceptions about welfare have changed fundamentally.

Within a few years of passage of the 1988 federal welfare reform act, poverty analysts were beginning to appreciate the heterogeneity of welfare families. Such families varied significantly with respect to the problems that led them to public assistance, including separation or divorce, a child's illness or disability, low education, unemployment, teen pregnancy, intergenerational dependency, and the like. It followed that approaches for helping welfare families become economically independent would be more effective if they reflected the diversity of families' circumstances, as opposed to presuming they were all the same. In the early 1990s, the welfare researcher Thomas Corbett likened the problem to peeling an onion: an optimal approach to welfare reform consisted of removing one layer after another. Corbett described various subgroups of welfare families and then proposed different strategies for adults and children (table 6.1). A reasonable approximation would be that the outer layer, consisting of the working-poor and short-term welfare recipients, comprises 30 percent of the welfare caseload, the middle layer 40 percent, and the most welfare-dependent core, 30 percent.[4]

Similarly, Rebecca Blank proposed three tiers for poverty policy: (1) evaluation and short-term assistance, (2) job search and training assistance, and (3) cash support. A focus in her scheme is an initiative similar to an apprenticeship. Combining education, training, and socialization, programs like Chicago's Employment Training Center and San Jose's Center for Employment Training offer positive inducements to the working-poor. Blank sees incentives as preferable to meting out punitive sanctions to poor families: "Any policymaker who believes that setting rigid time limits will guarantee that current clients find jobs and become self-sufficient is badly misinformed and has not faced up to the new set of social problems and costs that such a policy will create."[5]

Along the same lines, Donna Franklin has presented a four-level scheme for serving black families (table 6.2).[6] By acknowledging that work is a common denominator among successful families and that a host of problems are associated with dependence on welfare, Corbett and Franklin not only presented a more nuanced portrait of the welfare-poor but also suggested

145

Table 6.1   Matching Reforms with Subgroups

Subgroups	Programs for Adults	Programs for Children
	Foundation Reforms	
Outer layer:		
Working poor and those on welfare less than 2 years	Refundable personal tax credits	Refundable child tax credits
	Expand tax credit with cash value of food stamps	Assured child support
	Other tax reforms	
	Earnings Supplements	
	Earned Income Tax Credit indexed and based on family size	Refundable childcare credit
	Direct earnings supplement	
	Indexed minimum wage	
	Transitional Supports	
	Assured medical coverage	Assured childcare
Middle layers:		
Those with limited options and very low earnings capacity (on welfare 2–8 years)	Welfare-to-work training programs	Education reform programs
	Wage-bill subsidies	"Soft" learnfare
	Social contract service options	School-to-jobs transition
		Youth capital account
The core		
The system-dependent: those with very low earning capacity and additional barriers— chemical dependence, depression, etc. (long-term and chronic users of welfare	Work requirements	"Hard" learnfare
	Intensive services	Teen pregnancy prevention
	Time-limited financial assistance	Intensive services
	Guaranteed job	

Source: Thomas Corbett, "Child Poverty and Welfare Reform," *Focus* 15 (Spring 1993), p. 9.

how to add rungs on the ladder of upward mobility. Herein lies a warning for those who enthuse about "Work First" but fail to realize the importance of developing its sequel. The dilemma is simple: further integration of low-income families with the mainstream is unlikely as long as the programs and infrastructure of public welfare remain. Insofar as welfare behaviorism further elaborates and reinforces the welfare bureaucracy, the poor will remain socially and economically segregated. Eventually, welfare reform will founder on the shoals of low-wage work and the welfare bureaucracy unless public welfare is deconstructed.

In all likelihood, the limits of welfare reform, as it is presently configured, have been reached. Despite the modest gains in the form of increased earnings and welfare savings, important warning signs are already evident. The

Table 6.2   African American Family Assessment and Intervention

Level	Description	Intervention Strategy	Intervention Techniques
I	Age-condensed, multigenerational system; adolescent childbearing and welfare dependency; matrifocal household (never-married mothers)	Focus on strengths, not problems; mobilize available supports to bolster executive capacity.	Family preservation; case management; gathering resources from extended family and community agencies; professional acting as convener, advocate, teacher, role model
II	Weak attachment to the labor force; no multigenerational welfare dependency; matrifocal; probably divorced or separated	Focus on strengths; develop a coalition of those in charge against those needing control; increase clarity of expectation.	Ecosystems-oriented; setting limits; clear communication; social learning: written contracts, behavioral reinforcers, and task assignments
III	Two-parent family structure (may be divorced or separated); labor force participation (may be temporarily unemployed); no history of welfare dependency	Focus on problems; clarify the "ideal" family structure in conformity with family expectations; increase generational clarity.	Defending family and individual boundaries; balancing triangles, rebuilding alliances; developing generational boundaries, task assignments, and communication skills
IV	Two-parent family structure, with father or stepfather in the home; patriarchal or egalitarian marital dyad; strong labor force participation	Focus on problems, clarification and resolution of legacies and historical trauma, insight, and yearnings.	Focusing on cognition, affect, communication, interpersonal relationships, and structural issues in the family

Source: Donna Franklin, *Ensuring Inequality* (New York: Oxford University Press, 1997), p. 230.

struggle of welfare mothers with the responsibilities of work and family tasks, already undermined by welfare diversion strategies, will be abruptly subverted by time limits. In summarizing the experience of welfare reform to date, Timothy Bartik concluded:

> So far, welfare reform has had it easy: pushing the most employable welfare recipients into a job, any job, in a booming economy. The harder challenges are how to reach the rest of the welfare recipients, either with a job or with some sort of safety net or disability program, and how to get welfare recipients to get and keep full-time, full-year jobs with adequate pay. Political realities suggest that it will be difficult to develop policies to do this that are not part of broader policies meant to help many more persons than just welfare recipients. Any employment policy for welfare recipients must be part of overall employment policies that benefit all Americans who have irregular jobs or low pay.[7]

Thus, any honest review of welfare reform will incorporate a reconsideration of the relationship between the economy and poverty—in other words, between capitalism and the poor.

CAPITALISM FOR THE POOR

For many Americans, the idea of promoting capitalism through welfare policy seems counterintuitive. Welfare philosophy in America has, more often than not, seen these concepts as reflecting contradictory dynamics in the nation's culture. Capitalism, after all, skews the distribution of resources, making welfare necessary in the first place. This view was driven home by the Great Depression, whose magnitude eclipsed previous market failures and justified the introduction of the American welfare state. The Progressive impulse in welfare policy was to replace capitalism for the poor with socialism for the poor, as is evident in the creation of the public welfare bureaucracy. More affluent segments of the population would struggle individually with capitalism, while the poor enjoyed the collective benefits of socialized welfare—a contradiction that many American welfare philosophers elided.

The idea that capitalism had any constructive relevance for the poor was simply not a matter for serious conjecture. The major welfare theories that evolved in America—socialist egalitarianism, social insurance theory, the culture of poverty, institutional residualism, the maternalist welfare state, the new paternalism[8]—portrayed markets, at best, as opportunity structures that the poor might be able to use, given proper guidance, and at worst, as the antithesis of social progress. The combination of socialist romanticism and the chronic poverty that blighted regions of the country during the industrial era largely accounted for the distributional impulses that marked American social philosophy after the Progressive era. For the half-century following the creation of the American welfare state with the Social Security Act of 1935, students of social welfare were taught that economic redistribution consisted of taxing the rich and transferring wealth to the poor through social programs; the notion that economic redistribution might also consist of systematically extending the benefits of capitalism to the poor was not worth taking seriously.

Nor were the prospects of capitalism for the poor advanced by the ideological conventions that defined American politics through the twentieth century. After all, the American welfare state was *the* liberal project, providing the rationale for the employment of tens of thousands of civil servants and spawning the human service professions that populated the institutions that accompanied Progressivism: education, health care, and social services. For liberals, the mutual exclusiveness of welfare and capitalism meant government jobs essential for the smooth functioning of the welfare state; for conservatives, the calculus was more oblique, yet no less compelling. Conservative ideology held that markets themselves were optimal distributive vehicles and that interfering in them, through government regulation or direct provision of commodities, introduced inefficiencies. By minimizing welfare, conservatives preached the virtues of lower wages for business to pay as well as lower taxes for the working public.

There were, of course, exceptions to the ideological conventions that served to separate welfare and capitalism. Many immigrant groups, including blacks, established their own market-related institutions as a means to rise into the American mainstream. "Our country has a long history of the successful development of 'immigrant banks' that served ethnic neighborhoods and helped transform them from low-income to middle-income communities," observed researchers of the Jerome Levy Economics Institute.[9] Community savings and loans, mutual assistance funds, and businesses that distributed essential goods and services all functioned within the context of capitalism, and it is not parenthetical that the groups most adept at this choreography came to define American business and finance.[10] Not only did markets work to enhance opportunities for poor immigrants, but welfare also helped middle-class families prosper. Though rarely considered in discussions of social welfare, the forgiveness of taxes on wealth—tax expenditures for mortgage interest, health insurance, and retirement pensions—has contributed greatly to the wealth of more affluent families. Thus, welfare and capitalism have been wed, but most often in ways that have advantaged more affluent American families.

In contrast to government welfare, the benefits of bootstrap capitalism are derived from the market. Prior to the New Deal, when government assumed responsibility for social welfare, taking over from a foundering business community and inadequate nonprofit agencies, "welfare capitalism" enjoyed popularity among captains of industry and better-paid workers as well. While the conventional history of American social welfare often deletes constructive business influences, this revisionism is hardly accurate. Model company towns were the most complete incarnation of corporate welfare. In the 1820s, the utopian businessman Robert Owen transformed a bankrupt Scottish mill town, New Lanark, into a model community by abolishing child labor, providing housing for workers, and instituting an incentive-based wage system. Having realized a substantial profit from the New Lanark experiment, Owen attempted (but failed) to replicate the experience in New Harmony, Indiana. During the 1880s the Pullman Company, a manufacturer of railroad passenger cars, planned and built a company town for 8,000 people; it featured a hotel, markets, landscaped parks, and factories in addition to residences. Contemporary innovations in worker-ownership plans can be traced to Nelson Olsen Nelson, who not only built the planned community of Leclair, Illinois, replicating the latest in city planning, but also transferred ownership of his company to his employees.[11] Speaking on behalf of the United States Chamber of Commerce, John D. Rockefeller sounded more like a welfare advocate than an industrial titan when he asked,

> Shall we cling to the conception of industry as an institution, primarily of private interest, which enables certain individuals to accumulate wealth, too often irrespective of the well-being, the health and happiness of those engaged in its production? Or shall we adopt the modern viewpoint and *regard industry as being a form of social service*, quite as much as a revenue-producing process? . . . The soundest industrial policy is that which has constantly in mind the welfare of employees as well as the making of profits, and which, when human considerations demand it, *subordinates profits to welfare.*[12]

Gerald Swope, president of General Electric and planner of the Social Security Act, learned about the value of social policy while he lived at Hull House under the tutelage of Jane Addams. Mary Parker Follett, also a settlement worker, derived her management theory from industrial psychology, presaging the idea of union-management collaboration.[13]

The Progressive era and the New Deal both evolved under the influence of American commerce. Before the New Deal, workplace injuries were so frequent and jury settlements so large that employers persuaded legislators in virtually all the states to institute Worker Compensation programs. Unemployment Compensation, one of the social insurances included in the Social Security Act, provided for laidoff workers by mandating that their employers pay premiums that were calibrated according to their unemployment history. Social Security, the foundation of the American welfare state, was modeled on private pension programs, the primary difference being that, because it was *social* insurance, workers and employers were required to participate.[14]

As Neil Gilbert observed, "Industry's attending to the social needs of workers through an assortment of medical and funeral benefits, as well as provisions for recreational, educational, housing, and social services," accounted for a substantial measure of social and economic security in industrial America.[15] As a corporate initiative, however, welfare capitalism was not solely a manifestation of altruism on the part of the business community. "Welfare capitalism, in the form of company unions and other employee benefit packages, further undermined organized labor and proponents of governmental intervention in social welfare," noted Michael Reisch. "It effectively promoted the image of the socially responsible corporation whose profits were linked to American progress and well-being."[16] Postwar prosperity served to justify expanding welfare capitalism, so that skilled and professional workers in industry, government, and the nonprofit sector would take for granted those job benefits which were a desirable condition of employment.

Retrospectively, then, the relationship between capital and social welfare has been less antagonistic than current ideological convention would suggest. Indeed, if the prosperity of the American mainstream is any indication, greater integration of the welfare-poor with capitalism is likely to enhance their opportunities. This will not happen, however, without creating new opportunity structures for poor American families. This is why renewed interest has been expressed in "bootstrap capitalism,"[17] the application of market principles to enhance social welfare.

THE RENAISSANCE OF BOOTSTRAP CAPITALISM

While renewed interest in bootstrap capitalism is the immediate consequence of conservative impulses in welfare reform, broader cultural forces contributed to this renaissance. Foremost was a political shift within the Democratic party that institutionalized neoliberalism as an orientation to social policy. The emergence of neoliberal thought can be traced to the failed candidacies of traditional liberals—Michael Dukakis and Walter Mondale—whose endorsement of social entitlements made them vulnerable to conservative attack. Subsequently, an insurgency of centrist Democrats established the Democratic Leadership Council (DLC) to pull Democrats to the center, in the process creating the Progressive Policy Institute (PPI) to incubate ideas toward that end.[18] The election and reelection of Bill Clinton and Al Gore, two founders of the DLC, consolidated and furthered the infusion of neoliberalism within the party. For a decade now, the DLC and PPI have called for welfare reform that stipulates work requirements, family integrity, and time limits on receipt of assistance.[19]

A second force was communitarianism. As sociologists expressed renewed appreciation for the importance of civic activities in healthy communities, a "communitarian" movement of moderate intellectuals raised questions about the corrosive consequences of unfettered individualism, when it took the form of ostentatious consumption among the wealthy or unconditional benefits for the poor. Instead of unconditional welfare benefits that are indiscriminate with respect to morality, communitarians favor policies that reward intact families.[20] Under the leadership of Amitai Etzioni, communitarian thought has grown from a cabal of university-based scholars to a broad crusade including leaders of community-based organizations, elected officials, and media personalities.[21] According to the communitarian critique of traditional welfare, unconditional benefits allow the poor to engage in immoral behavior—substance abuse, unwed pregnancy, and crime—subsidized perversely by government in the name of social welfare. By insisting on specific standards of conduct in exchange for public assistance, welfare reform thus reasserts a measure of social control. For Robert Putnam, the critical ingredient in community development is a civic tradition that fosters "social capital." According to Putnam, "part of the problem facing blacks and Latinos in the inner city is that they lack 'connections' in the most literal sense." Alleviating poverty, then, requires building community institutions, the social infrastructure without which the poor cannot expect to prosper.[22]

Proponents of bootstrap capitalism contend that during the last decade neoliberalism and civic sociology have provided the impetus for a range of new possibilities in poverty policy. These can be classified under three general headings: wage supplements, asset building, and community capitalism.

WAGE SUPPLEMENTS

The most established form of bootstrap capitalism consists of supplements to wages. Currently, tax credits for low-wage workers and their employers are the primary means toward this end. Through tax credits, the Internal Revenue Service (IRS) reimburses poor workers and the employers who hire them, thus reinforcing the work ethic and strengthening the relationship between welfare and the labor market. Since its inception in 1975, the federal Earned Income Tax Credit has paid refunds to low-wage workers with children. The EITC was intended to reduce the tax burden on low-income workers, effectively supplementing their wages and making work more attractive than welfare.[23] By the late 1990s, the EITC had eclipsed AFDC and TANF and vied with SSI as the largest cash benefit welfare program. The EITC is a de facto negative income tax for low-wage workers. Single or married people who work full- or part-time qualify, depending on their earnings, and the amount of the refund varies according to family composition. A worker raising one child with a family income less than $25,078 can receive up to $2,152, while a worker raising more than one child with a family income less than $28,495 can receive up to $3,556. The EITC heavily favors families, however. Workers between 25 and 64 years of age who are not raising children and have incomes below $9,500 are eligible only for payments up to $332.[24]

The EITC could be an important support for the transition from welfare to work. Analysts have estimated that between 75 and 90 percent of those eligible apply, although welfare researchers place the percentage of working welfare mothers who obtain an EITC refund between 28 and 42 percent.[25] Assuming a 76 percent usage rate still leaves 3.4 million taxpayers without EITC benefits to which they are entitled.[26] Low use may be partly attributed to the program's complexity, which causes many poor taxpayers to resort to tax preparers for assistance. Jeffrey Liebman studied EITC use and found that the program increased the labor market participation of women with children and did not decrease hours of work for workers already in the labor force.[27]

Several states augment the EITC with supplemental Earned Income Credits (EICs). Nine states—Iowa, Maryland, Massachusetts, Minnesota, Oregon, New York, Rhode Island, Vermont, Wisconsin—have EICs calibrated from the federal EITC. Minnesota and Wisconsin are the most generous, refunding qualified taxpayers 25 percent and 43 percent of the EITC, respectively.[28] A few states have enacted tax credits for rent, utilities, childcare, and health insurance. Minnesota, for example, has a working family credit, a child and dependent care credit, and a property tax refund for renters, all part of the state's ongoing effort to integrate tax and welfare systems, reduce the complexity of overlapping programs, and increase work incentives. Minnesota also subsidizes health insurance for poor persons not on Medicaid.[29]

The primary problem with the federal EITC and state EICs as a bridge from welfare to work is their low use among women negotiating this transition. Historically, welfare has provided strong incentives not to report earned income, and, as a result, a large portion of wages have been paid under the table, essentially undetected by the IRS. Some welfare mothers may have incurred various forms of debt and had their EITC refund attached; if their mates are in arrears in child support payments, EITC refunds are intercepted. For beneficiaries working underground to make ends meet, the EITC is of little value, at least until they are full participants in the formal economy. Another practical defect of this wage supplement strategy is that the vast majority of low-wage earners elect to receive their refund in a lump sum. Monthly reimbursement of up to 60 percent of the total refund is available but rarely chosen. Lump-sum refunds subvert financial planning and exacerbate the problem of irregular income. Making matters worse, commercial tax preparers often persuade financially pressed tax filers to sign for "refund anticipation loans," the interest on which can be astronomical, often between 50 and 200 percent.[30]

Tax credits have also been extended to employers to encourage them to hire low-income workers. Between 1979 and 1994 the Targeted Jobs Tax Credit (TJTC) offered employers who hired target-group employees up to 50 percent of first-year and 25 percent of second-year wages, up to $6,000. By 1991, TJTC paid employers $245 million for 428,000 workers, an average of $570 per employee. Workers averaged $5.00 an hour and worked about 30 hours a week. An assessment of TJTC concluded that "40 to 52 percent of the jobs receiving TJTC subsidies reflected net employment additions for economically disadvantaged twenty-three to twenty-four-year-olds at a cost of approximately $1,500 (1991 dollars) per net job created."[31] A related program offering employers subsidies of up to 50 percent of wages during the first six months of employment—the Job Training and Partnership Act (JTPA)—found that adult women participants increased their earnings $2,292 over 30 months, a figure in line with the welfare-to-work programs.[32] The TJTC was followed by the Work Opportunity Tax Credit (WOTC), which took effect in 1996. Initially, WOTC was limited to 35 percent of a maximum of $6,000 in wages, or a credit of no more than $2,100 per worker.[33] Subsequently, the credit became more generous, applying to the first $20,000 of eligible wages during the first two years of employment. The credit increases from 35 percent of the first $10,000 in the first year to 50 percent of the first $10,000 of eligible wages in the second year, with a maximum credit of $8,500 per qualified worker.[34]

The primary problem with employer tax credits is that prospective employees have to count on their bosses to sort through the tax code, prepare the necessary paperwork, and then wait for a refund from the IRS. The employer is, of course, reimbursed in part for this nuisance through the tax credit, but this may be insufficient, especially for small employers. In low-income communities with a surfeit of job-seekers, employers can simply offer lower wages and avoid contending with the IRS altogether.

Edmund Phelps has suggested a direct employment subsidy as a replacement for tax credits. By subsidizing the work of low-wage earners, Phelps proposes to reinforce the value of the work ethic while providing incentives to employers to hire them.

> The subsidy is thus like a matching grant rewarding the firm for as many workers as it employs, particularly workers whose private productivity is low (as evidenced by the low hourly labor cost that firms are willing to pay for their services). It is the low productivity workers whose possibility of self-support and cohesion with the mainstream of society is impaired and whose job attachment and social responsibility are undermined when they are paid a wage to match their low productivity, so it is these workers especially to whom the subsidies are to be targeted.[35]

Phelps proposes a graduated scale through which the wage subsidy gradually declines from $3.00 supplementing a $4.00 base wage (for a total wage of $7.00 an hour) to $0.06 augmenting $12.00 (for a total wage of $12.06).[36] He estimates that a wage subsidy could be implemented at a cost of $125 billion, an amount attained by collapsing the EITC, employer tax credits, and welfare, and preventing future costs related to social control.[37]

A more radical departure from current thinking about welfare reform would be to aggregate all welfare programs as well as tax expenditures for the poor into an income ladder whose rungs would be constructed of wages, benefits, and refundable tax credits. As conceived by Jonathan Forman, such an arrangement would ensure a basic income floor that would be augmented through "a comprehensive system of refundable tax credits." Essentially, wages would be supplemented through the tax code according to a tax filer's special requirements, including health care, childcare, education, and training.[38] Such an arrangement would not only greatly simplify the present confusion of welfare programs but also destigmatize the receipt of aid.

ASSET DEVELOPMENT

Students of poverty are accustomed to considering social justice in relation to income distribution. Because poverty has been a chronic feature of the American experience, advocates for the poor can assess progress toward economic equality by examining family income over time. Between 1947 and 1995 the income share of the poorest quintile of the population has fallen from 5.0 to 4.4 percent, while the share controlled by the top quintile has risen from 43.0 to 46.5 percent.[39] Since 1970, moreover, wages have remained static or declined, forcing many families to dispatch a second wage-earner to meet higher living expenses,[40] while the wage spread between higher- and lower-wage workers has widened. In 1982, the highest decile of workers earned $24.80 an hour, 3.95 times the rate of the lowest decile ($6.28). In 1996, the highest decile earned $25.74 an hour, 4.72 times as much as the lowest decile ($5.46). Including the value of benefits actually worsens the disparity. The total wage and benefit package of high-wage workers in 1982 was worth 4.56 times as much as that of the lowest; by 1996 the discrepancy was greater, a factor of 5.56.[41]

Yet the distribution of wealth may be a better indicator of social justice than income distribution. While the top quintile controls 43.0 percent of the income, it owns 86.9 percent of the society's net financial assets. In the late 1980s, the median net financial assets for white Americans were $6,999; for black Americans, they were zero. While 25.3 percent of whites reported zero or negative net financial assets, 60.9 percent of blacks did so.[42] Changes in the distribution of wealth during the past three decades are shown in table 6.3. The distribution of wealth is significantly more skewed than the distribution of income. Moreover, the distribution of wealth shows a problem among the poor that is not revealed by income distribution data alone: because of chronic debt, the lowest quintile has *negative* wealth. Note that between 1962 and 1983, a period of major expansion of welfare state entitlement benefits, the negative wealth of the lowest quintile was cut in half but remained negative.

The intractability of poverty can be attributed to the focus of welfare policy on subsidizing consumption as opposed to building wealth. As Michael Sherraden has observed, the entire focus of welfare programs has been on

Table 6.3   Changes in the Distribution of Wealth, 1962–1992

Quintile	Share of wealth				Change 1983–1992 %
	1962	1983	1989	1992	
Top	81.0%	81.3%	84.6%	83.8%	2.5%
Fourth	13.4	12.6	11.5	11.5	−1.1
Middle	5.4	5.2	4.6	4.4	−0.8
Second	1.0	1.2	0.8	0.9	−0.3
Bottom	−0.7	−0.3	−1.4	−0.5	−0.2

Note: Wealth is defined as net worth, equal to a household's assets less its debt.
Source: Derived from Lawrence Mishel, Jared Bernstein, and John Schmitt, *The State of Working America* (Washington, D.C.: Economic Policy Institute, 1997).

income support.[43] Conventional welfare theorists argue that the responsibility of government is to provide temporary support for those in need, and the best way to do that is to give the poor cash that they can spend, or in-kind benefits they can use for other necessities. Programs like AFDC and Food Stamps are surrogates for lost earnings—hence their label, "income maintenance." A poverty policy that emphasizes income without addressing asset-building errs fundamentally: income supports barely allow the poor to keep their heads above water. A close examination of disadvantaged families that escape poverty reveals that they behave economically very much like middle-income families: the escape from poverty depends on accumulating assets.

A long-range strategy for getting people out of poverty is a program of Individual Development Accounts (IDAs). An IDA is a dedicated account in which an external source matches an individual's contribution; it is tax-exempt if funds are expended for four purposes: finishing college or vocational school, buying a home, starting a business, or supplementing a pension.[44] The amount of the match varies with an individual's income. IDAs could be inherited, thus helping poor families become more prosperous over generations.[45] So posed, IDAs are antithetical to neoclassical economic thought, which holds that the poor are simply incapable of saving significant amounts of capital, that this is a capacity reserved for, and therefore the proper province of, financial institutions. Traditionally, economic thought has valued saving largely for its deferred-consumption aspect, ignoring the quite substantial psychological and social value of owning assets.[46] Research on shelter, for example, indicates that "home ownership does have a significant [positive] effect on the life satisfaction of low-income people."[47] A more extensive analysis of attitudes and behaviors in relation to assets among participants in the Panel Study of Income Dynamics from 1968 to 1972 confirmed that "assets have a positive effect on expectations and confidence about the future; influence people to make specific plans with regard to work and family; induce more prudent and protective personal behaviors; and lead to more social connectedness with relatives, neighbors, and organizations."[48] Wendell Berry's tale of Mr. John Jones of North Middleton, Kentucky, makes the point nicely. As president of the local bank, Jones persisted in making tuition loans to enable any graduate of the town's high school to attend the university, even if collateral was unavailable. Despite the consternation of bank examiners, Jones "never lost a dime on a one of them."[49]

Within a decade of the publication of Sherraden's seminal *Assets and the Poor*, momentum was building to extend IDAs nationally. Although the 1996 federal welfare reform act makes provisions for IDAs, no direct funding was authorized. Consequently, IDA advocates hustled to locate resources from state and local governments or the private sector. After passage of PRWORA, 24 states planned to incorporate IDAs into their welfare reform plans. An additional 40 community-based organizations undertook IDA programs, most of which included "economic literacy as well as financial and personal counseling to develop investment plans" for poor families.[50] IDA account-holders were expected to save $5.00 to $20.00 a month, and every dollar of earned income was matched $0.50 to $4.00.[51]

By encouraging the poor to capitalize, IDAs promise access to the modest but primary avenues of upward mobility. Although the public perception of capitalism is that it is dominated by mammoth corporations, in actuality much commerce is on a smaller scale. Accordingly, education and home ownership can be leveraged with relatively low levels of savings. For example, half of all businesses started in the United States each year are capitalized with less than $5,000; the average down payment on homes purchased by low- and moderate-income families is less than $3,000; and the average annual tuition at a community college is less than $1,200.[52]

The IDA concept is now being tested in 13 sites across the nation in the "Downpayments on the American Dream" demonstration, funded with $15 million from a consortium of foundations.[53] The Corporation for Enterprise Development and the Washington University Center for Social Development have advocated a national IDA demonstration, an objective that was partially met late in 1998 with passage of the Assets for Independence Act, which allocated $125 million for that purpose.[54] Pursuing the idea further, in the spring of 1999 President Clinton proposed Universal Savings Accounts, where deposits of couples earning less than $80,000 a year would be matched using $38 billion of the Social Security "surplus."[55]

Microenterprise is another strategy for asset building.[56] Imported from the Third World, where microloans demonstrated a surprising capacity to pull peasant women out of poverty, microenterprise has evolved gradually in the United States.[57] Historically, commercial financial institutions have justified denying loans to the poor because of the high risk of nonpayment and the inefficiencies of negotiating small loans. Since their emergence in developing nations during the 1970s, however, microenterprise financiers have developed a repayment track-record far better than that of commercial banks, typically exceeding 90 percent.[58] By the mid-1980s, several microenterprise ventures were established in America.[59] Within a few years the Institute for Social and Economic Development reported on the provision of assistance to 138 poor families: 86 percent of supported businesses were still operating, compared with 50 percent of other businesses of comparable scale; 122 of the businesses had been started by AFDC recipients; and 33 percent of these had left welfare.[60] Researchers from the Institute for Women's Policy Research found that a significant minority of poor women used microenterprise to complement income from other sources, particularly wages. Among former AFDC recipients who were part of a national data base, hourly earnings from self-employment were $4.37 (in 1990 dollars); however, women who had participated in the Self Employment Learning Project reported hourly wages averaging more than $5.00 per hour.[61] It is encouraging that microenterprise resources that were not associated with welfare have become more accessible; in 1996, the federal government made available $130 million for microcredit programs.[62]

Yet despite the enthusiasm of proponents, microenterprise has yet to demonstrate applicability to more than a narrow band of poor families. Lisa Servon conducted in-depth interviews with participants and managers of three microenterprise programs and concluded that "while microenterprise programs clearly play a critical role in growing and stabilizing the self-employment activity of low-income people, self-employment is neither a certain nor an easy route off of welfare."[63]

Public welfare remains the primary obstacle to alleviating poverty through asset building. For more than a half-century, poor families were denied capital because of restrictions on assets as part of the means test attached to public assistance benefits. To become eligible for programs like AFDC, Food Stamps, Medicaid, and SSI, poor families had to liquidate their assets down to approximately $1,500; if that level was exceeded, welfare benefits would be terminated. With the welfare waivers encouraged by the 1981 OBRA, many states increased their asset limits.

COMMUNITY CAPITALISM

During the past few decades, a new generation of community development agencies evolved as federal aid to the cities fell. Between 1980 and 1993 the number of people living in poverty increased from 29 million to 39 million, yet government aid to cities dropped 19.4 percent.[64] Increasing poverty compounded by rescissions in federal aid required community development advocates to consider alternative sources of support, particularly the private sector. The Ford Foundation's Local Initiative Support Corporation (LISC) experimented with strategies designed to make urban development organizations self-supporting; the Rouse Company created the Enterprise Foundation in order to rehabilitate ghetto neighborhoods. Soon community activists were collaborating with the private sector, often through local community development corporations (CDCs), to mount neighborhood projects.[65] Since these initial explorations, some 2,000 CDCs have sprung up in the United States. Illustrative of grassroots partnership between the public and private sectors, CDCs have been lauded as the philosophical if not the programmatic manifestation of a new era in urban policy.[66] The communitarian Antonin Wagner contends that "community-based welfare capitalism constitutes a historically rooted, technically workable, and morally attractive arrangement for the future of our societies."[67]

Specialized CDCs, such as community development banks and credit unions, have been organized in several cities—Chicago's South Shore Bank, Ithaca's Alternatives Credit Union, Durham's Self-Help Credit Union, and the Marshall Heights Community Development Organization in Washington, D.C.—in order to provide more extensive financial services to low-income families. The capacity of these CDCs to leverage capital is not inconsequential. Conceived as a housing restoration venture, Chicago's South Shore Bank was so successful that it served as the exemplar for the Clinton administration's Empowerment Zone initiative, which pumped $3.5 billion into economically distressed cities and regions.[68] Begun in 1983 with $77 raised from a bake sale, Self-Help Credit Union was the fifth-largest community development credit union in 1996, making $6.6 million in home loans (58 percent to minority households and 33 percent to female-headed households), $3.6 million in assistance from its community facilities fund (37 childcare loans created spaces for 1,459 children), and $14.4 million in commercial loans (55 percent to minorities and 53 percent to women).[69] In addition to the five satellite offices of Self-Help Credit Union, North Carolina boasted 13 minority-community-based credit unions; 14 of these boasted 20,000 members, assets of over $35 million, and loans of $12 million; and an additional three community development credit unions are planned, so that every region of the state will offer financial services to low-income residents.[70] In response to the Community Reinvestment Act (CRA), Fleet Financial Group of the Eastern United States has made $3.9 billion in mortgage loans to low- and moderate-income families, established a CDC through which $5.2 million in assistance was granted, and instituted related projects in seven states as well as a $1 million mortgage loan pool for residents of the Seneca Nation.[71] Since 1985, the Delaware Valley Reinvestment Fund, located in Philadelphia, has used $90 million to leverage $350 million to finance 3,000 low-income housing units, generating 5,000 jobs in the process.[72] By the mid-1990s, the First Nations Development Institute, an indigenous peoples' community development advocate, had invested $1 million to enhance the financial capacity of Native Americans in six western states by organizing community development credit unions and banks.[73] Such ventures represent a departure from the social entitlement orientation associated with traditional liberalism: "Rather than focus solely on providing a social safety net, the federal and state governments are trying to connect the poor to the dominant economic world of saving, borrowing, and plastic money."[74]

All these community development ventures reflect a shift in aid to disadvantaged areas: away from a social model focused on the deficits of individuals and funded by income redistribution, toward an economic model emphasizing investment and financed through the generation of wealth. Proponents of community capitalism have observed that the poorest of neighborhoods display the essential ingredients of revitalization: a decaying social and physical infrastructure; redundant labor, as evident in high rates of unemployment and underemployment; and significant volumes of capital in the form of benefits from social programs. Michael Porter has noted that "inner city consumers, in fact, represent a major growth market of the future, and companies based in the inner city have a unique ability to understand and address these needs."[75] The problem has been the failure to deploy financial institutions that capture capital and put it to constructive use locally. "The depressed areas are great sources of funds (social security checks, welfare payments, earnings, private pensions, and so on), but these have been flowing into megabanks that use them elsewhere."[76]

The prospects of community capitalism brightened with passage of the Bank Enterprise Act of 1994, which, in response to President Clinton's vow to deploy 100 community development banks across the nation, authorized $382 million for community financial institutions.[77] For 1996, $50.3 million was awarded to 69 organizations; the following year, 102 applicants received $54.4 million.[78] Meanwhile, Porter convened the Initiative for a Competitive Inner City "to develop programs to involve companies, professional service firms, and graduate business schools in assisting and creating inner-city companies in cities around the country"; Bank of America, Citibank, and John Hancock are involved in this project.[79] Soon, the Coalition of Community Development Financial Institutions (the CDFI Coalition) was established as a nonprofit organization representing over 350 CDFIs in all 50 states,[80] managing between $2 billion and $3 billion in capital.[81] Between 1990 and 1996, the 46 CDFIs making up the National Association of Community Development Loan Funds increased outstanding loans from $30.7 million to $152.6 million. While loans increased fivefold, CDFI efficiency improved. Between 1994 and 1996, for example, total expenses per dollar lent decreased from $0.24 to $0.11.[82] Including nonmember CDFIs, the CDFI Coalition estimates that such institutions now manage about $1.8 billion "and have loaned nearly $4 billion in disadvantaged communities around the country."[83] The National Community Capital Association reported that its members generated $750 million in direct financing in 1997. Member CDFIs financed 72,609 housing units, of which 94 percent were for low-income people, and 44,221 jobs, of which 61 percent went to low-income workers, 39 percent to women, and 14 percent to minorities.[84]

NETWORKING CAPITAL

By the late 1990s a paradox was evident in American community development. Although an infrastructure for economic development had been constructed through CDCs as well as community development credit unions and banks across the nation, some 10 million recipients of federal income benefits were without bank accounts[85]—even though the PRWORA time limits made it imperative for the poor to manage their meager resources carefully. The unbanked consisted largely of poor families—almost half of African American families are without bank accounts, as are one of four renters, one of six persons under age 35, and 15 percent of those earning between $10,000 and $25,000 annually.[86] According to a Federal Reserve study, 41 percent of families with incomes below $12,000 a year have no deposit account.[87]

The unbanked must rely on fringe banks—check-cashing outlets and pawnshops—to manage their financial affairs for exploitative fees. Fees for cashing checks, for example, range from 1 to 20 percent of the value of the check.[88] The fringe banking industry sees a steady stream of welfare checks: "In a study of three New Jersey counties, it was found that almost half of all AFDC checks issued in the counties were cashed at check-cashing facilities; of the users interviewed as they left the facility after cashing an AFDC check, it was found that 92 percent did not have a bank account."[89] The fees for such transactions cut into already meager resources. "A family of four with an income of $24,000 per year would pay $396 annually if it cashed its paychecks at a check-cashing store and bought six money orders per month."[90] Yet mainstream commercial banks, with income increasingly generated by account-related fees, could charge low-income account holders even more.[91]

The parasitic relationship of fringe banks to poor families was interrupted by passage of the Debt Collection Improvement Act of 1996, which mandated that federal income benefits must be direct-deposited by 1999, through electronic benefit transfer (EBT). The virtue of EBT lay initially in its efficiency: while it required $0.43 to generate each paper check, EBT reduced the cost to $0.02 per transaction. EBT brought other benefits as well: it was destigmatizing, since beneficiaries could use ATM cards to obtain cash and purchase food, thus eliminating Food Stamp coupons; fraud and stolen checks were virtually eliminated.[92] Treasury Secretary Robert Rubin speculated that EBT could also bring the unbanked into the financial mainstream: "If we can figure out a way to get them into the banking system for the first time, not only will it give them a more efficient way to cash checks and access to other financial services, but it may also encourage people to save, to plan financially, and therefore, to improve their economic life over time."[93] In light of the efficiencies afforded by EBT, federal and state governments rushed to contract out the service. By 1995, $111 billion in government benefits was being distributed electronically; Citibank, the largest intermediary, served more than a dozen states.[94]

While government has been quick to take advantage of EBT efficiencies, less attention has been directed at providing financial services to the unbanked. "This relationship between the move to an all-electronic benefit delivery system and welfare reform needs to be better appreciated by the policy and advocacy communities," contended Michael Stegman. "It is hard to imagine a mother moving from welfare to work, and staying off welfare, without a bank account and without building up some cash reserves for emergencies."[95] As one way to address this deficiency, Stegman suggested coupling IDAs with EITC refunds through an arrangement that would encourage low-wage earners to earmark their tax refund for a savings account, the balance of which would be matched up to $300 per year.[96] But this identifies only a narrow band of the possibilities afforded the welfare- and working-poor through community capitalism.

A more radical way to network capital would not only provide financial services to the poor, but also leverage capital for community development. The fulcrum for this would be "community financial services," an expanded and dynamic form of community development financial institution. In addition to traditional services, such as savings and checking, community financial services would include other financial products developed with low-income account-holders in mind. Economic literacy would be chief among these and would include "money management skills, cost comparisons for fringe banking services, the economics of rent-to-own contracts, and credit planning."[97] Economic literacy courses would be geared toward particular financial products, to prepare consumers for various investment programs. For example, a course in the fundamentals of personal finance would be required for basic membership; beyond that, consumers would be required to attend a more specialized course on IDAs, how to use microcredit for business startup, or how to purchase a home through a subsidized loan. An important component would be financial planning, which would acquaint consumers with the need to supplement Social Security with private savings and encourage them to invest in select mutual funds. Assistance in tax preparation would be a financial service that would encourage taxpayers to access the EITC and related tax credits, in the process helping them view various income sources in relation to long-range planning. For consumers who are not account-holders, money orders would be offered at cost or for a modest fee. In addition, employers of low-income workers would receive tax assistance enabling them to take advantage of the WOTC.

The capital formation side of community financial services would derive assets from several sources. Because "in most . . . urban ghetto neighborhoods more than half of the population is *not* poor," a significant source of capital would be the income of neighborhood residents.[98] In even the poorest neighborhoods, 62.2 percent of households report work-related income, accounting for 72 percent of total neighborhood revenues.[99] As a depository, community financial services have access to the wages of neighborhood residents as well as their EBT benefits. Although many of these accounts would be drawn down between deposits, community financial services would be able to capture the "float"—interest on unexpended balances—estimated to be $0.19 per account each month, a small amount that would supplement revenue from more significant sources.[100] Commercial banks could be solicited for token deposits in a financial services center, which could then be credited toward their Community Reinvestment Act obligations. Community-based nonprofits could be persuaded to use community financial services for payroll purposes, an opportunity to make a direct investment in local neighborhoods and in the process add to the center's reserves. Finally, localities obtain community development funds from federal and state governments; there is no reason why unexpended community development funds should not be deposited in community financial services.

A final consideration regarding capitalizing networks pertains to the welfare bureaucracy. During the past decade criticism of public welfare has been building up, and critics from the left and the right have voiced similar complaints. The conservative sociologists Peter and Brigitte Berger argued that social services were the vehicle through which middle-class professionals evangelized among lower-class clients;[101] Herbert Gans suggested that one of the functions of poverty is "the creation of new job opportunities for the better-off populations in the many professions and occupations that exist to isolate, control, or punish the poor."[102] "We have become a careless society," John McKnight contended, "populated by impotent citizens and ineffectual communities dependent on the counterfeit of care called human services."[103]

Communities could begin to deconstruct the welfare bureaucracy by allowing nonprofit organizations to charter community financial services. Demonstrations in East St. Louis[104] and New Orleans[105] indicate that universities have not only the resources but also the missionary spirit to undertake such innovations. Working with representatives of poor neighborhoods, faculty and students could perfect a communitarian approach to poverty policy, one that "is neither exclusively market-oriented nor dominated by government."[106] Government would reserve the right to determine program eligibility, but once that is affirmed, consumers could choose the financial institution from which they wish to receive their benefits via EBT. The financial institutions would then be required to provide a basic financial service package, including economic literacy training, and would be reimbursed by the government on a per capita basis. The current welfare monopoly held by welfare departments, in other words, would be largely disassembled, the savings divided by the number of beneficiaries, and the resulting revenues distributed to financial institutions in relation to their subscription lists of account-holders who are receiving public aid. If consumers are unhappy with the fees or services of one financial institution, they would be free to select another. Financial institutions receiving per capita revenues from the government would have to provide annual reports on their expenditures as well as the experience of account-holders over time. They would also be required to post summaries of customer evaluations so that prospective members can learn from the experience of those currently receiving services.

Community financial services staff would offer services qualitatively different from those now provided through public welfare. Activities would revolve around "account managers" trained in microeconomics; they would be familiar not only with basic financial services but also with programs for the welfare- and working-poor. Their role is significant enough that they should hold a college degree in a discipline related directly to microeconomics, such as business or human ecology. To promote service integration, account managers would cycle through economic literacy training programs. To enhance their knowledge of account-holders, the number of accounts assigned would be limited. Use of laptop computers would allow managers to go out into the community. Account managers' performance would be assessed periodically through account-holder surveys and longitudinal tracking of accounts, with incentive awards for those who provide exceptional service. So reconfigured, community financial services would offer the poor opportunities by exploiting the technological and organizational innovations that typify a postindustrial environment.

A NEW PARADIGM FOR POVERTY POLICY?

Bootstrap capitalism runs contrary to social welfare as it has been known. A tacit assumption of AFDC had been that, unless they demonstrated otherwise, welfare mothers either evidenced insurmountable barriers to employment or were better off at home taking care of their children. Work was considered a modest supplement to welfare; the latter provided a family's income. Until states began to experiment with raising the asset limit, public welfare disallowed any but the meagerest indication of wealth. The idea that poor communities would use markets to propel revitalization contradicted liberal orthodoxy, which held that capitalism was responsible for the economic disparities between the haves and have-nots and that only an alternative governmental distribution scheme could address poverty and its attendant problems.[107] As Michael Porter has observed, "Rethinking the inner city in economic rather than social terms will be uncomfortable for many who have devoted years to social causes and who view profit and business in general with suspicion."[108]

Yet it would be premature to propose bootstrap capitalism as a replacement for public welfare. A fundamental question is, to what extent will bootstrap capitalism ameliorate poverty? Central to this question is the adequacy of the labor market. Rebecca Blank noted that 63 percent of poor families reported a member working during the previous year, yet a variety of circumstances—low wages, sickness, erratic jobs—meant that welfare benefits continued to be needed.[109] The welfare-poor have often worked, Joel Handler concurred, and the issue of poverty can only be approached by addressing structural flaws in the labor market. "The 'problem' of welfare dependency is not the recipients. Rather, the problems are the job market and the conditions of work. In addition to poorly paying, unsteady, increasingly part-time work, are difficulties of a lack of benefits, especially critical health insurance, and child care."[110]

The adequacy of government funding to ameliorate poverty is a related issue. Consider tax credits as a vehicle for wage supplements. The EITC, the largest tax credit for the poor, is dwarfed by tax expenditures for the middle class. In 1999, for example, the larger tax expenditures—$337 billion for pension contributions made by employers, $352 billion for health insurance premiums paid by business, and $169 billion for mortgage interest deductions—are projected to eclipse those for low-income populations: $28 billion for EITC, $3.5 billion for low-income housing, and $2.9 billion for dependent care.[111] Including the social insurance programs, Social Security and Medicare, which provide substantial benefits to the nonpoor, further diminishes the proportion of antipoverty expenditures, even if ancillary programs such as Food Stamps, Medicaid, and SSI are included. For purposes of fairness *and* equity, poverty policy must be comparable in scale to the tax expenditures granted middle-income and wealthy Americans.

If a case can be made for bootstrap capitalism, it will not be as a replacement for public welfare, but rather as its sequel. Destitute families will surely require income maintenance assistance, and the most troubled of them will need it for protracted periods. For such families, public welfare will be essential to family survival. Beyond this basic level of support, bootstrap capitalism offers rungs on the ladder of upward mobility, not only for individual families but also for communities. In applying bootstrap capitalism, advocates of the poor could exploit the very structures and processes of capitalism to alleviate poverty. In this respect, bootstrap capitalism steals a page from the immigrant experience. Many immigrant groups established their own market-related institutions as a means to join the American mainstream, as did some African American leaders, like Maggie Walker, mentioned in Chapter 2. The bank she established in a black Richmond neighborhood in 1899 provided capital that would not otherwise have been available to African Americans in that city for decades.

While the application of capitalism to reduce poverty may be viewed as a contradiction by orthodox leftists, proponents of economic justice actually have little time in which to work. A predatory "poverty industry" has recently emerged, a rapidly expanding commercial sector consisting of check-cashing outlets, high-rate loan companies, and others eager to serve the poor and bankless. Michael Hudson, an investigative journalist, has speculated about the scale of the poverty industry: "Add up all the businesses that bottom-feed on the 'fringe economy' and you'll come up with a market of $200 to $300 billion a year."[112] The recent expansion of "fringe banking" has been attributed to several factors, but the economist John Caskey noted that the increasing competition induced by deregulation led banks to withdraw from less profitable neighborhoods, leaving a large number of low-income consumers deprived of traditional financial services.[113] In the absence of institutions that contribute to community capitalism, in other words, the continual need for financial services by poor residents will be met by "fringe banks," which not only exploit the welfare- and working-poor but also suck capital out of neighborhoods toward absentee corporate headquarters.

Finally, bootstrap capitalism may serve as a counterpoint to conservatives' welfare behaviorism experiments. Although the outcomes of welfare behaviorism are disputed, it enjoys much public support, primarily because of widespread disenchantment with traditional welfare. Nonetheless, welfare behaviorism is rife with inconsistencies. By nature, it tends to be condescending, paternalistic, and invasive; its implementation requires sufficient elaboration of the welfare bureaucracy to give even conservatives pause. By contrast, bootstrap capitalism emphasizes work, savings, and civic betterment—themes that have resonated with Americans since the founding of the Republic and undergird the most popular social policies, such as Social Security and the GI Bill. In this respect, bootstrap capitalism builds on welfare-to-work by offering individuals additional income, families upward mobility, and communities stronger economies.

Notes
Index

Notes

PREFACE

1. Mickey Kaus, "The Work Ethic State," *New Republic* (July 7, 1986), p. 8; see also *The End of Equality* (New York: Basic Books, 1992).
2. For a more detailed discussion of the theoretical base of this thesis, see David Stoesz, "A Theory of Social Welfare," *Social Work* 34, no. 2 (1989), pp. 101–7.
3. Linda Gordon, *Pitied but Not Entitled* (Cambridge: Harvard University Press, 1994), pp. 103–4.
4. Harry Specht and Mark Courtney, *Unfaithful Angels* (New York: Free Press, 1994).

CHAPTER 1. THE END OF WELFARE

1. This was providential in that the 1996 welfare reform denied cash benefits to convicted drug felons, unless a state legislated otherwise.
2. Assuming 50 working weeks per year.
3. Leon Dash, *Rosa Lee* (New York: Basic Books, 1996).
4. Rosemary Bray, *Unafraid of the Dark* (New York: Random House, 1998), p. viii.
5. Although they are black and the majority of welfare recipients are white.
6. Indeed, Wilson's *The Truly Disadvantaged* (Chicago: University of Chicago Press, 1987) introduced the contention that the intellectual reaction to Moynihan's thesis dissuaded liberal academics from examining the most negative aspects of increasing minority poverty; he reiterated it a decade later in *When Work Disappears* (New York: Knopf, 1996).
7. Herbert Gans, *The War Against the Poor* (New York: Basic Books, 1995).
8. Mickey Kaus, *The End of Equality* (New York: Basic Books, 1992).
9. Carey Goldberg, "Welfare's Missing-in-Action," *New York Times*, 2 May 1999.
10. James Q. Wilson, "Two Nations" (Washington, D.C.: American Enterprise Institute, 1997).
11. For a good illustration of limited vision, see Mark Elliott, Don Spangler, and Kathy Yorkeivitz, "What's Next after Work First" (Philadelphia: Public/Private Ventures, 1998).

12. Michael Sherraden, *Assets and the Poor* (Armonk, N.Y.: M. E. Sharpe, 1991).

13. Alfred Kahn and Sheila Kamerman, *Big Cities in the Welfare Transition* (New York: Columbia University School of Social Work, 1998), p. 83.

14. General Accounting Office, *Welfare Reform* (Washington, D.C.: GAO, 1998), p. 11.

15. Quoted in Walter Trattner, *From Poor Law to Welfare State* (New York: Free Press, 1974), p. 86.

16. H. L. Mencken, *Minority Report* (New York: Knopf, 1956), p. 153.

17. Roy Lubove, *The Professional Altruist* (New York: Atheneum, 1975).

18. Personal conversation with Aaron Heffron of Independent Sector, April 21, 1999.

19. The conservatives' substitution proposal betrays a naivete about the increasing reliance of government on the nonprofit sector for service delivery. See Steven Smith and Michael Lipsky, *Nonprofits for Hire* (Cambridge: Harvard University Press, 1993).

20. Marvin Olasky, "Beyond the Stingy Welfare State," *Policy Review* (Fall 1990), p. 14.

21. Marvin Olasky, *Renewing American Compassion* (Washington, D.C.: Regnery Publishing, 1997), p. 3. See also *Tragedy of American Compassion* (Washington, D.C.: Regnery Gateway, 1992), and James Payne, *Overcoming Welfare* (New York: Basic Books, 1998).

22. Lester Salamon, *Partners in Public Service* (Baltimore: Johns Hopkins University Press, 1995), p. 196.

23. Rebecca Blank, *It Takes a Nation* (New York: Russell Sage Foundation, 1997), p. 205.

24. Judith Havemann, "Army of Volunteers Doesn't Answer Call," *Washington Post*, 26 April 1998.

25. Dirk Johnson, "Powell's Youth Drive Gains Steam after Sputtering," *New York Times*, 14 June 1998.

26. Michael Katz, *In the Shadow of the Poorhouse* (New York: Basic Books, 1986), p. 26.

27. Linda Gordon, *Pitied but Not Entitled* (Cambridge: Harvard University Press, 1994).

28. "Number of Programs in Eight Social Policy Domains" (Richmond, n.d.).

29. Wilson, "Two Nations," p. 6.

30. Sharon Parrott, "The Cato Institute Report on Welfare Benefits" (Washington, D.C.: Center on Budget and Policy Priorities, 1996).

31. Diana Furchtgott-Roth and Christine Stolba, *Women's Figures* (Washington, D.C.: American Enterprise Institute, 1996), p. 47.

32. Not adjusted for inflation, but the point remains valid.

33. Committee on Ways and Means, House of Representatives, *Overview of Entitlement Programs* (Washington, D.C.: GPO, 1998), p. 714.

34. Rob Green, Shelley Boots, and Karen Tumlin, *The Cost of Protecting Vulnerable Children* (Washington, D.C.: Urban Institute, 1999), p. 5.

35. David Stoesz, "Corporate Welfare," *Social Work* 31 (July/August 1986); How-

ard Karger and David Stoesz, *American Social Welfare Policy*, 3rd ed. (New York: Longman, 1998), ch. 7.

36. Karger and Stoesz, *American Social Welfare Policy*, ch. 7.

37. John Caskey, *Fringe Banking* (New York: Russell Sage Foundation, 1994).

38. For a nonideological discussion of the underclass, see "Special Issue: Defining and Measuring the Underclass," *Focus* 12, no. 1 (Spring/Summer 1989).

39. Phil Dearborn, "Fiscal Conditions in Large American Cities, 1971–1984," in Michael McGeary and Laurence Lynn, eds., *Urban Change and Poverty* (Washington, D.C.: National Academy Press, 1988), p. 256.

40. John Kasarda, "Industrial Restructuring and the Consequences of Changing Job Locations," in Reynolds Farley, ed., *Changes and Challenges: America 1990* (New York: Russell Sage Foundation, 1995), p. 156.

41. Ibid., p. 178.

42. Wilson, *When Work Disappears*, pp. 29–30.

43. David Remnick, "Dr. Wilson's Neighborhood," *New Yorker* 29 April and 6 May 1996, p. 98.

44. Jeanne Brooks-Gunn, Greg Duncan, and Nancy Maritato, "Poor Families, Poor Outcomes," in Greg Duncan and Jeanne Brooks-Gunn, eds., *Consequences of Growing Up Poor* (New York: Russell Sage Foundation, 1997), p. 12.

45. Sanders Korenman and Jane Miller, "Effects of Long-Term Poverty on Physical Health of Children in the National Longitudinal Survey of Youth," in Duncan and Brooks-Gunn, *Consequences of Growing Up Poor*, p. 94.

46. Jay Teachman et al., "Poverty During Adolescence and Subsequent Educational Attainment," in Duncan and Brooks-Gunn, *Consequences of Growing Up Poor*, p. 413.

47. Quoted in William Raspberry, "Before the Deluge," *Washington Post*, 8 March 1999.

48. Edward Murphy, "Survival Strategies of Low-Income Young Men" (Boston: Heller School, Brandeis University, 1998), pp. 3, 2.

49. Paul Jargowsky, *Poverty and Place* (New York: Russell Sage Foundation, 1997), p. 30.

50. Douglas Massey and Nancy Denton, *American Apartheid* (Cambridge: Harvard University Press, 1993).

51. Ibid., p. 145.

52. Ronald Ostrow, "New Report Echoes 'Two Societies' Warning of 1968 Kerner Commission," *Los Angeles Times*, 28 February 1993.

53. *Statistical Abstract of the United States*, 108th ed. (Washington, D.C.: GPO, 1988), pp. 260, 337.

54. Committee on Ways and Means, House of Representatives, *Overview of Entitlement Programs* (Washington, D.C.: GPO, 1990), p. 1311.

55. Robert Greenstein and Paul Leonard, *Bush Administration Budget* (Washington, D.C.: Center on Budget and Policy Priorities, 1990), p. 21, table 1.

56. David Stoesz and Howard Karger, *Reconstructing the American Welfare State* (Lanham, Md.: Rowman and Littlefield, 1992), p. 51.

57. Committee on Ways and Means, House of Representatives, *Overview of Government Programs* (Washington, D.C.: GPO, 1985), p. 376.

58.   Robert Mofitt and Douglas Wolf, "The Effect of the 1981 Omnibus Budget Reconciliation Act on Welfare Recipients and Work Incentives," *Social Service Review* 61 (1987), pp. 247–48.

59.   John Schwarz, *Illusions of Opportunity* (New York: Norton, 1997), p. 91.

60.   Committee on Ways and Means, *Overview*, 1996, pp. 1179, 1184.

61.   Robert Haveman, Barbara Wolfe, and Kathryn Wilson, "Childhood Poverty and Adolescent Schooling and Fertility Outcomes," in Duncan and Brooks-Gunn, *Consequences of Growing Up Poor,* p. 422.

62.   Jerome Miller, *Search and Destroy* (New York: Cambridge University Press, 1996), p. 85.

63.   Ibid., p. 54.

64.   Ibid., pp. 7–8, emphasis in original.

65.   Donna Franklin, *Ensuring Inequality* (New York: Oxford University Press, 1997), p. 207.

66.   Robert Merton, *Social Theory and Social Structure* (Glencoe, Ill.: Free Press, 1957), p. 144.

67.   Ibid., p. 160.

68.   Committee on Ways and Means, *Overview*, 1996, p. 473.

69.   Lawrence Mishel, Jared Bernstein, and John Schmitt, *The State of Working America* (Washington, D.C.: Economic Policy Institute, 1997), p. 51.

70.   Committee on Ways and Means, *Overview*, 1996, p. 872.

71.   "Food Stamps for the Dead," *Washington Post,* 11 March 1998.

72.   Committee on Ways and Means, *Overview*, 1996, p. 497.

73.   Kathryn Edin and Christopher Jencks, "Reforming Welfare," in Christopher Jencks, *Rethinking Social Policy* (Cambridge: Harvard University Press, 1992), pp. 207, 208.

74.   Kathryn Edin and Laura Lein, *Making Ends Meet* (New York: Russell Sage Foundation, 1997).

75.   Peter Edelman, "The Worst Thing Bill Clinton Has Done," *Atlantic Monthly,* March 1997, p. 56.

76.   Ibid., p. 53.

77.   Paul Peterson, Mark Rom, and Kenneth Scheve, Jr., "State Welfare Policy: A Race to the Bottom?" (paper presented at the National Association for Welfare Research and Statistics annual research conference, Jackson, Wyoming, September 10–13, 1995), p. 16.

78.   Iris McNichol and Iris Lav, "Will States Maintain the Safety Net?" (Washington, D.C.: Center on Budget and Policy Priorities, February 20, 1996); "Governors' Proposals Could Lead to Sharp State Funding Reductions in Medicaid and AFDC" (Washington, D.C.: Center on Budget and Policy Priorities, February 21, 1996).

79.   The author stated similar apprehensions about welfare reform: David Stoesz, "Welfare Reform Will Victimize Children," *Richmond Times-Dispatch,* 12 October 1995.

CHAPTER 2. THE OLD MATERNALISM

1. A fictitious name.

2. June Axinn and Herman Levin, *Social Welfare: A History of the American Response to Need*, 2nd ed. (New York: Harper and Row, 1982), p. 105.

3. Ibid., p. 106.

4. Theda Skocpol, *Protecting Soldiers and Mothers* (Cambridge: Harvard University Press, 1992), pp. 326, 332.

5. Quoted ibid., p. 331.

6. Ibid., pp. 348–49.

7. Jane Addams, *Twenty Years at Hull House* (Cutchogue, N.Y.: Buccaneer Books, 1994).

8. Bruce Jansson, *The Reluctant Welfare State* (Pacific Grove, Calif.: Brooks/Cole, 1993), p. 114.

9. William Trattner, *From Poor Law to Welfare State* (New York: Free Press, 1974), p. 189.

10. Linda Gordon, *Pitied but Not Entitled* (Cambridge: Harvard University Press, 1994), p. 55.

11. Allen Davis, *American Heroine* (New York: Oxford University Press, 1973), p. 276.

12. John Hope Franklin, *From Slavery to Freedom* (New York: Knopf, 1980), pp. 288–89.

13. Jill Quadagno, *The Color of Welfare* (New York: Oxford University Press, 1994), p. 20; Franklin, *From Slavery*, p. 396.

14. Barbara Machtinger, "The U.S. Children's Bureau and Mothers' Pensions Administration, 1912–1930," *Social Service Review* 73 (1999), pp. 105–18.

15. Skocpol, *Protecting*, p. 470.

16. Quoted in Gordon, *Pitied*, p. 105.

17. Ibid., p. 22.

18. Donna Franklin, *Ensuring Inequality* (New York: Oxford University Press, 1997), p. 55.

19. Gordon, *Pitied*, p. 276.

20. Deborah Stone, "Work and Moral Woman," *American Prospect* (November/December 1997), p. 80.

21. Franklin, *From Slavery*, p. 143.

22. Phyllis Day, *A New History of Social Welfare* (Englewood Cliffs, N.J.: Prentice Hall, 1989), pp. 246–47.

23. Lawrence Mishel, Jared Bernstein, and John Schmitt, *The State of Working America* (Washington, D.C.: Economic Policy Institute, 1997), pp. 232, 153.

24. Frances Fox Piven and Richard Cloward, *Regulating the Poor* (New York: Vintage, 1971), p. 133.

25. Ibid., pp. 124–25.

26. Mary Jo Bane and David Ellwood, *Welfare Realities* (Cambridge: Harvard University Press, 1994), p. 13.

27. Charles A. Reich, "Individual Rights and Social Welfare," *Yale Law Review* 74 (1965), p. 1255.

28. Charles A. Reich, "The New Property," *Yale Law Review* 73 (1964), pp. 785–86.

29. Reich, "Individual Rights," p. 1256.

30. *Social Security Bulletin Annual Statistical Supplement* (Washington, D.C.: Social Security Administration, 1975), p. 186.

31. Michael Sosin, "Legal Rights and Welfare Change," in Sheldon Danziger and Daniel Weinberg, eds., *Fighting Poverty* (Cambridge: Harvard University Press, 1986), p. 274.

32. Gary Lowe and P. Nelson Reid, eds., *The Professionalization of Poverty* (Hawthorne, N.Y.: Aldine de Gruyter, 1999).

33. Trattner, *From Poor Law,* pp. 199–200.

34. Machtinger, "Children's Bureau," p. 109.

35. Gordon, *Pitied,* p. 164.

36. Ibid., p. 262.

37. Marti Bombyk, "Progressive Social Work," in *Encyclopedia of Social Work,* 19th ed. (Washington, D.C.: National Association of Social Workers Press, 1995), pp. 1933, 1937.

38. William Epstein, "Social Efficiency and Social Work Research" (manuscript), pp. 25, 1.

39. The University of Wisconsin Institute for Research on Poverty is the exception. Of the more than 200 social work programs in the United States, only this one has developed an institutional capacity for first-class poverty research.

40. In counting articles, dissertation abstracts, government reports, and works about other nations were excluded.

41. Michael Lipsky, *Street-Level Bureaucracy* (New York: Russell Sage Foundation, 1980), p. xiii.

42. Michael Goodman, "Just Another Day in Paradise," *Los Angeles Times Magazine,* 19 December 1993, p. 30.

43. Frederick Wiseman, *Welfare* (Zipporah Films: Cambridge, Mass., 1975).

44. Rebecca Blank, *It Takes a Nation* (New York: Russell Sage Foundation, 1997), p. 158.

45. Theresa Funiciello, *Tyranny of Kindness* (New York: Atlantic Monthly Press, 1993), p. 252, emphasis in original.

46. Similarly, research in child welfare is inadequate; see Lela Costin, Howard Karger, and David Stoesz, *The Politics of Child Abuse in America* (New York: Oxford University Press, 1996).

47. Oddly, in 1961 the city manager of Newburgh, New York, proposed welfare reforms quite similar to those introduced by the 1996 federal legislation. In the flap that followed, the *New York Times* (June 24) reported that "more than a dozen administrative employees of the New York City Department of Welfare, 'endorse every item' of the Newburgh plan"—but social work paid little mind.

48. "It's Not Like They Say" (Washington, D.C.: Southport Institute for Policy Analysis, n.d.).

49. Marcia Meyers, Bonnie Glaser, and Karin MacDonald, "On the Front Lines of Welfare Delivery," *Policy Analysis and Management* 17 (Winter 1998), p. 18.

50. Irene Bush and Katherine Kraft, "Women on Welfare: What They Have to

Say about Becoming Self-Sufficient" (New Brunswick, N.J.: Rutgers University School of Social Work, 1997), pp. vii, iii, emphasis in original.

51. Ibid., p. 25.

52. Ibid.

53. Ibid., p. 24.

54. "Inhuman Services," *Harper's,* June 1997, p. 16.

55. Bush and Kraft, "Women on Welfare," pp. 19–26.

56. Evelyn Brodkin, "The State Side of the 'Welfare Contract'" (Chicago: University of Chicago School of Social Service Administration, 1995), p. 12.

57. Blank, *It Takes a Nation,* p. 157, emphasis in original.

58. Harry Specht and Mark Courtney, *Unfaithful Angels* (New York: Free Press, 1994), p. 4.

59. Daniel Bonevac, "Manifestations of Illiberalism in Philosophy," *Academic Questions* 12 (Winter 1998), p. 17.

60. Leslie Doty Hollingsworth, "Promoting Same-Race Adoption for Children of Color," *Social Work* 43 (March 1998), pp. 104–16.

61. Rita Simon and Howard Altstein, "The Case for Transracial Adoption," *Children and Youth Service Review* 18, nos. 1/2 (1996), pp. 20–21.

62. In contrast to its lack of interest in the poor, social work has pursued empirical research in two areas of professional activity: (1) the effectiveness of direct practice—research that generates continual doubts about professional efficacy; and (2) the publications of the faculties of schools of social work. Neither area well reflects social work's traditional concerns: family poverty and child welfare. The former raises profound questions about the value of professional intervention; the latter is an exercise in self-absorption.

63. Shelby Steele, *The Content of Our Character* (New York: Harper Perennial, 1990), pp. 16–17.

64. Paul Jargowsky, *Poverty and Place* (New York: Russell Sage Foundation, 1997), p. 189.

65. Daniel Patrick Moynihan, "The Negro Family: The Case for National Action" (Washington, D.C.: U.S. Department of Labor, 1965); Aage Sorensen and Seymour Spilerman, ed., *Social Theory and Social Policy* (Westport, Conn.: Praeger, 1993).

66 William Julius Wilson, *The Truly Disadvantaged* (Chicago: University of Chicago Press, 1987).

67. Richard Rorty, *Achieving Our Country* (Cambridge: Harvard University Press, 1998), pp. 14, 15.

68. The concept of involution was introduced by Clifford Geertz in *Agricultural Involution in Indonesia.* As a manifestation of professional involution, social work developed special journals to address the circumstances of special populations. As a result, social work academics who pursued preoccupations internal to the profession achieved promotion, tenure, and lifetime sinecures to promote cultural politics. While cultural politics thrived in American social work, interest in traditional concerns—the poor and children—correspondingly withered.

69. Smith notes that "American law had long been shot through with forms of second-class citizenship, denying personal liberties for political participation to most of the adult population on the basis of race, ethnicity, gender, and even religion." See

Rogers Smith, *Civic Ideals* (New Haven: Yale University Press, 1997), p. 2. I would argue that social work maintained an archaic welfare bureaucracy at the expense of the poor in order to further its pursuit of cultural politics.

70.   T. H. Marshall, *Class, Citizenship and Social Development* (Chicago: University of Chicago Press, 1964); Albert O. Hirschman, *The Rhetoric of Reaction* (Cambridge: Harvard University Press, 1991), pp. 3–4.

71.   Harold Wilensky and Charles Lebeaux, *Industrial Society and Social Welfare* (New York: Free Press, 1965), p. 127.

72.   Richard Titmuss, *Commitment to Welfare* (New York: Pantheon, 1968), p. 127.

73.   James Midgley, "The American Welfare State in International Perspective," in Howard Karger and David Stoesz, *American Social Welfare Policy*, 3rd ed. (New York: Longman, 1998), pp. 441, 444.

74.   Leon Ginsberg, *Conservative Social Welfare Policy* (Chicago: Nelson Hall, 1998), p. 70.

75.   Respectively: Michael Katz, *In the Shadow of the Poorhouse* (New York: Basic Books, 1986); Jansson, *The Reluctant Welfare State*.

76.   Arthur Schlesinger, Jr., *The Cycles of American History* (Boston: Houghton Mifflin, 1986), p. 47.

77.   William Julius Wilson, *When Work Disappears* (New York: Knopf, 1996), p. 172.

78.   Isaiah Berlin, *Two Concepts of Liberty* (Oxford: Clarendon Press, 1958), p. 42.

79.   Jeffrey Pressman and Aaron Wildavsky, *Implementation* (Berkeley: University of California Press, 1973).

80.   Quoted in Randall Rothenberg, *The Neoliberals* (New York: Simon and Schuster, 1984), pp. 68–69.

81.   Charles Peters, "A New Politics," *Public Welfare* 18 (1983), p. 36.

82.   *New Democrat*, a monthly of the Democratic Leadership Council, disseminates neoliberal policy proposals (Progressive Policy Institute, Washington, D.C.).

83.   Fay Cook and Edith Barrett, *Support for the American Welfare State* (New York: Columbia University Press, 1992), p. 62.

84.   Ibid., p. 163.

85.   Theodore Marmor, Jerry Mashaw, and Philip Harvey, *America's Misunderstood Welfare State* (New York: Basic Books, 1990), p. 57.

86.   Lisbeth Schorr, *Within Our Reach* (New York: Anchor Books, 1988).

87.   Sylvia Ann Hewlett, *When the Bough Breaks* (New York: Harper Perennial, 1992).

88.   Jonathan Kozol, *Savage Inequalities* (New York: Harper Perennial, 1991); *Amazing Grace* (New York: Harper Perennial, 1995).

89.   William Epstein, *Welfare in America* (Madison: University of Wisconsin Press, 1997).

90.   James Glassman, "Nanny-Statists Perpetuate the Myth of the Ignorant American," *Richmond Times-Dispatch*, 5 June 1998.

91.   William Ryan, *Blaming the Victim* (New York: Pantheon, 1971).

92. Irving Howe, *Beyond the Welfare State* (New York: Schocken Books, 1982), p. 10.

93. David Ellwood and Lawrence Summers, "Poverty in America," in Sheldon Danziger and Daniel Weinberg, eds., *Fighting Poverty* (Cambridge: Harvard University Press, 1986), p. 78.

94. Frances Fox Piven and Richard Cloward, *The New Class War* (New York: Pantheon, 1982), p. ix.

95. Fred Block, Richard Cloward, Barbara Ehrenreich, and Frances Fox Piven, *The Mean Season* (New York: Pantheon, 1987), p. ix.

96. Ibid., p. xiv.

97. Lawrence Mead, "The New Welfare Debate," *Commentary* (March 1988), p. 46.

98. Philip AuClaire, "Public Attitudes toward Social Welfare Expenditures," *Social Work* 29 (March/April 1984), p. 141.

99. Hugh Heclo, "The Political Foundations of Antipoverty Policy," in Danziger and Weinberg, *Fighting Poverty*, p. 330, emphasis in original.

100. John Doble and Keith Melville, "The Public's Social Welfare Mandate," *Public Opinion* 11 (January/February 1989), p. 59.

101. Steve Farkas and Jean Johnson, "The Values We Live By" (New York: Public Agenda, 1996), p. 24. Welfare recipients' sentiments regarding time limits on welfare paralleled those of the general public.

102. Ibid., p. 34.

103. Quoted in Richard Harwood, "At a Loss for a Label," *Washington Post*, 13 April 1998.

104. Rorty, *Achieving*, p. 99.

105. Ibid.

106. Quoted in David Broder, "Reagan's Policies Are Standard for Would-Be Successors," *Omaha World-Herald*, 24 January 1988.

107. Quoted in Michael Kelly, "You Say You Want a Revolution," *New Yorker* 21 November 1994, p. 58.

108. "Are States Improving the Lives of Poor Families?" (Medford, Mass.: Tufts University Center on Hunger and Poverty, 1998), p. 7.

109. Ibid., p. 21.

110. Orlando Patterson, "The Liberal Millennium," *New Republic*, 8 November 1999, p. 59.

CHAPTER 3. THE NEW PATERNALISM

1. A fictitious name.

2. Daniel Patrick Moynihan, "The Negro Family: The Case for National Action" (Washington, D.C.: U.S. Department of Labor, 1965); *Maximum Feasible Misunderstanding* (New York: Free Press, 1969).

3. Henry Aaron, *Politics and the Professors* (Washington, D.C.: Brookings Institution, 1978).

4. Paul Weyrich, the conservative guru of fundraising, evidently had a similar epiphany in 1969; see Karen Paget, "Lessons of Right-Wing Philanthropy," *American Prospect* (September/October 1998), p. 89.

5. James Smith, *The Idea Brokers* (New York: Free Press, 1991).

6. Robert Kaiser and Ira Chinoy, "How Scaife's Money Powered a Movement," *Washington Post,* 2 May 1999.

7. Sally Covington, *Moving a Public Agenda* (Washington, D.C.: National Committee for Responsive Philanthropy, 1997), p. 3.

8. Ibid., pp. 3, 5.

9. Quoted ibid., p. 35.

10. William Baroody, Jr., "The President's View," *AEI Annual Report 1981–1982* (Washington, D.C.: American Enterprise Institute, n.d.), p. 2.

11. Peter Berger and Richard John Neuhaus, *To Empower People* (Washington, D.C.: American Enterprise Institute, 1977).

12. See Brigitte Berger and Peter Berger, *The War Over the Family* (Garden City, N.Y.: Anchor, 1984).

13. Michael Balzano, *Federalizing Meals on Wheels* (Washington, D.C.: American Enterprise Institute, 1979), p. 37.

14. Michael Novak, *Toward a Theology of the Corporation* (Washington, D.C.: American Enterprise Institute, 1981), p. 5.

15. Ibid., p. 50.

16. Ibid., p. 28.

17. Smith, *Idea Brokers*, p. 204.

18. Interview with Stuart Butler at the Heritage Foundation, 4 October 1984.

19. Stuart Butler, "Enterprise Zones," in George Sternlieb and David Listokin, eds., *New Tools for Economic Development* (Piscataway, N.J.: Rutgers University Press, 1981); Peter Ferrara, *Social Security Reform* (Washington, D.C.: Heritage Foundation, 1982); *Rebuilding Social Security* (Washington, D.C.: Heritage Foundation, 1984).

20. Charles Murray, *Losing Ground* (New York: Basic Books, 1984), pp. 226–27.

21. Chuck Lane, "The Manhattan Project," *New Republic,* 25 March 1985.

22. Martin Anderson, "Welfare Reform," in Peter Duignan and Alvin Rabushka, eds., *The United States in the 1980s* (Stanford: Hoover Institution, 1980), p. 145.

23. Ibid., pp. 171–75.

24. Irving Horowitz, *Communicating Ideas* (New York: Oxford University Press, 1986), p. 43.

25. P. Thomas, "In Washington's Marketplace of Ideas, Think Tanks Are the Strongest Sellers," *Los Angeles Times,* 6 November 1988.

26. Cregg Easterbrook, "Ideas Move Nations," *Atlantic Monthly,* January 1986, p. 66.

27. James Smith, foreword in Covington, *Moving a Public Agenda,* p. 1.

28. Lee Edwards, *The Conservative Revolution* (New York: Free Press, 1999).

29. Burton Pines, *Back to Basics* (New York: William Morrow, 1982), p. 254.

30. Kaiser and Chinoy, "Scaife's Money."

31. Paget, "Lessons of Right-Wing Philanthropy," pp. 92, 94.

32. Ibid., pp. 91, 92.

33. E. J. Dionne, Jr., *They Only Look Dead* (New York: Simon and Schuster, 1997), pp. 187–91.

34. A more sophisticated analysis of various poverty-reduction programs conducted by liberal analysts revealed that the inclusion of Social Security actually reduces the official poverty measure by higher percentages than the conservatives' figures indicated. See Sheldon Danziger, Robert Haveman, and Robert Plotnick, "Antipoverty Policy," in Sheldon Danziger and Daniel Weinberg, eds., *Fighting Poverty* (Cambridge: Harvard University Press, 1986), p. 56. Subsequent retrospective analysis by the Census Bureau traced the value of noncash benefits from 1979 to 1994, documenting that the inclusion of noncash benefits reduced the poverty rate between 33.8 percent (in 1980) and 29.0 percent (in the early 1990s). See Committee on Ways and Means, House of Representatives, *Overview of Entitlement Programs* (Washington, D.C.: GPO, 1996), pp. 1228–31.

35. Michael Novak, ed., *The New Consensus on Family and Welfare* (Washington, D.C.: American Enterprise Institute, 1987), p. 45.

36. Ibid., p. 5.

37. Ibid., p. xiv.

38. George Gilder, *Wealth and Poverty* (New York: Basic Books, 1981), p. 118.

39. Lawrence Mead, *Beyond Entitlement* (New York: Free Press, 1986).

40. Michael Katz, *In the Shadow of the Poorhouse* (New York: Basic Books, 1986), ch. 2.

41. Linda Gordon, *Pitied but Not Entitled* (Cambridge: Harvard University Press, 1994).

42. Joel Handler, *The Poverty of Welfare Reform* (New Haven: Yale University Press, 1995), p. 3.

43. Lawrence Mead, *The New Politics of Poverty* (New York: Basic Books, 1992), p. 181.

44. Lawrence Mead, "Are Welfare Employment Programs Effective?" in Jonathan Crane, ed., *Social Programs That Really Work* (New York: Russell Sage Foundation, 1997), pp. 14, 15; Lawrence Mead, *The New Paternalism* (Washington, D.C.: Brookings Institution, 1997).

45. Douglas Besharov, "Statement before the Select Committee on Hunger," U.S. House of Representatives, Washington, D.C., 21 May 1992, pp. 11–13.

46. Dan Balz, "Ready, or Not?" *Washington Post Magazine*, 25 October 1998, p. 21.

47. Douglas Besharov, "Statement before the Select Committee on Hunger."

48. David Stoesz and Howard Karger, *Restructuring the American Welfare State* (Lanham, Md.: Rowman and Littlefield, 1992), pp. 62, 147.

49. David Ellwood, *Poor Support* (New York: Basic Books, 1988), p. 153.

50. Elizabeth Shogren and Ronald Brownstein, "GAO Says JOBS Plan Not Working," *Los Angeles Times*, 19 December 1994.

51. Will Marshall and Martin Schram, eds., *Mandate for Change* (New York: Berkley Books, 1993); Elaine Kamarck, "The Welfare Wars," *New Democrat*, July 1992.

52. Committee on Ways and Means, *Overview*, p. 714.

53. Tom Morganthau, "The Entitlement Trap," *Newsweek*, 13 December 1993.

54. "Charge to the Working Group on Welfare Reform, Family Support and Independence" (Washington, D.C.: n. p., n.d.).

55. Mickey Kaus, *The End of Equality* (New York: Basic Books, 1992), p. 135.

56. Elizabeth Shogren, "Child Care a Key Hurdle to Clinton Welfare Plan," *Los Angeles Times*, 6 March 1994; Paul Offner, "Day Careless," *New Republic*, 18 April 1994.

57. Paul Offner, "Solid Noncitizens," *New Republic*, 20 June 1994.

58. Ronald Brownstein and Elizabeth Shogren, "Welfare Reform Planners in Deadlock," *Los Angeles Times*, 22 March 1994.

59. Jason DeParle, "States' Eagerness to Experiment on Welfare Jars Administration," *New York Times*, 14 April 1994.

60. Elizabeth Shogren, "2 Florida Counties to Test Clinton-Style Welfare Plan," *Los Angeles Times*, 28 January 1994.

61. An overview of the various state TANF programs is afforded by the Assessing the New Federalism project of the Urban Institute. See L. Jerome Gallagher et al., *One Year after Federal Welfare Reform* (Washington, D.C.: Urban Institute, 1998).

62. Barbara Vobejda, "Most States Are Shaping Their Own Welfare Reform," *Washington Post*, 3 February 1996.

63. House Resolution 3500, 103rd Congress, 1st session.

64. Paul Offner, "Realistic and Affordable Welfare Reform: Target the Teen Mothers," *San Diego Union Tribune*, 10 January 1994; see also Paul Offner, "Target the Kids," *New Republic*, 24 January 1994.

65. Jason DeParle, "Plan May Not Satisfy Demands for Basic Change," *San Diego Union-Tribune*, 15 June 1994.

66. Ronald Brownstein, "Polarization Politics Seen as Key Obstacle to Welfare Proposal," *Los Angeles Times*, 15 June 1994.

67. DeParle, "Plan."

68. "Clinton's Secret Weapon," *New Republic*, 20 June 1994.

69. DeParle, "Plan"; Elizabeth Shogren, "Clinton Unveils Welfare Reform," *Los Angeles Times*, 15 June 1994.

70. Ronald Brownstein, "Clinton's Welfare Reform Shaped by Predecessors' Frustrated Efforts," *Los Angeles Times*, 14 June 1994.

71. Edwards, *Conservative Revolution*, p. 293.

72. Quoted in Leon Ginsberg, *Conservative Social Welfare Policy* (Chicago: Nelson Hall, 1998), p. 97.

73. Quoted ibid., p. 122.

74. Ann Devroy and Barbara Vobejda, "Clinton Faces 'Huge Heat' on Welfare," *Washington Post*, 4 November 1995.

75. David Super et al., "The New Welfare Law" (Washington, D.C.: Center on Budget and Policy Priorities, 1996), p. 2.

76. Bob Herbert, "Throw Them Out," *New York Times*, 2 August 1996.

77. Elizabeth Drew, *Whatever It Takes* (New York: Penguin, 1998), p. 131.

78. Mark Shields, "Last President of the Conservative Era?" *Washington Post*, 4 November 1997.

CHAPTER 4. WELFARE BEHAVIORISM

1. David Firestone, "Clinton to Sign Welfare Bill That Ends U.S. Aid Guarantee and Gives States Broad Power," *New York Times*, 1 August 1996; Barbara Vobejda, "Clinton to Sign Bill Overhauling Welfare," *Washington Post*, 1 August 1996.

2. *Welfare Reform: States Are Restructuring Programs to Reduce Welfare Dependency* (Washington, D.C.: General Accounting Office, 1998), p. 4.

3. Michael Novak, *The New Consensus on Family and Welfare* (Washington, D.C.: American Enterprise Institute, 1987).

4. Charles Murray, *Losing Ground* (New York: Basic Books, 1984), pp. 227–28.

5. Lawrence Mead, *Beyond Entitlement* (New York: Free Press, 1986).

6. George Gilder, *Wealth and Poverty* (New York: Basic Books, 1981), p. 118.

7. "Replace Welfare with 'Tough Love,' Dole Says," *Richmond Times-Dispatch*, 22 May 1996.

8. Marian Wright Edelman, "Say No to This Welfare 'Reform,'" *Washington Post*, 3 November 1995.

9. "A Children's Veto," *Washington Post*, 25 July 1996.

10. Daniel Patrick Moynihan, "When Principle Is at Issue," *Washington Post*, 4 August 1996.

11. Judith Gueron and Edward Pauley, *From Welfare to Work* (New York: Russell Sage Foundation, 1991).

12. Greater Avenues for Independence is California's welfare-to-work program.

13. Judith Gueron, "Welfare Programs and Welfare Reform," *Public Welfare* 53 (Summer 1995), p. 10.

14. Randall Eberts, "Welfare to Work" (Kalamazoo, Mich.: Upjohn Institute, 1995), p. 4.

15. Mary Jo Bane and David Ellwood, *Welfare Realities* (Cambridge: Harvard University Press, 1994), ch. 1.

16. Rachel Swarns, "Welfare Policies of the City Face Federal Scrutiny," *New York Times*, 8 November 1998.

17. Rachel Swarns, "In an Odd Turn, Officials Are Pushing Welfare," *New York Times*, 22 November 1998.

18. Bradley Schiller, "State Welfare-Reform Impacts" (Washington, D.C.: School of Public Affairs, American University, February 1998), pp. 13–14.

19. James Riccio and Yeheskel Hasenfeld suggest that sanctions contribute to welfare savings: GAIN programs that emphasized the formal penalty process tended to achieve greater reductions in average welfare payments to the experimental group relative to the control group average. Conversely, welfare savings tended to be lower when personalized attention was more strongly emphasized. Some savings are a direct result of sanctions; however, the threat of sanctions may also have influenced the behavior of recipients who were not actually sanctioned—for example, by encouraging them to leave AFDC sooner than they might have otherwise. See "Enforcing a Participation Mandate in a Welfare-to-Work Program," *Social Service Review* 70 (1996), p. 534.

20. Gaye Hamilton et al., *National Evaluation of Welfare-to-Work Strategies: Two-Year Findings on the Labor Force Attachment and Human Capital Development*

Programs in Three Sites (Washington, D.C.: Department of Health and Human Services, 1997).

21. Ibid., pp. ES4–6.

22. This was evident in an earlier evaluation of GAIN conducted by MDRC: "Simply maximizing participation in basic education and in vocational training or postsecondary education, which tend to be expensive program elements, offers no guarantee of success. Also, investing large amounts of expensive staff time in very personalized treatment of recipients, hoping that this support would lead to greater achievements, may not be essential for producing earnings gains and welfare savings." See James Riccio and Alan Orenstein, "Understanding Best Practices for Operating Welfare-to-Work Programs," *Evaluation Review* 20 (February 1996), p. 23.

23. This generalization is affirmed by Riccio and Hasenfeld, "Enforcing a Participation Mandate."

24. Susan Scrivener et al., *National Evaluation of Welfare-to-Work Strategies: Implementation, Participation Patterns, Costs, and Two-Year Impacts of the Portland (Oregon) Welfare-to-Work Program* (Washington, D.C.: Department of Health and Human Services, 1998), pp. ES2–3.

25. Ibid., p. ES23.

26. Lois Quinn and Robert Magill, "Politics Versus Research in Social Policy," *Social Service Review* 68 (1994), pp. 503–20.

27. Dan Bloom, Veronica Fellerath, David Long, and Robert Wood, "LEAP: Interim Findings of a Welfare Initiative to Improve School Attendance among Teenage Parents" (New York: Manpower Demonstration Research Corporation, 1993).

28. Robert Wood, Dan Bloom, Veronica Fellerath, and David Long, "Encouraging School Enrollment and Attendance among Teenage Parents on Welfare," *Children and Youth Services Review* 17 (1995), p. 289.

29. Ibid., p. 292.

30. Larry Mead, personal communication, 1999.

31. Wood et al., "Encouraging," p. 283.

32. Johannes Bos and Veronica Fellerath, *LEAP: Final Report* (New York: Manpower Research Demonstration Research Corporation, 1997), pp. ES4–5.

33. Ibid., pp. 112–13.

34. Denise Polit, Janet Quint, and James Riccio, "The Challenge of Serving Teenage Mothers" (New York: Manpower Demonstration Research Corporation, 1988).

35. Robert Granger and Rachel Cytron, *Teenage Parent Programs* (New York: Manpower Demonstration Research Corporation, 1998), pp. 7, 10, 16.

36. Ibid., pp. 19, 20.

37. Ibid., p. 22.

38. Ibid., p. 21.

39. Janet Quint, Johannes Bos, and Denise Polit, *New Chance: Final Report* (New York: Manpower Demonstration Research Corporation, 1997), p. ES3.

40. Ibid., pp. ES10–11.

41. Ibid., p. ES16.

42. Ibid., p. ES30.

43. Ibid., p. ES13.

44. Rutgers University, "A Final Report on the Impact of New Jersey's Family Development Program" (http://www.state.nj.us/humanservices/rutfdp.html).

45. Judith Havemann, "Fewer Births for N.J. Welfare Mothers," *Washington Post*, 3 November 1998.

46. Committee on Ways and Means, House of Representatives, *Overview of Entitlement Programs* (Washington, D.C.: GPO, 1998), p. 629.

47. Ibid., p. 599.

48. Ibid., p. 609.

49. Ibid., p. 549.

50. Mark Turner and Elaine Sorensen, "Noncustodial Fathers and Their Child Support Payments" (Washington, D.C.: Urban Institute, 1995).

51. Reynolds Farley, *The New American Reality* (New York: Russell Sage Foundation, 1996), p. 98.

52. Kathryn Edin, "Single Mothers and Child Support," *Children and Youth Services Review* 17 (1995), pp. 214–15.

53. Committee on Ways and Means, House of Representatives, *Overview of Entitlement Programs* (Washington, D.C.: GPO, 1996), p. 580.

54. Dan Bloom and Kay Sherwood, "Matching Opportunities to Obligations" (New York: Manpower Demonstration and Research Corporation, 1994).

55. Fred Doolittle et al., "Building Opportunities, Enforcing Obligations" (http://www.mdrc.org/Reports/Paren's%20Fair%20Share/WEB-PFS-ExecSum.html; New York: Manpower Demonstration Research Corporation, 1998).

56. David Super et al., "The New Welfare Law" (Washington, D.C.: Center on Budget and Policy Priorities, 1996), p. 2.

57. Patricia Smith and W. Jean Young, "Childhood Welfare Receipt and the Implications of Welfare Reform," *Social Service Review* 72 (1998), p. 13.

58. Johanne Boisjoly, Kathleen Harris, and Greg Duncan, "Trends, Events, and Duration of Initial Welfare Spells," *Social Service Review* 72 (1998), pp. 487–88.

59. Anthony Halter, "State Welfare Reform for Employable General Assistance Recipients," *Social Work* 41 (January 1996), p. 106.

60. "Welfare Reform: Where Virginia Stands" (Richmond, Va.: Senate Finance Committee, 1997).

61. Dan Bloom, Mary Farrell, James Kemple, and Nandita Verma, *FTP: The Family Transition Program* (New York: Manpower Demonstration Research Corporation, 1997), pp. ES1–15.

62. Ibid., p. ES18.

63. Ibid., pp. 100–101.

64. Ibid., p. ES14.

65. Tom Corbett, "Welfare Reform in Wisconsin," in Donald Norris and Luke Thompson, eds., *The Politics of Welfare Reform* (Thousand Oaks, Calif.: SAGE, 1995).

66. Lawrence Mead, "The Decline of Welfare in Wisconsin" (Milwaukee: Wisconsin Policy Research Institute, March 1996), p. 3.

67. Michael Wiseman, "State Strategies for Welfare Reform: The Wisconsin Story" (Madison: Institute for Research on Poverty, 1995), p. 19.

68. Ibid., p. 14.

69. Ibid., p. 22.

70. Mickey Kaus, "Tommy's New Tune," *New Republic,* 18/25 September 1995, p. 25.

71. Ibid., pp. 25–26.

72. Jason DeParle, "Getting Opal Caples to Work," *New York Times Magazine,* 24 August 1997, pp. 34–35.

73. Lawrence Mead, "The Decline of Welfare in Wisconsin" (New York: NYU Department of Politics, 1997), p. 7.

74. Sarah Archibald, "New Hope for Wisconsin Works," *LaFollette Policy Report* 9 (Spring/Summer 1998), p. 13.

75. Hans Bos et al., "New Hope for People with Low Incomes" (New York: Manpower Demonstration Research Corporation, 1999), p. 3.

76. Ibid., pp. 3–4.

77. Ibid., p. 26.

78. Wiseman, "State Strategies," p. 6.

79. Mead, "Decline" (1996), p. 8.

80. Ibid., p. 19.

81. Ibid., pp. 24–25.

82. Kathryn Edin and Laura Lein, *Making Ends Meet* (New York: Russell Sage Foundation, 1997), ch. 2.

83. Demonstrating this hypothesis would require a detailed analysis of all poor families, a subject well beyond most welfare reform research as it is presently conceived. See Lawrence Mead, "Are Welfare Employment Programs Effective?" (New York: NYU Department of Politics, 1997).

84. Joint Legislative Audit and Review Commission, *Virginia's Welfare Reform Initiative* (Richmond, Va.: Commission, 1999), p. 12.

85. Kathleen Maloy et al., "Diversion as a Work-Oriented Welfare Reform Strategy and Its Effect on Access to Medicaid" (Washington, D.C.: Georgetown University Center for Health Policy Research, 1999), p. iv.

86. Barbara Vobejda and Judith Havemann, "States' Welfare Shift: Stop It Before It Starts," *Washington Post,* 12 August 1998.

87. Kathleen Maloy et al., *A Description and Assessment of State Approaches to Diversion Programs and Activities Under Welfare Reform* (Washington, D.C.: Georgetown University Center for Health Policy Research, 1998), p. v.

88. "Deflecting Welfare Applicants," *Washington Post,* 17 August 1998.

89. The absence of systematic data on the impact of welfare reform makes an accurate assessment of the 1996 federal legislation impossible, at least for the moment. See Barbara Vobejda and Judith Havemann, "State's Welfare Data in Disarray," *Washington Post,* 13 April 1998.

90. Mark Greenberg, "Welfare-to-Work Grants and Other TANF-Related Provisions in the Balanced Budget Act of 1997" (Washington, D.C.: Center for Law and Social Policy, 1998).

91. Conversation with Ed Lazere of the Center on Budget and Policy Priorities, 20 May 1998.

CHAPTER 5. THE DYNAMICS OF WELFARE AND WORK

1. Committee on Ways and Means, House of Representatives, *Overview of Entitlement Programs* (Washington, D.C.: GPO, 1996), p. 504.

2. The data are derived from different studies, but there is no reason to doubt that FSA made work, not (re)marriage, the primary way out of welfare.

3. House Ways and Means Committee, *Overview*, 1996, p. 505.

4. LaDonna Pavetti, *Questions and Answers on Welfare Dynamics* (Washington, D.C.: Urban Institute, 1995), p. 4.

5. Committee on Ways and Means, *Overview*, 1996, pp. 510–11.

6. David Stoesz, *Small Change: Domestic Policy Under the Clinton Presidency* (White Plains, N.Y.: Longman, 1996), p. 59.

7. Pamela Loprest and Gregory Acs, "Profile of Disability among Families on AFDC" (Washington, D.C.: Urban Institute, 1995), p. 3.

8. Ibid., p. 16.

9. Gregory Acs and Pamela Loprest, "The Effect of Disabilities on Exits from AFDC," *Policy Analysis and Management* 18 (Winter 1999), p. 39.

10. Ibid., p. 41.

11. Ibid., pp. 43–44.

12. Krista Olson and LaDonna Pavetti, *Personal and Family Challenges to the Successful Transition from Welfare to Work* (Washington, D.C.: Urban Institute, 1997), p. 25.

13. Ibid., pp. 35–36.

14. These figures almost certainly understate the degree of disability, if only insofar as those who have communication difficulties are less able to transmit their circumstances to inquisitors. William Epstein observed "that a large proportion of welfare recipients, especially the long term dependent, have some serious problems, but outside of the eligibilities of SSI, mental health programs, drug and alcohol rehab, and Medicaid" (personal communication, September 9, 1998). Such deficits make exiting welfare through work even less likely.

15. James K. Galbraith, "Dangerous Metaphor: The Fiction of the Labor Market," in *Public Policy Brief* (Annandale-on-Hudson, N.Y.: Jerome Levy Economics Institute, 1997), p. 1.

16. Randy Albelda and Chris Tilly, *Glass Ceilings and Bottomless Pits: Women's Work, Women's Poverty* (Boston, Mass.: South End Press, 1997), pp. 15–16. The entire list is italicized in the original.

17. E.g., George Gilder, *Wealth and Poverty* (New York: Basic Books, 1981), p. 118.

18. Sheldon Danziger, Robert Haveman, and Robert Plotnick, "Antipoverty Policy," in Sheldon Danziger and Daniel Weinberg, eds., *Fighting Poverty* (Cambridge: Harvard University Press, 1986), p. 75.

19. Sheldon Danziger and Jeffrey Lehman, "How Will Welfare Recipients Fare in the Labor Market?" *Challenge* 39 (March/April 1996), p. 31.

20. Lawrence Mishel, Jared Bernstein, and John Schmitt, *The State of Working America* (Washington, D.C.: Economic Policy Institute, 1997), p. 44.

21. E. J. Dionne, Jr., "Up from the Bottom," *Washington Post Weekly*, 3 August 1998, p. 27.

22. A detailed discussion of the relationship between locality and poverty can be found in Paul Jargowsky, *Poverty and Place* (New York: Russell Sage Foundation, 1997).

23. Harry Holzer, "Black Employment Problems," *Journal of Policy Analysis and Management* 13 (1994), p. 715; see Chapter 1 in this book for references to Kasarda and Wilson.

24. John Fitzgerald, "Local Labor Markets and Local Area Effects on Welfare Duration," *Journal of Policy Analysis and Management* 14 (1995), p. 61.

25. Robert Solow, "Who Likes Workfare," in Amy Gutman, ed., *Work and Welfare* (Princeton: Princeton University Press, 1998), p. 42.

26. Ibid., p. 10.

27. Richard Sennett, *The Corrosion of Character* (New York: Norton, 1998), p. 141.

28. Daniel Meyer and Maria Cancian, "Life after Welfare," *Public Welfare* 54 (Fall 1996), p. 27.

29. Ibid.

30. Daniel Meyer and Maria Cancian, "Economic Well-Being Following an Exit from AFDC" (Madison: Institute for Research on Poverty, 1997), p. 8.

31. Ibid., pp. 9–10.

32. Ibid., table 1.

33. Cathy Born et al., "Life after Welfare: An Interim Report" (Baltimore: University of Maryland School of Social Work, 1997), p. iv.

34. Cathy Born et al., "A Life after Welfare: An Early Report on Maryland's Reform Efforts" (Baltimore: University of Maryland School of Social Work, 1997), pp. 6–7.

35. Born et al., "Interim Report," pp. 25–26.

36. Ibid., pp. 38–40.

37. Robert Pear, "Most States Meet Work Requirement of Welfare Law," *New York Times*, 30 December 1998. Paradoxically, states were unable to comply with the requirement that both parents be employed in 75 percent of two-parent households.

38. Sheldon Danziger and Jeffrey Lehman, "The Employment and Earnings Prospects of Welfare Recipients" (Ann Arbor: University of Michigan Population Studies Center, 1995), p. 8.

39. Jared Bernstein, "Welfare Reform and the Low-Wage Labor Market" (Washington, D.C.: Economic Policy Institute, 1997), pp. 8, 9.

40. Ibid.

41. Lawrence Mishel and John Schmitt, "Cutting Wages by Cutting Welfare" (Washington, D.C.: Economic Policy Institute, 1995), p. 5.

42. Harry Holzer, *What Employers Want* (New York: Russell Sage Foundation, 1996), p. 58.

43. Ibid.

44. Ibid.

45. Ibid., pp. 104–5, 112–13.

46. Vicki Lens, "Welfare Mothers and Work: Myth Versus Reality," *Jewish Social Work Forum* 33 (Winter/Spring 1997–98), p. 15.

47. Jan Hagen and Liane Davis, "The Participants' Perspective on the Job Opportunities and Basic Skills Training Program," *Social Service Review* 69 (1995), p. 661.

48. Gary Burtless, "The Employment Experiences and Potential Earnings of Welfare Recipients" (Washington, D.C.: Brookings Institution, 1997), p. 3.

49. "Economy Gives Some Black Women a Boost," *Richmond Times-Dispatch,* 18 August 1998.

50. Burtless, "Employment Experiences," p. 8.

51. The inclusion of time limits in welfare reform is an ironic replication of Unemployment Compensation. Time limits under TANF are much longer than those of Unemployment Compensation, but it could be argued that the benefits are inferior.

52. Roberta Spalter-Roth, Beverly Burr, Heidi Hartmann, and Lois Shaw, *Welfare That Works* (Washington, D.C.: Institute for Women's Policy Research, 1995), p. 18.

53. Bradley Schiller, *The Economics of Poverty and Discrimination,* 7th ed. (Upper Saddle River, N.J.: Prentice Hall, 1998).

54. Bradley Schiller, "Moving Up: The Training and Wage Gains of Minimum-Wage Entrants," *Social Science Quarterly* 75 (1994), p. 629.

55. Ibid., p. 627.

56. Ibid., p. 634.

57. Bradley Schiller, "Relative Earnings Redux," *Review of Income and Wealth,* series 40, no. 4 (1994), p. 447.

58. Ibid.

59. Ibid., pp. 448–52.

60. Bradley Schiller and C. Nielsen Brasher, "Effects of Workfare Saturation on AFDC Caseloads," *Contemporary Policy Issues* 11 (1993), pp. 39–49.

61. Frances Riemer, "Quick Attachments to the Workforce," *Social Work Research* 21 (December 1997), pp. 227–28.

62. Felice Perlmutter, *From Welfare to Work* (New York: Oxford University Press, 1997), p. 74.

63. Thomas Karier, "Welfare Graduates" (Annandale-on-Hudson, N.Y.: Jerome Levy Economics Institute, 1998), p. 4.

64. Perlmutter, *From Welfare to Work,* p. 27.

65. David Howell and Elizabeth Howell, "The Effects of Immigrants on African American Earnings" (New York: New School for Social Research, 1997), p. 23.

66. Daniel McMurer and Isabel Sawhill, *Getting Ahead* (Washington, D.C.: Urban Institute, 1998), p. 33.

67. "Poverty Short-Lived for Most, Study Finds," *Richmond Times-Dispatch,* 10 August 1998.

68. Kathryn Edin and Christopher Jencks, "Reforming Welfare," in Christopher Jencks, *Rethinking Social Policy* (Cambridge: Harvard University Press, 1992), p. 208.

69. Kathryn Edin, "The Myths of Dependence and Self-Sufficiency," *Focus* 17 (Fall/Winter 1995), p. 3.

70. Ibid., pp. 6, 5.

71. Kathryn Edin and Laura Lein, *Making Ends Meet* (New York: Russell Sage Foundation, 1997), pp. 101, 109.

72. Ibid., p. 130.

73. Ibid., p. 140.

74. Katherine Newman, *No Shame in My Game* (New York: Knopf, 1999), p. 258.

75. Ibid., p. 201.

76. Ibid., p. 111.

77. Edin and Lein, *Making Ends Meet*, p. 220.

78. This was also reported in an evaluation of five years of participation in Chicago's Project Match. *"What did people do once they started working?* Simply put, they left jobs, and rather quickly. Among the 296 in the longitudinal sample who ever worked, 55 percent lost or quit their first job within six months and 71 percent left it within a year. And they left subsequent jobs, too: on average, people in the longitudinal sample who worked had five jobs during their follow-up period." Suzanne Wagner et al., *Five Years on Welfare* (Chicago: Erikson Institute, 1998), pp. 10, 13.

79. Ann Rangarajan and Anne Gordon, "The Transition from Welfare to Work" (Princeton: Mathematica Policy Research, 1997), pp. 8–10.

80. Ibid., p. 36.

81. Ibid., p. 3.

82. Ibid., p. 29.

83. Jason DeParle, "Newest Challenges for Welfare," *New York Times*, 20 November 1997.

84. Michael Grunwald, "How She Got the Job," *American Prospect*, July/August 1997, pp. 25–29.

85. Alan Finder, "Some Private Efforts See Success in Job Hunt for Those on Welfare," *New York Times*, 16 June 1998.

86. Jason DeParle, "Tougher Welfare Limits Bring Surprising Results," *New York Times*, 30 December 1997.

87. The Project Match researchers came to this conclusion, as well: "Many welfare recipients have considerably more work experience than previously suspected." Wagner et al., *Five Years*, p. 8.

88. Hasenfeld notes this in his critical review of the Riverside GAIN program: "In fact, Riverside may be only getting the experimentals to switch from the informal to the formal economy." Yeheskel Hasenfeld, "Welfare Reform and Social Services" (Ann Arbor: University of Michigan, 1998), p. 21.

CHAPTER 6. BOOTSTRAP CAPITALISM

1. The expression is similar to that used by Michael Meeropol, *Surrender: How the Clinton Administration Completed the Reagan Revolution* (Ann Arbor: University of Michigan Press, 1998); Daniel Yergen and Joseph Stanislaw, *The Commanding Heights* (New York: Simon and Schuster, 1998).

2. Rebecca Blank, *It Takes a Nation* (New York: Russell Sage Foundation, 1997), p. 232, emphasis in original.

3. Judith Havemann and Barbara Vobejda, "The Welfare Alarm That Didn't Go Off," *Washington Post,* 1 October 1998.

4. Thomas Corbett, "Child Poverty and Welfare Reform," *Focus* 15 (Spring 1993), pp. 1–17.

5. Blank, *It Takes a Nation,* p. 259.

6. Donna Franklin, *Ensuring Inequality* (New York: Oxford University Press, 1997), p. 230.

7. Timothy Bartik, "Employment as a 'Solution' to Welfare," *Employment Research* 7 (April 2000), p. 3

8. Michael Weiss, "Theories of the Social Contract," *World and I* 7 (September 1992), pp. 36–49.

9. Hyman Minsky, Dimitri Papadimitriou, Ronnie Phillips, and L. Randall Way, "Community Development Banking" (Annandale-on-Hudson, N.Y.: Jerome Levy Economics Institute, 1993), p. 22.

10. The more extensive histories of American social welfare include references to immigrant ventures in capitalism, though these are usually subordinated to discussions of the grinding poverty that was alleviated by government social programs. See, for example, Bruce Jansson, *The Reluctant Welfare State,* 2nd ed. (Pacific Grove, Calif.: Brooks/Cole, 1993).

11. Howard Karger and David Stoesz, *American Social Welfare Policy,* 3rd ed. (New York: Longman, 1998), ch. 7.

12. Quoted in Norman Furniss and Timothy Tilton, *The Case for the Welfare State* (Bloomington: Indiana University Press, 1977), p. 156, emphasis in original.

13. Sanford Jacoby, *Modern Manors* (Princeton: Princeton University Press, 1997), pp. 19–20.

14. Karger and Stoesz, *American Social Welfare Policy,* ch. 7.

15. Neil Gilbert, *Capitalism and the Welfare State* (New Haven: Yale University Press, 1983), p. 3.

16. Michael Reisch, "The Sociopolitical Context and Social Work Method, 1890–1950," *Social Service Review* (1998), pp. 170–71; see also Stanley Wenocur and Michael Reich, *From Charity to Enterprise* (Urbana: University of Illinois Press, 1989), pp. 84–85.

17. As described by Esping-Andersen, bootstrap capitalism assumes integration and complementarity between the welfare state and market economics. He classifies the American welfare state as "liberal" insofar as entitlements are strictly circumscribed and benefits are often means-tested and related to the work ethic. Unlike many American welfare philosophers, Esping-Andersen views even the more comprehensive and well-provisioned welfare states as engaged in forms of bootstrap capitalism. See Gosta Esping-Anderson, *The Three Worlds of Welfare Capitalism* (Princeton: Princeton University Press, 1990). One qualification: bootstrap capitalism should not be mistaken for corporate welfare, the government's provision of artificial supports to business.

18. David Stoesz, *Small Change: Domestic Policy under the Clinton Presidency* (White Plains, N.Y.: Longman, 1996), ch. 1.

19. Concomitantly, the incursion of fundamentalist Christians into the Republican party effectively marginalized any moderate influences that had remained after the Reagan revolution.

20. Amitai Etzioni, *The Spirit of Community* (New York: Pantheon, 1993).

21. See Amitai Etzioni, ed., *The Essential Communitarian Reader* (Lanham, Md.: Rowman and Littlefield, 1998). In advocating the revitalization of community institutions, communitarians echo the "mediating structures" initiative that conservative policy institutes had orchestrated to accuse federal social programs of robbing communities of sustenance while exacerbating individual alienation. See Peter Berger and Richard John Neuhaus, *To Empower People* (Washington, D.C.: American Enterprise Institute, 1977).

22. Robert Putnam, "The Prosperous Community," *American Prospect* (Spring 1993), p. 39.

23. Committee on Ways and Means, House of Representatives, *Overview of Entitlement Programs* (Washington, D.C.: GPO, 1996); Michael Cabellero, "The Earned Income Tax Credit," *Tax Lawyer* 48 (1995), pp. 435–69; Ed Lazere, "State Earned Income Tax Credits Build on the Strengths of the Federal EITC" (Washington, D.C.: Center on Budget and Policy Priorities, 1998).

24. Committee on Ways and Means, *Overview*, 1996, pp. 804–5.

25. John Scholz, "Earned Income Tax Credit," *National Tax Journal* 47 (March 1994), pp. 63–88.

26. George Yin and Jonathan Forman, "Redesigning the Earned Income Tax Credit Program to Provide More Effective Assistance for the Working Poor," *Tax Notes* 61 (May 17, 1993), p. 954.

27. Jeffrey Liebman, *The Impact of the Earned Income Tax Credit on Incentives and Income Distribution* (Cambridge: Harvard University Press, 1997).

28. Lazere, "State Earned Income Tax Credits."

29. Paul Wilson and Robert Cline, "State Welfare Reform," *National Tax Journal* 17 (1994), pp. 655–76; David Stoesz and David Saunders, "From Welfare to Tax Credits," *Community Tax Law Report* 2 (October 1997), pp. 5–6.

30. Michael Hudson, *Merchants of Misery* (Monroe, Maine: Common Courage, 1996), p. 10.

31. Lawrence Katz, "Wage Subsidies for the Disadvantaged," in Richard Freeman and Peter Gottschalk, eds., *Generating Jobs* (New York: Russell Sage Foundation, 1998), p. 40.

32. Ibid., p. 41; David Stoesz, "Welfare Behaviorism," *Society* 34 (March/April 1997), pp. 68–77.

33. Committee on Ways and Means, *Overview*, 1996, pp. 813–14.

34. David Saunders and David Stoesz, "Welfare Capitalism in a Global Economy" (Richmond: Virginia Commonwealth University School of Social Work, 1998), p. 9.

35. Edmund Phelps, *Rewarding Work* (Cambridge: Harvard University Press, 1997), p. 106.

36. Ibid., p. 113.

37. Matthew Miller, "How to End Poverty for the Working Poor," *Washington Post*, 1 February 1998.

38. Jonathan Forman, "Administrative Savings from Synchronizing Social Welfare Programs and Tax Provision," *Journal of the National Association of Administrative Law Judges* 13 (Spring 1993), pp. 5–71.

39. Lawrence Mishel, Jared Bernstein, and John Schmitt, *The State of Working America* (Washington, D.C.: Economic Policy Institute, 1997), p. 53.

40. Reynolds Farley, *The New American Reality* (New York: Russell Sage Foundation, 1996), p. 134.

41. Peter Passell, "Benefits Dwindle Along with Wages for the Unskilled," *New York Times,* 14 June 1998.

42. Wealth is defined as "net financial assets" excluding equity from a home or other source. See Melvin Oliver and Thomas Shapiro, *Black Wealth/White Wealth* (New York: Routledge, 1997), pp. 58, 69, 86–87.

43. Michael Sherraden, "Stakeholding: A New Direction in Social Policy" (Washington, D.C.: Progressive Policy Institute, 1990).

44. Robert Friedman and Dorothy Broadman, "IDAs . . . What Are They?" *Community Investments* (Winter 1998), pp. 5–8.

45. Michael Sherraden, *Assets and the Poor* (Armonk, N.Y.: M. E. Sharpe, 1991).

46. Michael Sherraden, personal communication, 21 September 1998.

47. William Rohe and Michael Stegman, "The Effects of Homeownership," *Journal of the American Planning Association* 60 (Spring 1994), p. 180.

48. Gautam Yadama and Michael Sherraden, "Effects of Assets on Attitudes and Behaviors," *Social Work Research* 20 (March 1996), p. 10.

49. Wendell Berry, *What Are People For?* (New York: Northpoint, 1997), p. 119.

50. "Summary of Assets for Independence Act S. 1255" (Washington, D.C.: Corporation for Enterprise Development, n.d.).

51. Ibid.

52. Ray Boshara and Robert Friedman, "20 Promising Ideas for Savings Facilitation and Mobilization in Low-Income Communities in the U.S." (Washington, D.C.: Corporation for Enterprise Development, 1997), p. 4.

53. "Reclaiming the American Dream" (Washington, D.C.: Corporation for Enterprise Development, 1998).

54. "Assets for Independence Act" (Washington, D.C.: Corporation for Enterprise Development, 1998).

55. George Hager and Amy Goldstein, "Clinton Details Plan for New Retirement Savings Accounts," *Washington Post,* 15 April 1999.

56. By the mid-1990s a journal of microenterprise had begun publication: *Journal of Developmental Entrepreneurship,* Norfolk State University, Norfolk, VA 23504.

57. David Stoesz, Charles Guzzetta, and Mark Lusk, *International Development* (Needham Heights, Mass.: Allyn & Bacon, 1998), ch. 12.

58. "Micro-enterprise Peer Lending," *Journal of Cooperative Development* 1 (Spring 1998).

59. Alex Counts, *Give Us Credit* (New Delhi, India: Research Press, 1996).

60. John Else and Salome Raheim, "AFDC Clients as Entrepreneurs," *Public Welfare* 50 (Fall 1992), p. 37.

61.   Roberta Spalter-Roth, Enrique Soto, Lily Zandniapour, and Jill Braunstein, *Micro-Enterprise and Women* (Washington, D.C.: Institute for Women's Policy Research, 1994), p. 38.

62.   Lisa Servon, "Helping Poor Women Achieve Self-Sufficiency Through Self-Employment" (Washington, D.C.: Research Institute for Small and Emerging Business, 1998), p. 1.

63.   Diane Meyerhoff, "Federal Funding Opportunities for Microenterprise Programs," *Journal of Developmental Entrepreneurship* 2 (Fall/Winter 1997), pp. 99–109.

64.   "Comprehensive Approaches to Community Development" (Washington, D.C.: GAO, 1995), p. 2.

65.   John Accordino, "Community-Based Development" (Richmond, Va.: Federal Reserve Bank, 1997).

66.   Michael Sandel, *Democracy's Discontent* (Cambridge: Harvard University Press, 1996); Fred Siegel, *The Future Once Happened Here* (New York: Free Press, 1997).

67.   Antonin Wagner, "Reassessing Welfare Capitalism," *Journal of Community Practice* 2, no. 3 (1995), p. 61.

68.   Lori Montgomery, "Fed's Urban Aid Plan Shows Few Triumphs So Far," *Albuquerque Journal,* 31 December 1995.

69.   "Annual Report, 1996" (Durham, N.C.: Self-Help Credit Union).

70.   "Building Community Wealth" (Raleigh: North Carolina Minority Support Center, 1996).

71.   "Promoting Progress through Partnerships: Fleet Community Reinvestment Act Report, 1996–1997" (Providence, R.I.: Fleet Community Development Bank).

72.   "Banking on the Poor," *The Economist,* 24 June 1998, p. 28.

73.   "Biennial Report, 1994–95" (Fredericksburg, Va.: First Nations Development Institute).

74.   Rochelle Stanfield, "Capitalism for the Poor," *National Journal* (July 11, 1998), p. 1618.

75.   Michael Porter, "Competitive Advantage in the Inner City," *Harvard Business Review* 73 (May/June 1995), p. 59.

76.   Minsky et al., "Community Development Banking," p. 15.

77.   Michael Kelly, "The High Road to Scandal," *Washington Post,* 10 June 1998; Accordino, "Community-Based Development," p. 25.

78.   "Review of Management Practices at the Treasury Department's Community Development Financial Institutions Fund" (Washington, D.C.: Subcommittee on General Oversight and Investigations of the Committee on Banking and Financial Services, House of Representatives, 1998), p. 1.

79.   Michael Porter, "New Strategies for Inner-City Economic Development," *Economic Development Quarterly* 11 (February 1997), p. 9.

80.   Testimony of Christine Gaffney, Mary Mathews, and Rita Haynes on behalf of the Coalition of Community Development Financial Institutions before the House of Representatives Subcommittee on VA, HUD, and Independent Agencies Appropriation, May 1, 1997. Momentum behind the CDFI movement faltered in June 1998 when a scandal within the Treasury's CDFI office resulted in the resignation of

the executive director and associate director of the CDFI Fund. Federal support for the economic development of poor neighborhoods remains intact.

81. "Banking on the Poor," p. 28.

82. Katherine Stearns and Valerie Threlfall, "A Report on the Membership" (Philadelphia: National Community Capital Association, 1997), pp. 4, 16.

83. Mark Pinsky and Valerie Threlfall, "The Parallel Banking System and Community Reinvestment" (Philadelphia: National Community Capital Association, 1996), p. 15.

84. Katherine Stearns, Valerie Threlfall, and Beth Lipson, "Charting CDFI Progress" (Philadelphia: National Community Capital Association, 1998), pp. 8, 9.

85. Michael Stegman, "Electronic Benefit Transfer's Potential to Help the Poor" (Washington, D.C.: Brookings Institution, 1998), p. 7; William Sessums, "'Unbanked' Citizens Draw Government Attention," *Community Investments* 9 (Fall 1997), pp. 7–12.

86. Michael Stegman, "EFT '99" (Chapel Hill, N.C.: Center for Community Capitalism, 1997), p. 3.

87. Caskey, *Fringe Banking* (New York: Russell Sage Foundation, 1994), p. 71.

88. Stegman, "EFT '99," p. v.

89. Dimitri Papadimitriou, Ronnie Phillips, and L. Randall Wray, "A Path to Community Development" (Annandale-on-Hudson, N.Y.: Jerome Levy Economics Institute, 1993), p. 24.

90. Hudson, *Merchants of Misery*, p. 55.

91. Stegman, "EFT '99," p. 20.

92. Jerry Reynolds, "Electronic Funds Transfer," *Shelterforce* 96 (November/December 1997), pp. 8–9.

93. Quoted in Stegman, "EFT '99," p. i.

94. "Treasury Names Citibank for Major EBT Project in 8 States" (New York: Citibank, 1995).

95. Stegman, "Electronic Benefit Transfer's Potential," p. 5.

96. Ibid., p. 7.

97. Ibid.

98. Blank, *It Takes a Nation*, p. 28.

99. Paul Jargowsky, *Poverty and Place* (New York: Russell Sage Foundation, 1997), p. 101.

100. Stegman, "EFT '99," p. 17; the float from 10,000 EBT deposits would generate $22,800.

101. Brigitte Berger and Peter Berger, *The War Over the Family* (Garden City, N.Y.: Anchor, 1984).

102. Herbert Gans, *The War Against the Poor* (New York: Basic Books, 1995), p. 7.

103. John McKnight, *The Careless Society* (New York: Basic Books, 1995), p. x.

104. Kenneth Reardon, "Enhancing the Capacity of Community-Based Organizations in East St. Louis," *Journal of Planning Education and Research* 17 (1998), pp. 323–33; Kenneth Reardon, "Participatory Action Research as Service Learning," *New Directions for Teaching and Learning* 73 (Spring 1998), pp. 57–64.

105. Sarah Kreutziger et al., "The Campus Affiliates Program," *American Behavioral Scientist* 42 (February 1999), pp. 827–39.

106. Wagner, "Reassessing Welfare Capitalism," p. 46.

107. A change in this predilection is evident in Phillip Fellin, "Development of Capital in Poor, Inner-City Neighborhoods," *Journal of Community Practice* 5, no. 3 (1998), pp. 87–98.

108. Porter, "Competitive Advantage," p. 71.

109. Blank, *It Takes a Nation*, p. 31.

110. Joel Handler, *The Poverty of Welfare Reform* (New Haven: Yale University Press, 1995), p. 55.

111. Committee on Ways and Means, *Overview*, 1996, pp. 777–79.

112. Hudson, *Merchants of Misery*, pp. 17, 2.

113. John Caskey, *Fringe Banking*, p. 8.

Index